英国文学史及经典作品选读

主　编　张　扬
副主编　李曼丽　周　洁　金晓玲
　　　　王艳薇　陈　姝　武玲慧
主　审　李　雪　董　霖　李慧杰

哈尔滨工业大学出版社

内容简介

《英国文学史及经典作品选读》是将文学史与文学作品结合论述的教材,全书各章节按照英国文学史的时间顺序进行组织布局,介绍了英国文学早期、中世纪到20世纪的历史文化、文学史背景特点,以及具有代表性的作家与作品。每个章节都以作家为独立单元,首先提炼出具有思政意义的评论与精彩引文、译文;其次介绍其生平事件、作品内容概要、作品选文原文以及内容注释,并在注释中体现了与国际化语言考试对标的雅思与托福词汇;最后结合作品选文提出思辨题目及本章节需掌握的文学专有词汇。

本教材框架清晰,章节内容编写思路明确,适合我国高校非英语专业本硕博学生使用。

图书在版编目(CIP)数据

英国文学史及经典作品选读/张扬主编. —哈尔滨:
哈尔滨工业大学出版社,2023.4
ISBN 978-7-5603-9555-5

Ⅰ.①英… Ⅱ.①张… Ⅲ.①英语-阅读教学-高等学校-教材②英国文学-文学史 Ⅳ.①H319.37

中国版本图书馆 CIP 数据核字(2021)第122380号

策划编辑	常 雨
责任编辑	张凤涛 常 雨
出版发行	哈尔滨工业大学出版社
社 址	哈尔滨市南岗区复华四道街10号 邮编150006
传 真	0451-86414749
网 址	http://hitpress.hit.edu.cn
印 刷	哈尔滨市石桥印务有限公司
开 本	787mm×960mm 1/16 印张 22.25 字数 570 千字
版 次	2023年4月第1版 2023年4月第1次印刷
书 号	ISBN 978-7-5603-9555-5
定 价	48.00元

(如因印装质量问题影响阅读,我社负责调换)

前　言

　　文学对于民族精神和人文素养的滋养至关重要,是人文学科的重要组成部分。文学具有一切时间、一切地点的一切人类文化的特征。文学是语言和文化的结晶,没有国界,世界文学的经典之作具有认知历史与现实、启迪人生、陶冶情操和支撑内在生命的价值。习近平总书记提出:"高校哲学社会科学有重要的育人功能,要面向全体学生,帮助学生形成正确的世界观、人生观、价值观,提高道德修养和精神境界,养成科学思维习惯,促进身心和人格健康发展。"习近平总书记在哈尔滨工业大学百年校庆"贺信精神"中也明确提出"坚持社会主义办学方向,紧扣立德树人根本任务,在教书育人、科研攻关等工作中,不断改革创新、奋发作为、追求卓越"。

　　《英国文学史及经典作品选读》一书,以习近平总书记"贺信精神"为指引,立足我国高校外语教学;以教材为载体,将习总书记在贺信中强调的"坚持社会主义办学方向,紧扣立德树人根本任务,追求卓越"贯彻到文学教材与思政育人实践中,建构"3V"文学思政教材育人体系,打造《英国文学史及经典作品选读》教材思政典型范例,提倡"教材知识学以致用,思政育人实践先行";在讲授文学专业知识、培养学生国际交流、国际视野的同时,提升学生的3V认知——即Visions 国际视野、家国情怀,Values 世界观、人生观、价值观,Virtues 道德思想、人格培养(具体为爱国爱家、法制意识、社会责任、人文精神、仁爱之心等);最终培养学生成长为会语言、懂文化、通文学、爱国家、精专业的卓越国际化人才,以良好的中国国家民族形象骄傲地站在世界舞台之上。

　　《英国文学史及经典作品选读》是面向我国高校非英语专业本硕博学生编写的核心素养系列教材之一,与《北美文学史及经典作品选读》教材一样,适合基于项目为驱动的高校本硕博英语混合式课堂教学模式以及任何新时代慕课课程背景下的创新教学形式。本教材以建构英语文学知识框架体系为基础,以培养学生人文核心素养为己任,力求帮助学生形成健康高尚的人格和健全的心性,并具有国际视野与家国情怀,建立正确的三观以及道德观念;在提升文学作品审美能力的同时,提升学生的思辨能力,帮助学生从不同角度思考问题,提升自身对不同历史及文化的认知能力。

本教材以"3V"文学思政教材育人体系为框架,旨在优化教材育人功能,全面系统地介绍影响英国文学发展的历史背景、社会背景及文化思潮;在追溯英国文学的发展历史、各个时期呈现出的文学发展特点、不同文学流派的主要特征以及重要作家及其代表作品的基础上,着重引导学生对国家、社会以及个人发展发表个人见解,并以英国文学作品为切入点,提升学生对历史背景、文本、人物的"3V"认知,同时结合文学文本,将英国文学史与作家作品进行横向(共时)与纵向(历时)分析,培养学生对中西方文学观点的思辨能力。本教材也介绍了文学批评的基本知识和方法,从而使学生了解英国文学的发展全貌,掌握英国文学知识、文学常识和文学批评的基本方法。教材选取各个阶段具有代表性的作家、作品进行细致的文本分析,通过阅读、赏析、讨论,理解英国文学原著,培养学生对英国文学作品的鉴赏能力和思辨能力。

张 扬
2023 年 1 月

Contents

Chapter 1	**Early and Medieval English Literature**	1
Unit 1	Geoffrey Chaucer	5
Unit 2	Thomas Malory	11
Chapter 2	**English Literature in the Renaissance**	22
Unit 1	Edmund Spenser	26
Unit 2	William Shakespeare	31
Chapter 3	**Literature of the English Revolution and Restoration**	68
Unit 1	John Milton	71
Unit 2	John Bunyan	78
Unit 3	John Donne	84
Unit 4	Henry Fielding	88
Chapter 4	**18th-Century English Literature**	98
Unit 1	Daniel Defoe	102
Unit 2	Jonathan Swift	113
Unit 3	William Blake	122
Unit 4	Robert Burns	128
Chapter 5	**Romanticism in English Literature**	136
Unit 1	William Wordsworth	138
Unit 2	Samuel Taylor Coleridge	141
Unit 3	George Gordon Byron	147
Unit 4	John Keats	156
Unit 5	Percy Bysshe Shelley	167
Unit 6	Jane Austen	172

Chapter 6 19th-Century English Literature ·········· 179
    Unit 1 Charles Dickens ·········· 181
    Unit 2 Charlotte Brontë ·········· 196
    Unit 3 Thomas Hardy ·········· 212
    Unit 4 William Makepeace Thackeray ·········· 223
    Unit 5 George Bernard Shaw ·········· 232
Chapter 7 20th-Century English Literature ·········· 249
    Unit 1 Joseph Conrad ·········· 252
    Unit 2 William Butler Yeats ·········· 256
    Unit 3 James Joyce ·········· 260
    Unit 4 Virginia Woolf ·········· 271
    Unit 5 David Herbert Lawrence ·········· 274
    Unit 6 Katherine Mansfield ·········· 281
    Unit 7 William Somerset Maugham ·········· 290
    Unit 8 David Lodge ·········· 298
    Unit 9 J. K. Rowling ·········· 320
Reference ·········· 348

Chapter 1

Early and Medieval English Literature

I. Historical Background

1. The Making of England

More than 7,000 years ago, when the Ice Age ended, melting ice flooded low-lying lands in continental Europe, creating the English Channel and the North Sea and turning Britain into an island. Around 3000BC, the first known settlers of Britain were the Iberians. More dramatic monuments were the henges, the most important of which was Stonehenge in Wiltshire.

1.1 The Native Celts 凯尔特人

The Celts may originally have come from eastern and central Europe (now called France, Belgium and southern Germany); they came to Britain in three main waves: Gaels, Britons and the Belgae. Celts, also called the Britons, are regarded as the natives of Great Britain. Celts began to move into Great Britain in about 700BC, and they are believed to be ancestors of the Highland Scots, the Irish and the Welsh people. Some of the Celtic words or sounds were later assimilated into the English language. Their languages, the Celtic languages, are the basis of Gaelic, Irish and Welsh.

1.2 Roman Britain

In 55BC, Julius Caesar sailed across the English Channel after he had conquered Gaul. In 43AD, the Romans occupied England by driving the native Celts into mountainous Scotland and Wales, and completely conquered the southern part of the island of Great Britain, including England and Wales. But they were never able to completely defeat or control what is now Scotland. For nearly 400 years, Britain was under Roman occupation. The Romans built many towns, roads, baths, temples and buildings. They made good use of Britain's natural resources. They also brought the new religion, Christianity, to Britain.

2. The Anglo-Saxon Period

In the mid-5th century, Jutes, Saxons and Angles came to Britain. A Jutish chief became the King of Kent in 449. Then the Saxons established their kingdom in Essex, Sussex and Wessex from the end of the 5th century to the beginning of the 6th century. In the second half of the 6th century, the Angles, who also came from northern Germany and were to give their name to the English people, settled in East Anglia, Mercia and Northumbria. These seven principal kingdoms of Kent, Essex, Sussex, Wessex, East Anglia, Mercia and Northumbria have been given the name of Heptarchy. The early Anglo-Saxons converted to Christianity.

Viking and Danish Invasions

The Norwegians and the Danes, the invaders, attacked various parts of England from the end of the 8th century. They even managed to capture York, an important center of Christianity in 867. By the middle of the 9th century, the Vikings and the Danes were posing a threat to the Saxon kingdom of Wessex.

Alfred (849 – 899), a king of Wessex, defeated the Danes and reached a friendly agreement with them in 879. He founded a strong fleet and is known as "the father of the British navy". All this earns him the title "Alfred the Great".

3. The Anglo-Norman Period

3.1 The Norman Conquest

It was said that King Edward had promised the English throne to William, the Duke of Normandy but the Witan chose Harold. In 1066, William defeated Harold and killed him during the important battle of Hastings. William was crowned king of England, thus beginning the Norman Conquest of England. The Norman Conquest is perhaps the best-known event in English history. The feudal system was completely established in England. Norman-French culture, language, manners and architecture were introduced. The Church was brought into closer connection with Rome. The English is a mixture of nationalities of different origins. The ancestors of many English people were the ancient

Angles and Saxons. Some English people are of the Norman-French origin.

3.2 The Hundred Years' War

The Hundred Years' War was a series of conflicts from 1337 to 1453 between the Kingdom of England and the Kingdom of France.

It was due to a dynastic disagreement to William the Conqueror, while remaining Duke of Normandy. As dukes of Normandy and other lands on the continent, the English kings owed homage to the King of France. The question of legal succession to the French crown was central to the war. Although primarily a dynastic conflict, the war gave impetus to ideas of French and English nationalism.

During the Hundred Years' War, Joan of Arc believed she could rescue the French people. She rallied the demoralized French troops, leading them in battle. Ultimately captured and imprisoned by the English, Joan was condemned as a heretic and a witch and stood trial before the Inquisition in 1431. She eventually became a martyr and was then burnt at the stake and became a national hero.

3.3 Wars of Roses

The Wars of the Roses in the 15th century were fought by the noble families of York and Lancaster between 1455 and 1485. They are called the Wars of the Roses because each family used a rose as its symbol—a white rose for York and a red rose for Lancaster. These wars were very bloody, full of battles, betrayals and murders. Finally the last Yorkist king, Richard III, was beaten by a Welsh noble, Henry Tudor in England who became King Henry VII, the first Tudor monarch. He made a Tudor rose—a red rose with a white rose in the middle. This came to symbolize the peace that had come after all the fighting. The House of Tudor subsequently ruled England and Wales for 117 years.

II. Literary Background

1. Anglo-Saxon Literature

Anglo-Saxon literature, that is, the Old English literature is almost exclusively a verse literature in oral form. It could be passed down by word of mouth from generation to generation. Its creators for the most part are unknown. It was only given a written form long after its composition.

Beowulf is the oldest poem in the English language, commonly cited as one of the most important works of Anglo-Saxon literature; and also the surviving heroic epic poem consisting of 3182 alliterative long lines. Alliteration is used for poetic effect, a repetition of the initial sounds of several words in a group. e. g. a. To his kin the kindest, keenest for praise; b. Sing a song of southern singer.

Beowulf, king of the Geats who live in Juteland, Denmark, comes to the help of Hrothgar, the king of the Danes, whose mead hall (Heorot) has been under attack by a monster known as Grendel. After Beowulf slays him, Grendel's mother attacks the hall and is also defeated. Beowulf goes home to Geatland in Sweden and later becomes king of the Geats. After a period of fifty years, Beowulf defeats a fire-spewing dragon, but Beowulf is severely wounded during the fight. He dies a heroic death. The poem ends with the funeral of the hero.

A lot of metaphors and understatements are used in the poem. For example, the sea is called "the whale-road" or "the swan road"; the soldiers are called "shield-men"; human-body is referred to as "the bone-house"; God is called "wonder-wielder"; monster is referred to as "soul-destroyer".

2. Medieval English Literature

Medieval literature covers about four century, which encompasses essentially all written works available in Europe and beyond during the Middle Ages. In the early part of the period (1066 up to the mid-14th century), there was not much about literature in English. The works of this time were composed of religious writings. In the second half (the 14th century), English literature started to flourish. Middle English literature deals with wider subjects and various styles, tones and genres.

2.1 The Romance

The most prevailing kind of literature in feudal England was the romance, which was a long composition, sometimes in verse, sometimes in prose, describing the life and adventures of a noble hero, often in the form of allegory. The knight was the central character of romances.

The romance of King Arthur (adventures of King Arthur and his Knights of the Round Table) is comparatively the most important for the history of English literature.

King Arthur is a legendary British leader of the late 5th and early 6th centuries, who led the defense of Britain against Saxon invaders in the early 6th century. Some Welsh and Briton tales and poems relating the story of Arthur date from earlier than this work. In these works, Arthur appears either as a great warrior defending Britain from human and supernatural enemies or as a magical figure of folklore, sometimes associated with the Welsh Otherworld, Annwn.

2.2 English Ballads

The most important department of English folk literature is the ballad. A ballad is a story told in song, usually in 4-line stanzas, with the second and fourth lines rhymed.

Popular folk literature occupies an important place in this period. The Middle English literature strongly reflects the principles of the medieval Christian doctrine, which are primarily concerned with the issue of personal salvation. An emphasis has also been placed on the humanity of Christ and the imagery of human passion. Love has largely superseded fear; and explorations into undiscovered regions of the heart offer fresh possibilities for introspection.

The most famous cycle of English ballads centers on the stories about a legendary outlaw called Robin Hood. In English history, Robin Hood is partly a real and partly a legendary figure. The ballads tell us that he lived during the reign of Richard Ⅰ. The dominant key in his character is his hatred for the cruel oppressors and his love for the poor and downtrodden. He was the leader of a band of outlaws, and they lived in the deep forest. They often attacked the rich, waged war against the bishops and archbishops, and helped the poor people. Therefore, Robin Hood and his followers were constantly hunted by the sheriffs.

Unit 1　Geoffrey Chaucer

Appreciation

When in April the sweet showers fall 春雨给大地带来了喜悦，
And pierce the drought of March to the root, and all 送走了土壤干裂的三月，
The veins are bathed in liquor of such power 沐浴着草木的丝丝经络，
As brings about the engendering of the flower 顿时百花盛开，生机勃勃。

Author

Geoffrey Chaucer is widely considered the greatest English poet of the medieval Ages. Chaucer rose in royal employment and became a knight of the shire for Kent. As a member of the king's household, Chaucer was sent on diplomatic errands throughout Europe. From all these activities, he gained the knowledge of society that made it possible to write *The Canterbury Tales*.

Although he wrote many works, which include *The Book of the Duchess*, *The House of Fame*, *The Legend of Good Women* and *Troilus and Criseyde*, and he is best remembered for his immortal *The Canterbury Tales*. Chaucer died in October 1400 and he was the first poet to have been buried in Poets' Corner of Westminster Abbey.

Chaucer is the first to use the rhymed couplet of iambic pentameter, which is to be called the heroic couplet. Iambic pentameter is the basic rhythmical pattern in English verse, with five feet in a line, usually an unaccented syllable followed by an accented syllable. Thus, he lays the foundation of the English tonic-syllabic verse.

He uses London dialect in his writings and he contributes to making it the foundation for modern English speech. Though drawing influence from French, Italian and Latin models, he is the first great poet who wrote in the English language. His production of so much excellent poetry was an important factor in establishing English as the literary language of the country. The spoken English of the time consisted of several dialects, and Chaucer did much in making the dialect of London the standard for the moden English speech. Chaucer is considered the source of the English vernacular tradition and "the father of modern English literature".

Brief Introduction

The Canterbury Tales is a collection of stories written in Middle English by Geoffrey Chaucer between 1387 and 1400. It is composed of humorous, bawdy, and poignant stories told by a group of fictional pilgrims, who travel together on a journey from Southwark to the shrine of Saint Thomas Becket at Canterbury Cathedral. They come from all layers of society, and tell stories to each other to kill time while travelling to Canterbury. Many of the stories seem to fit their individual characters and social standing; the innkeeper shares the name of a contemporary keeper of an inn in Southwark, and real-life identities for the Wife of Bath, the Merchant, the Man of Law and the Student have been suggested.

Incomplete as they are, these tales cover practically all the major types of medieval literature; courtly romance, folk tale, beast fable, story of travel and adventure, saint's life, allegorical tale, sermon, alchemical account, and others. Taking the stand of the rising bourgeoisie, Chaucer affirms men and women's right to pursue their happiness on earth and opposes the dogma of asceticism preached by the church. As a forerunner of humanism, he praises man's energy, intellect, quick wit and love of life. His tales expose and satirize the evils of the time. *The Canterbury Tales* is considered to be among the masterpieces of literature.

The Prologue provides a framework for the tales. It contains a group of vivid sketches of typical medieval figures. It supplies a miniature of the English society of Chaucer's time. Looking at his word-pictures, we know at once how people lived in that era. That is why Chaucer has been called "the founder of English realism".

Selected Reading

The Canterbury Tales
The Prologue[①]

<blockquote>
When in April the sweet showers fall
And pierce the drought of March to the root[②], and all
The veins are bathed in liquor of such power[③]
As brings about the engendering of the flower[④],
</blockquote>

---

①prologue[IELTS]：序言

②pierce... to the root：The gentle spring rain penetrates the very roots of the plants

③bathed in liquor of such power：liquor, 甘霖。The water of the spring rain moistening every rib of the leaves and endowing the plants with its power

④As brings about the engendering of the flower：engendering, 生长；发芽。With the power of the water, flowers begin to blossom

When also Zephyrus① with his sweet breath

Exhales② an air in every grove and heath③

Upon the tender shoots④, and the young sun⑤

His half-course in the sign of the Ram has run,

And the small fowl⑥ are making melody

That sleep away the night with open eye

(So nature pricks them and their heart engages⑦)

Then people long to go on pilgrimages

And palmers⑧ long to seek the stranger strands⑨

Of far-off saints, hallowed⑩ in sundry⑪ lands,

And specially, from every shire's end⑫

Of England, down to Canterbury⑬ they wend⑭

To seek the holy blissful martyr⑮, quick

To give his help to them when they were sick,

It happened in that season that one day

---

①Zephyrus: the west wind, 西风（在英国，春天里西风从大西洋上吹来，是温暖和煦的。）

②exhale: 呼出；吐出

③grove and heath: 树林和荒地

④shoots: 新芽

⑤the young sun/ His half-course in the sign of the Ram has run: Ram, 白羊宫，古代用于解释天体运行的黄道带十二宫中的一个。太阳经过白羊宫时正是春天，所以称太阳为 the young sun

⑥fowl: [复数]鸟

⑦So nature ... engages: So nature stimulates them and attracts their hearts

⑧palmers: 朝圣者；香客

⑨the strange strands: 异乡的海岸

⑩hallowed: 被奉为神圣的

⑪sundry: 各种各样的

⑫from every shire's end: from the farthest limit of every county

⑬Canterbury: 坎特伯雷。a town southeast of London, in the county of Kent

⑭wend: 行；走

⑮the holy blissful martyr: martyr, 殉道者，指坎特伯雷大主教 St. Thomas Becket, 他死后被葬于坎特伯雷

In Southwark①, at The Tabard, as I lay

Ready to go on pilgrimages and start

For Canterbury, most devout at heart,

At night there came into that hostelry②

Some nine and twenty in a company

Of sundry folk happening then to fall

In fellowship, and they were pilgrims all

That towards Canterbury meant to ride,

The rooms and stables of the inn were wide;

They made us easy; all was of the best,

And, briefly, when the sun had gone to rest,

I'd spoken to them all upon the trip

And was soon one with them in fellowship,

Pledged③ to rise early and to take the way

To Canterbury, as you heard me say.

But none the less, while I have time and space,

Before my story takes a further pace,

It seems a reasonable thing to say

What their condition was, the full array

Of each of them, as it appeared to me,

According to profession and degree④,

And what apparel⑤ they were riding in;

And at a Knight I therefore will begin.

---

①Southwark：当时伦敦的一个郊区
②hostelry：inn，旅店；客栈。这里指 Tabard
③pledged：发誓
④degree：社会地位
⑤apparel：服饰

Questions for Discussion

1. What is the importance of "The General Prologue" in *The Canterbury Tales*?
2. What are Chaucer's contributions to English literature and the English language?
3. Give a brief analysis of the quotation.

> When in April the sweet showers fall
> And pierce the drought of March to the root, and all
> The veins are bathed in liquor of such power
> As brings about the engendering of the flower,
> When also Zephyrus with his sweet breath
> Exhales an air in every grove and heath
> Upon the tender shoots, and the young sun
> His half-course in the sign of the Ram has run,
> And the small fowl are making melody
> That sleep away the night with open eye
> (So nature pricks them and their heart engages)
> Then people long to go on pilgrimages
> And palmers long to seek the stranger strands
> Of far-off saints, hallowed in sundry lands,
> And specially, from every shire's end
> Of England, down to Canterbury they wend
> To seek the holy blissful martyr, quick
> To give his help to them when they were sick.

Unit 2 Thomas Malory

Appreciation

King Arthur turned back the powers of darkness and raised the morale of his compatriots.
——William of Malmesbury

永远不蛮横无理,永远不滥杀无辜,永远不背信弃义;为人不可残暴,要宽恕那些乞求宽恕的人;对于贵妇、少女以及一切有身份的女人,都应该鼎力相助,否则处以极刑;任何人不得无视法律,不得为了世间财富与人争斗。尚义气、重然诺、见义勇为、慷慨大方、抑恶扬善、嫉恶如仇、彬彬有礼。

——马洛礼,摘自《亚瑟之死》

Author

Sir Thomas Malory was an English writer, the author or compiler of *Le Morte D'Arthur*, the classic English-language chronicle of the Arthurian legend, published by William Caxton in 1485. He likely wrote *Le Morte D'Arthur* (*The Death of Arthur*) based on Arthurian mythology, the first major work of English language prose. The entire work is eight romances that span twenty-one books with 507 chapters, which was said to be considerably shorter than the original French sources, despite its vast size. Malory was responsible for organizing these diverse sources and consolidating them into a cohesive whole

Brief Introduction

Le Morte D'Arthur (originally spelled *Le Morte Darthur*, ungrammatical Middle French for "The Death of Arthur") is a 15th-century Middle English prose reworking by Sir Thomas Malory of tales about the legendary King Arthur, Guinevere, Lancelot,

Merlin and the Knights of the Round Table—along with their respective folklore. Today, this is one of the best-known works of Arthurian literature. Many authors since the 19th-century revival of the legend have used Malory as their principal source.

Selected Reading

The Death of Arthur

BOOK XVII Chapter 19

So departed he from thence, and commended the brethren to God; and so he rode five days till that he came to the Maimed King. And ever followed Percivale the five days, asking where he had been; and so one told him how the adventures of Logris were enchieved. So on a day it befell that they came out of a great forest, and there they met at traverse with Sir Bors, the which rode alone. It is none need to tell if they were glad; and them he saluted, and they yielded him honour and good adventure, and everych told other. Then said Bors: It is mo than a year and a half that I ne lay ten times where men dwelled①, but in wild forests and in mountains, but God was ever my comfort.

Then rode they a great while till that they came to the castle of Carbonek. And when they were entered within the castle King Pelles knew them; then there was great joy, for they wist well by their coming that they had fulfilled the quest of the Sangreal②. Then Eliazar, King Pelles' son, brought to-fore them the broken sword wherewith Joseph was stricken through the thigh. Then Bors set his hand thereto, if that he might have soldered it again; but it would not be. Then he took it to Percivale, but he had no more power thereto than he. Now have ye it again, said Percivale to Galahad, for an it be ever enchieved by any bodily man ye must do it. And then he took the pieces and set them together,

---

①dwell[IELTS][TOEFL]:居住;栖息
②sangreal:圣杯;圣血

and they seemed that they had never been broken, and as well as it had been first forged. And when they within espied that the adventure of the sword was enchieved, then they gave the sword to Bors, for it might not be better set; for he was a good knight and a worthy man.

And a little afore even the sword arose great and marvellous[①], and was full of great heat that many men fell for dread. And anon alighted a voice among them, and said: They that ought not to sit at the table of Jesu Christ arise, for now shall very knights be fed. So they went thence, all save King Pelles and Eliazar, his son, the which were holy men, and a maid which was his niece; and so these three fellows and they three were there, no mo. Anon they saw knights all armed came in at the hall door, and did off their helms and their arms, and said unto Galahad: Sir, we have hied right much for to be with you at this table where the holy meat shall be departed. Then said he: Ye be welcome, but of whence be ye? So three of them said they were of Gaul, and other three said they were of Ireland, and the other three said they were of Denmark. So as they sat thus there came out a bed of tree, of a chamber, the which four gentlewomen brought; and in the bed lay a good man sick, and a crown of gold upon his head; and there in the midst of the place they set him down, and went again their way. Then he lift up his head, and said: Galahad, Knight, ye be welcome, for much have I desired your coming, for in such pain and in such anguish I have been long. But now I trust to God the term is come that my pain shall be allayed[②], that I shall pass out of this world so as it was promised me long ago. Therewith a voice said: There be two among you that be not in the quest of the Sangreal, and therefore depart ye.

Chapter 20

Then King Pelles and his son departed[③]. And therewithal beseemed them

---

①marvellous[IELTS]:极好的;非凡的
②allay:减轻(情绪方面)
③depart[IELTS][TOEFL]:离开;启程

that there came a man, and four angels from heaven, clothed in likeness of a bishop, and had a cross in his hand; and these four angels bare him up in a chair, and set him down before the table of silver where upon the Sangreal was; and it seemed that he had in midst of his forehead letters the which said: See ye here Joseph, the first bishop of Christendom, the same which Our Lord succoured① in the city of Sarras in the spiritual place. Then the knights marvelled, for that bishop was dead more than three hundred year to-fore. O knights, said he, marvel not, for I was sometime an earthly man. With that they heard the chamber door open, and there they saw angels; and two bare candles of wax, and the third a towel, and the fourth a spear which bled marvelously, that three drops fell within a box which he held with his other hand. And they set the candles upon the table, and the third the towel upon the vessel, and the fourth the holy spear even upright upon the vessel. And then the bishop made semblaunt as though he would have gone to the sacring of the mass. And then he took an ubblie which was made in likeness of bread. And at the lifting up there came a figure in likeness of a child, and the visage was as red and as bright as any fire, and smote himself into the bread, so that they all saw it that the bread was formed of a fleshly man; and then he put it into the Holy Vessel again, and then he did that longed to a priest to do to a mass. And then he went to Galahad and kissed him, and bade him go and kiss his fellows: and so he did anon. Now, said he, servants of Jesu Christ, ye shall be fed afore this table with sweet meats that never knights tasted. And when he had said, he vanished② away. And they set them at the table in great dread, and made their prayers.

Then looked they and saw a man come out of the Holy Vessel, that had all the signs of the passion of Jesu Christ, bleeding all openly, and said: My knights, and my servants, and my true children, which be come out of deadly life into spiritual life, I will now no longer hide me from you, but ye shall see

---

①succour:救助;救援
②vanish[IELTS][TOEFL]:消亡;绝迹

now a part of my secrets and of my hidden things: now hold and receive the high meat which ye have so much desired. Then took he himself the Holy Vessel and came to Galahad; and he kneeled down, and there he received his Saviour, and after him so received all his fellows; and they thought it so sweet that it was marvelous to tell. Then said he to Galahad: Son, wottest thou what I hold betwixt my hands? Nay, said he, but if ye we will tell me. This is, said he, the holy dish wherein I ate the lamb on Sheer Thursday. And now hast thou seen that thou most desired to see, but yet hast thou not seen it so openly as thou shalt see it in the city of Sarras in the spiritual place. Therefore thou must go hence and bear with thee this Holy Vessel; for this night it shall depart from the realm of Logris, that it shall never be seen more here. And wottest thou wherefore? For he is not served nor worshipped to his right by them of this land, for they be turned to evil living; therefore I shall disherit them of the honour which I have done them. And therefore go ye three to-morrow unto the sea, where ye shall find your ship ready, and with you take the sword with the strange girdles①, and no more with you but Sir Percivale and Sir Bors. Also I will that ye take with you of the blood of this spear for to anoint the Maimed King, both his legs and all his body, and he shall have his health. Sir, said Galahad, why shall not these other fellows go with us? For this cause: for right as I departed my apostles② one here and another there, so I will that ye depart; and two of you shall die in my service, but one of you shall come again and tell tidings. Then gave he them his blessing and vanished away.

Chapter 21

And Galahad went anon to the spear which lay upon the table, and touched the blood with his fingers, and came after to the Maimed King and anointed his legs. And therewith he clothed him anon, and start upon his feet out of his bed

---

①girdle：束缚物；腰带
②apostle：宗徒；使徒

as a whole man, and thanked Our Lord that He had healed him. And that was not to the worldward, for anon he yielded① him to a place of religion of white monks, and was a full holy man. That same night about midnight came a voice among them which said: My sons and not my chief sons, my friends and not my warriors, go ye hence where ye hope best to do and as I bade② you. Ah, thanked' be Thou, Lord, that Thou wilt vouchsafe to call us, Thy sinners. Now may we well prove that we have not lost our pains. And anon in all haste they took their harness and departed. But the three knights of Gaul, one of them hight Claudine, King Claudas' son, and the other two were great gentlemen. Then prayed Galahad to everych of them, that if they come to King Arthur's court that they should salute my lord, Sir Launcelot, my father, and all the fellowship of the Round Table; and prayed them if that they came on that part that they should not forget it.

Right so departed Galahad, Percivale and Bors with him; and so they rode three days, and then they came to a rivage, and found the ship whereof the tale speaketh of 1 So W. de Worde; Caxton "of them."

to-fore. And when they came to the board they found in the midst the table of silver which they had left with the Maimed King, and the Sangreal which was covered with red samite. Then were they glad to have such things in their fellowship; and so they entered and made great reverence③ thereto; and Galahad fell in his prayer long time to Our Lord, that at what time he asked, that he should pass out of this world. So much he prayed till a voice said to him: Galahad, thou shalt have thy request; and when thou askest the death of thy body thou shalt have it, and then shalt thou find the life of the soul. Percivale heard this, and prayed him, of fellowship that was between them, to tell him wherefore he asked such things. That shall I tell you, said Galahad; the other

---

①yield[IELTS][TOEFL]:屈服;产量
②bid[IELTS]:告辞;再见;出价
③reverence:尊敬;崇敬

day when we saw a part of the adventures of the Sangreal I was in such a joy of heart, that I trow① never man was that was earthly. And therefore I wot well, when my body is dead my soul shall be in great joy to see the blessed Trinity every day, and the majesty of Our Lord, Jesu Christ.

So long were they in the ship that they said to Galahad: Sir, in this bed ought ye to lie, for so saith the scripture. And so he laid him down and slept a great while; and when he awaked he looked afore him and saw the city of Sarras. And as they would have landed they saw the ship wherein Percivale had put his sister in. Truly, said Percivale, in the name of God, well hath my sister holden us covenant. Then took they out of the ship the table of silver, and he took it to Percivale and to Bors, to go to-fore, and Galahad came behind. And right so they went to the city, and at the gate of the city they saw an old man crooked. Then Galahad called him and bade him help to bear this heavy thing. Truly, said the old man, it is ten year ago that I might not go but with crutches. Care thou not, said Galahad, and arise up and shew thy good will. And so he assayed, and found himself as whole as ever he was. Than ran he to the table, and took one part against Galahad. And anon arose there great noise in the city, that a cripple② was made whole by knights marvellous that entered into the city.

Chapter 22

But as soon as they were there Our Lord sent them the Sangreal, through whose grace they were always fulfilled while that they were in prison. So at the year's end it befell that this King Estorause lay sick, and felt that he should die. Then he sent for the three knights, and they came afore him; and he cried them mercy of that he had done to them, and they forgave it him goodly; and he died anon. When the king was dead all the city was dismayed③, and wist not who might be their king. Right so as they were in counsel there came a voice among

---

①trow:相信
②cripple[TOEFL]:残疾人;跛脚
③dismay[TOEFL]:诧异;灰心

them, and bade them choose the youngest knight of them three to be their king: For he shall well maintain you and all yours. So they made Galahad king by all the assent of the holy city, and else they would have slain him. And when he was come to behold the land, he let make above the table of silver a chest of gold and of precious stones, that hilled the Holy Vessel. And every day early the three fellows would come afore it, and make their prayers.

Now at the year's end, and the self day after Galahad had borne the crown of gold, he arose up early and his fellows, and came to the palace, and saw tofore them the Holy Vessel, and a man kneeling on his knees in likeness of a bishop, that had about him a great fellowship of angels, as it had been Jesu Christ himself; and then he arose and began a mass of Our Lady. And when he came to the sacrament① of the mass, and had done, anon he called Galahad, and said to him: Come forth the servant of Jesu Christ, and thou shalt see that thou hast much desired to see. And then he began to tremble right hard when the deadly flesh began to behold the spiritual things. Then he held up his hands toward heaven and said: Lord, I thank thee, for now I see that that hath been my desire many a day. Now, blessed Lord, would I not longer live, if it might please thee, Lord. And therewith the good man took Our Lord's body betwixt his hands, and proffered it to Galahad, and he received it right gladly and meekly. Now wottest thou what I am? said the good man. Nay, said Galahad. I am Joseph of Aramathie, the which Our Lord hath sent here to thee to bear thee fellowship; and wottest thou wherefore that he hath sent me more than any other? For thou hast resembled me in two things; in that thou hast seen the marvels of the Sangreal, in that thou hast been a clean maiden, as I have been and am.

And when he had said these words Galahad went to Percivale and kissed him, and commended him to God; and so he went to Sir Bors and kissed him,

---

①dismay[TOEFL]:诧异;灰心

and commended him to God, and said: Fair lord, salute me to my lord, Sir Launcelot, my father, and as soon as ye see him, bid him remember of this unstable world. And therewith he kneeled①down to-fore the table and made his prayers, and then suddenly his soul departed to Jesu Christ, and a great multitude of angels bare his soul up to heaven, that the two fellows might well behold it. Also the two fellows saw come from heaven an hand, but they saw not the body. And then it came right to the Vessel, and took it and the spear, and so bare it up to heaven. Sithen was there never man so hardy to say that he had seen the Sangreal.

Chapter 23

When Percivale and Bors saw Galahad dead they made as much sorrow as ever did two men. And if they had not been good men they might lightly have fallen in despair. And the people of the country and of the city were right heavy. And then he was buried; and as soon as he was buried Sir Percivale yielded him to a hermitage out of the city, and took a religious clothing. And Bors was alway with him, but never changed he his secular clothing, for that he purposed him to go again into the realm of Logris. Thus a year and two months lived Sir Percivale in the hermitage② a full holy life, and then passed out of this world; and Bors let bury him by his sister and by Galahad in the spiritualities

When Bors saw that he was in so far countries as in the parts of Babylon he departed from Sarras, and armed him and came to the sea, and entered into a ship; and so it befell him in good adventure he came into the realm of Logris; and he rode so fast till he came to Camelot where the king was. And then was there great joy made of him in the court, for they weened all he had been dead, forasmuch as he had been so long out of the country. And when they had eaten, the king made great clerks to come afore him, that they should chronicle③of the

---

①kneel[IELTS]:跪着
②hermitage:隐居处;修道院
③chronicle:编年史

high adventures of the good knights. When Bors had told him of the adventures of the Sangreal, such as had befallen him and his three fellows, that was Launcelot, Percivale, Galahad, and himself, there Launcelot told the adventures of the Sangreal that he had seen. All this was made in great books, and put up in almeries at Salisbury. And anon Sir Bors said to Sir Launcelot: Galahad, your own son, saluted you by me, and after you King Arthur and all the court, and so did Sir Percivale, for I buried① them with mine own hands in the city of Sarras. Also, Sir Launcelot, Galahad prayed you to remember of this unsiker world as ye behight him when ye were together more than half a year. This is true, said Launcelot; now I trust to God his prayer shall avail me.

Then Launcelot took Sir Bors in his arms, and said: Gentle cousin, ye are right welcome to me, and all that ever I may do for you and for yours ye shall find my poor body ready at all times, while the spirit is in it, and that I promise you faithfully, and never to fail. And wit ye well, gentle cousin, Sir Bors, that ye and I will never depart asunder whilst our lives may last. Sir, said he, I will as ye will.

Questions for Discussion

1. Discuss the hidden meaning of the Holy Grail.
2. Discuss the characteristics of King Arthur.

Terms

1. Epic
2. Lambic pentameter
3. Heroic couplet
4. Alliteration

---

①bury[IELTS]:埋葬;安葬

5. English Ballads

6. Middle Ages

7. Romance

Chapter 2

English Literature in the Renaissance

I. Historical Background

In 1485, the Wars of Roses came to an end, and in 1492, Christopher Columbus's voyage to the America opened European eyes to the existence of the New World. New Worlds, both geographical and spiritual, are the key to the Renaissance, the rebirth of learning and culture, which reached the peak in Italy in the early sixteenth century and in Britain during the reign of Queen Elizabeth from 1558 to 1603.

1. The Reformation

England emerged from the Wars of Roses with a new dynasty in power, the Tudors. The greatest of the Tudor monarchs was Henry VIII (1509 – 1547) who established himself as both the head of Church and the head of state. England became Protestant, and the nation's political and religious identity had to be redefined.

2. The Reign of Queen Elizabeth I

Elizabeth Tudor, 7 September, 1533 – 24 March, 1603, the last Tudor monarch, was the daughter of Henry VIII and Anne Boleyn, his second wife, who was executed two and a half years after Elizabeth's birth. During Mary's reign, Elizabeth was imprisoned for nearly a year on suspicion of supporting Protestant rebels. In 1558, Elizabeth succeeded her half-sister to the throne and set out to rule by good counsel. Elizabeth's 45-year reign, known as the Elizabethan era, is generally considered one of the most glorious in English history.

Elizabeth was very well-educated and inherited intelligence, determination and shrewdness from both parents. She used her notoriously sharp tongue to settle any argument, usually in her favour. Her indecisiveness often infuriated her ministers; when faced with a difficult decision, she would busy herself with other matters for months on end. It could be argued that her legendary indecision helped to delay the inevitable and expensive war with Spain for many years, but history regards her as a wise ruler.

Elizabeth established an English church that helped shape a national identity and remains in place today but there were constant threats, plots and potential rebellions agaist her. Many Protestant extremists left the country for religious reasons to set up the first colony in Virginia and Pennsylvania, the beginnings of another New World. Elizabeth's reign did give the nation some sense of stability, national and religious triumph when the Spanish Armada, the fleet of the Catholic King Philip of Spain, was defeated in 1588.

Elizabeth followed a largely defensive foreign policy, and her reign raised England's status abroad. She believed that God was protecting her. Elizabeth chose never to marry. Elizabeth herself refused to make windows into men's souls. There is only one Jesus Christ and all the rest is a dispute over trifles. Elizabeth used her marriage prospects as a political tool in foreign and domestic policies. However, the Virgin Queen was presented as a selfless woman who sacrificed personal happiness for the good of the nation. The image of Elizabeth's reign is one of triumph and success.

She died at Richmond Palace on 24 March, 1603, having become a legend in her lifetime. The date of her accession was a national holiday for two hundred years. The arts flourished during Elizabeth's reign. The Elizabethan era is recorded in history as a time of great poets and writers such as Edmund Spenser, William Shakespeare and Christopher Marlowe; great adventurers like Sir Francis Drake and Sir Walter Raleigh; and also as an era of great statesmen.

3. Economic Movements

With this growth in wealth and political importance of the nation, London developed as the capital, and from the foundation of the first public theatre in London, the stage became the forum of debate, spectacle, and entertainment. The writer took his work to an audience, including the Queen herself and the lowliest of the subjects. With the growth in theatrical expression, the growth of Modern English went as a national language. Country houses such as Longleat and Hardwick Hall were built, miniature painting reached its high point, theatres thrived—the Queen attended the first performance of Shakespeare's *A Midsummer Night's Dream*.

The political and religious confusion of the age were the reflection of the changes of the national economy in England which developed at a slow but steady pace. With the Enclosure Movement from the 15th century on, England developed from a mere producer of wool to a manufacturer of cloth, which stimulated the development of the clothing industry on a capitalist line; also it produced helpless, dispossessed peasants who became hired labour for merchants.

4. The Renaissance

Renaissance refers to the period between the 14th and mid-17th century in western civilization and the movement marks the transition from the medieval to the modern world. It first started in Florence and Venice of Italy and went to embrace the rest of Europe, with the flowering of painting, sculpture and architecture.

The word "Renaissance", which means rebirth or revival, is usually regarded as the result of an emphasis upon the discovered Greek and Roman classics and the combination or compromise of a newly interpreted Christian tradition and an admired tradition of pagan classical culture, which was stimulated by a series of historical events, such as the rediscovery of ancient Roman and Greek culture, the new discoveries in geography and astronomy, the religious reformation and the economic expansion. Two striking features of Renaissance: People had a thirsting curiosity for the classical literature; the keen interest in the activities of humanity arose.

II. Literary Background

1. The Beginning of the English Renaissance

Renaissance was a cultural and artistic movement but its style and ideas were slow in penetrating England. In the days of Henry VIII, a group of scholars called Oxford Reformers introduced the classical literature to England and strove to reform education on a humanistic line. These English humanists were all churchmen, and the greatest was Thomas More, the author of *Utopia*, which may be thought of as the first literary masterpiece of the English Renaissance.

During the reign of Elizabeth I and then James I (1603 – 1625), a London-centred culture, both courtly and popular, produced great poetry and drama. The

Chapter 2 English Literature in the Renaissance

greatest and most distinctive achievement of Elizabethan literature is the drama. Christopher Marlowe was the greatest playwright before Shakespeare and the most gifted of the "University Wits".

2. The height of the English Renaissance—the Elizabethan era

English literature in the Renaissance Period is usually regarded as the highlight in the history of English literature. After 1588, the flourishing period of English drama arrived, and the summit was Shakespeare's works. Other important figures in Elizabethan theatre include Christopher Marlowe, Ben Jonson, Thomas Dekker, John Fletcher and Francis Beaumont.

English literature developed with a great speed and made a magnificent achievement. Marlowe's subject focuses on the moral drama of the Renaissance man. He introduced the story of *Faust* to England in his play *Doctor Faustus*, which is about a scientist and magician who, obsessed by the thirst of knowledge and the desire to push man's technological power to its limits, sells his soul to the Devil. *Faustus* makes use of "the dramatic framework of the morality plays the story of temptation, fall, and damnation, and its free use of morality figures such as the good angel and the bad angel and the seven deadly sins, along with the devils Lucifer and Mephistopheles." Marlowe first made blank verse (unrhymed iambic pentameter) the principal instrument of English drama.

Elizabethan lyrical poetry is remarkable for its variety, its freshness, its youthfulness and its romantic feeling. A group of great poets appeared, and a large number of noble poetry was produced. In that period, writing poetry became a fashion. England then became "a nest of singing birds".

Edmund Spenser is often referred to as "the poets' poet", who is the author of *The Faerie Queene*, an epic poem and fantastical allegory celebrating the Tudor dynasty and Elizabeth Ⅰ. He is generally acknowledged to be the greatest non-dramatic poet of the Elizabethan Age. Spenser employs the archaic language of Chaucer but the modern pronunciation of the Renaissance and the biblical allegory poem to tell his story, whose purpose is to educate, to turn a young man into a gentleman. Spenser influenced many of the poets who followed him, including John Milton, Percy Shelley, John Keats, Lord Byron, and Lord Tennyson.

Francis Bacon wrote more than fifty excellent essays, which make him one of the best essayists in English.

Unit 1　Edmund Spenser

Author

Edmund Spenser ranks as the foremost English poet of the 16th century in the Elizabethan age. He is recognized as one of the premier craftsmen of Modern English verse, and one of the greatest poets in the English language, and his work reflects the religious and humanistic ideals as well as the intense but critical patriotism of Elizabethan England. His contributions to English literature—in the form of a heightened and enlarged poetic vocabulary, a charming and flexible verse style, and a rich fusing of the philosophic and literary currents of the English Renaissance—entitle him to a rank not far removed from that of William Shakespeare and John Milton.

Spenser was the son of a London tailor, but his family seems to have had its origins in Lancashire. The poet was admitted to the newly founded Merchant Taylors' School in about 1561 as a "poor scholar". The curriculum at Mulcaster's school included Latin, Greek, and Hebrew; music and drama were stressed; the English language was also a subject of study—then a novelty. In 1569 he went to Cambridge, where he entered Pembroke College as a sizar (a student who earns his tuition by acting as a servant to wealthy students). Spenser's health was poor but he had an excellent reputation as a student. He studied Italian, French, Latin, and Greek; read widely in classical literature and in the poetry of the modern languages; and authored some Latin verse. He read Plato and Aristotle and was influenced by Puritan moral beliefs. Though Spenser strove to emulate such ancient Roman poets as Virgil and Ovid, many of his best-known works are notably divergent from those of his predecessors. The language of his poetry is purposely archaic, reminiscent of earlier works such as *The Canterbury Tales* of Geoffrey Chaucer and Ⅱ *Canzoniere* of Francesco Petrarca. His works includes *The Shepheardes Calender*, *The Faerie Queene*, *Amoretti*.

Famous as the author of the unfinished epic poem, he is the poet of an ordered yet passionate Elizabethan world. *The Faerie Queene* is a masterpiece of English literature written in the Spenserian stanza. The Elizabethans hailed him as their "Prince of Poets". Edmund Spenser is the most outstanding poet who lived between the age of Chaucer and that of Shakespeare.

★ **The Spenserian stanza and sonnet**

Spenser used a distinctive verse form, called the Spenserian stanza, in several works including *The Faerie Queene*. The stanza's main meter is iambic pentameter with a final line in iambic hexameter (having six feet or stresses, known as an Alexandrine), and the rhyme scheme is ababbcbcc. He also used his own rhyme scheme for the sonnet.

The chief qualities of Spenser's poetry: a perfect melody, a rare sense of beauty, a splendid imagination, a lofty moral purity and seriousness, and a dedicated idealism. In addition, Spenser uses strange forms of speech and obsolete words in order to increase the rustic effect.

Brief Introduction

The Faerie Queene is an English epic and fantastical allegory celebrating the Tudor dynasty and Elizabeth I, which is a vast patriotic celebration of English culture set in a mystical fairy tale world.

Spenser gives the allegorical presentation of virtues through Arthurian knights in the mythical "Faerieland". Arthur represents the virtue of Magnificence and *the Faerie Queene* herself represents Glory (hence her name Gloriana). At last spenser only managed to cover six of the virtues: Holiness, Temperament, Chastity, Friendship, Justice, and Courtesy. The incomplete seventh book appears to represent the virtue of Consistency.

The selection from Book I of *The Faerie Queene* illustrates the virtue of Holiness, telling the tale of Red Cross Knight of Holiness, and reveals his virtue through adventures to protect the Virgin Una, and relieve her kingdom from a menacing dragon. He sets out on the orders of the Glorious Queen of Faerie to kill the dragon who has imprisoned Una's parents. Una accompanies him, concealing her face behind a veil to keep her dazzling beauty. She mounts on a donkey and leads by a cord a milk-white lamb. They are made victims by the subtle tricks of the devil himself. The Red Cross Knight kills Sansfoy (without faith), but is deceived by false Fidessa, whose real name is Dussa, symbol of sin. The Knight manages to escape her seduction. However, Una is taken prisoner by Sansloy and left for a moment at mercy of his rage and lust. At the mansion of Lucifer, a daughter of Pluto and Porserpina, he fights a fierce battle with Sansjoy and is tricked by Duessa into a luckless combat with the giant Orgoglio, who represents fleshly and irrational presumption and diabolical vainglory. King Arthur comes and rescues him from the dragon's place at this crucial moment. Book I ends with the happy marriage between Una and the Red Cross Knight.

Spenser's aim was to "fashion a gentleman or noble person in virtuous and gentle discipline", including elements of the romance of chivalry, the handbook of manners and morals, and the national epic.

Canto 1

Archimago has escaped from his imprisonment and is intent on revenge upon Redcrosse. When he meets the knight Guyon and his squire, Palmer, Archimago tells that a wicked knight who bears the cross of Christ on his shield has just recently attacked a virgin and is intent on despoiling her. During the journey, they meet the alleged virgin who is actually Duessa in disguise. She confirms Archimago's story, inflaming Guyon to righteous anger, finally they encounter Redcrosse. Guyon balks at attacking a knight bearing a red cross. The two knights become friends.

Later, they meet Amavia who stabs herself in the chest as they approach but find the woman holding a newborn baby and lying next to the body of a dead man, and her husband Mordant who was seduced by Acrasia. The enchantress lures men to her Bower of Bliss with the promise of sex and magically turns them into beasts. Mordant is able to free himself of the enchantment, but Acrasia exerts revenge upon him by poisoning him, and finally she dies in Guyon's arms.

Selected Reading

The Faerie Queene

1
A Gentle Knight was pricking① on the plain,

---

①prick: 鞭策，策马

Clad in mighty arms and sliver shield,
Wherein old dints① of deep wounds did remain,
The cruel marks of many a bloody field;
Yet arms② till that time did he never wield③:
His angry steed④ did chide⑤ his foaming bitt⑥,
As much disdaining to the curb⑦ to yield:
Full jolly⑧ knight he seemed, and fair did sit,
As one for knightly joust⑨ and fierce encounters fit.

2

But on his breast a bloody Cross he bore,
The dear remembrance of his dying Lord,
For whose sweet sake that glorious badge⑩ he wore,
And dead as living ever him adored⑪:
Upon his shield the like was also scored,
For soveraine⑫ hope, which in his help he had:
Right faithful true he was in deed and word,
But of his cheer did seem too solemn⑬ sad;
Yet nothing did he dread, but ever was dreaded⑭.

3

Upon a great adventure he was bond,

---

①dints：凹痕
②arms：武器，兵种
③wield[IELTS]：挥舞（剑等）
④steed：[诗]马，战马
⑤chide：斥责，责骂
⑥bitt：缆柱，系于缆柱
⑦curb[IELTS]：抑制
⑧jolly：欢乐的，高兴的，快活的
⑨joust：骑马用长矛打斗；持矛比武
⑩badge[IELTS]：徽章，证章
⑪adored[IELTS]：爱慕者，崇拜者
⑫soveraine：sovereign,至高无上的，君主的，独立自主的，完全的
⑬solemn[TOEFL][IELTS]：庄严的，隆重的，严肃的
⑭dread[TOEFL][IELTS]：恐惧，恐怖，可怕的人（或物），畏惧；惧怕，担心

That greatest Gloriana to him gave,
That greatest Glorious① Queen of Faerie Land,
To win him worship②, and her grace to have,
Which of all earthly things he most did crave③;
And ever as he rode, his heart did yearn
To prove his puissance④ in battle brave
Upon his foe⑤, and his new force to learn
Upon his foe, a Dragon horrible and stern⑥.

Questions for Discussion

1. What's the knight's name in this part?
   What does the knight stand for?
   The knight set out on his quest to rescue the parents of Una, a beautiful lady.
   What does she symbolize?
   Analyze the writing features of the poem.
2. What more than anything else on earth does the knight want?
3. What do we learn about the Lady?
4. Please briefly analyze Edmund Spenser's *The Faerie Queen*.
5. What was Spenser's primary purpose in writing *The Faerie Queene*?
6. How is the virtue of Holiness depicted in *The Faerie Queene*?

---

①Glorious[IELTS]:光荣的,显赫的
②worship[IELTS]:崇拜,礼拜,尊敬
③crave:恳求,渴望
④puissance:(马的)越障能力测试,<古>权力,权势,力量,影响
⑤foe:反对者,敌人,危害物
⑥stern[TOEFL][IELTS]:严厉的,苛刻的

Unit 2 William Shakespeare

Appreciation

To be, or not to be; that is the question: 生存还是毁灭，这是一个值得考虑的问题；
Whether 'tis nobler in the mind to suffer 这两种行为，哪一种更高贵？
The slings and arrows of outrageous fortune, 默然忍受命运的暴虐的毒箭，
Or to take arms against a sea of troubles, 或是挺身反抗人世的无涯的苦难，
And by opposing end them? 通过斗争把它们扫清？

Author

William Shakespeare is the greatest of all English authors and one of the greatest authors in world literature. He is generally considered the greatest dramatist in human history and the supreme poet of the English language.

Shakespeare was born in Stratford-on-Avon in 1564. He got education in a local grammar school for a few years. There he picked up "small Latin and less Greek". In 1582 Shakespeare married Anne Hathaway, the daughter of a peasant family, eight years older than her husband. A few years later, Shakespeare went to London and became an actor and a writer. During the twenty-two years of his literary career, he produced 37 plays, 154 sonnets and some long poems. Shakespeare wrote 11 tragedies: *Hamlet*, *Othello*, *King Lear*, and *Macbeth* and etc. All of these plays express a profound dissatisfaction with life. They show the struggle and conflicts between good and evil of the tune, between justice and injustice. In these plays, Shakespeare condemns the dark and evil society. Comedies are, *As You like It*, *The Merchants of Venice*, *Much Ado About Nothing*, *A Midsummer Night's Dream*. Histories are *Henry* Ⅳ, *Henry* Ⅴ, *Richard* Ⅱ, *Richard* Ⅲ, *Henry* Ⅷ.

In the 20th century, his works were repeatedly adopted and rediscovered by new movements in scholarship and performance. His plays remain highly popular today and are constantly studied, performed, and reinterpreted in diverse cultural and political contexts throughout the world.

Brief Introduction

Hamlet is Shakespeare's longest play and among the most powerful and influential tragedies in English literature. The protagonist of *Hamlet* is Prince Hamlet of Denmark, son of deceased King Hamlet and Queen Gertrude. The play dramatizes how Hamlet exerts revenge on his uncle Claudius, who has murdered Hamlet's father—the King, and then taken the throne and married Hamlet's mother.

Hamlet's character is one of virtue and integrity at the beginning of the play, fearing the consequences of his actions. As the play unfolds, Hamlet becomes more and more confused and his inner struggle seems to be getting worse. Hamlet finally wins the battle within himself, causing him to act against his own inhibitions to dutifully avenge the murder of his father. This speech connects many of the play's main themes, including the idea of suicide and death, the difficulty of knowing the truth in a spiritually ambiguous universe, and the connection between thought and action. In addition, this speech reveals the quality of Hamlet's mind. His deeply passionate nature is complemented by a relentlessly logical intellect, which works furiously to find a solution to his misery.

Selected Reading

Hamlet

Act III   Scene I

To be, or not to be[①]**; that is the question:**
Whether 'tis nobler in the mind to suffer
The slings and arrows of outrageous fortune,
Or to take arms against a sea of troubles,

---

① To be, or not to be: 生还是死, 生存还是死亡; 是反抗还是屈从; 是耐心地忍受这样的痛苦和折磨更显得高尚, 还是奋起反抗, 去终结给人带来痛苦和折磨的原因?

And by opposing end them? To die: to sleep;
No more; and by a sleep to say we end
The heart-ache and the thousand natural shocks
That flesh is heir to[①], 'tis a consummation[②]
Devoutly to be wish'd. To die, to sleep;
To sleep: perchance[③] to dream: ay, there's the rub[④];
For in that sleep of death what dreams may come
When we have shuffled off this mortal coil[⑤],
Must give us pause: there's the respect[⑥]
That makes calamity of so long life;
For who would bear the whips and scorns of time,
The oppressor's wrong, the proud man's contumely,
The pangs of despised love, the law's delay,
The insolence of office and the spurns
That patient merit of the unworthy takes,
When he himself might his quietus make
With a bare bodkin[⑦]? who would fardels[⑧] bear,
To grunt and sweat under a weary life,
But that the dread of something after death,
The undiscover'd country from whose bourn
No traveler returns, puzzles the will
And makes us rather bear those ills we have
Than fly to others that we know not of[⑨]?

---

①That flesh is heir to：人类注定要承受的苦难
②consummation：事件、生命的完成，终结
③perchance：也许
④rub：obstacle，阻拦、麻烦
⑤When we have shuffled off this mortal coil：当我们摈弃了这一切的人生烦恼
⑥respect：考虑
⑦With a bare bodkin：出鞘的匕首
⑧fardels：重负
⑨fly to others that we know not of：进入了我们不知道的地域（暗指死亡）

Thus conscience does make cowards of us all;
And thus the native hue of resolution①
Is sicklied② o'er with the pale cast of thought,
And enterprises of great pith③ and moment
With this regard their currents turn awry,
And lose the name of action. Soft you now!
The fair Ophelia! Nymph, in thy orisons
Be all my sins remember'd.

Questions for Discussion

1. What's the essence of Hamlet's most exhaustively discussed soliloquy "To be or not to be"? Write an essay with any topic of your choice.
2. Is Hamlet a frail and weak-minded youth? A thought-sick dreamer? A man active in thought but passive and slow in action? Why does he delay taking revenge for his father?
3. Examine Hamlet's passionate enumeration of life's calamity: "the whips and scorns of time" is parallel structure and antithecal structure: "To be or not to be". How does the language help present the sense of pain of life? Why would people rather bear suffering of the world instead of ending their life according to *Hamlet*?
4. Analyze Hamlet's character through this soliloquy and list the possible reasons for his melancholy and dely.
5. What is the theme of *Hamlet*?
6. Please ananlyze the image of *Hamlet*.
7. Suppose you were Hamlet, what would you do?

---

① the native hue of resolution: hue, n. 色调，样子，颜色。resolution, 坚定，决心，决定。西方通常认为脸色泛红表示人的坚强决心。这句话指人脸上表示决心的天然色晕
② sicklied: 受到损害；露出病态(指失去了表示决心的红晕)
③ enterprises of great pith: enterprise, 事业心，进取心。pith, (植物的)木髓，骨髓，重要部分。对崇高事业的追求

Appreciation

So long as men can breathe or eyes can see，只要人类还在呼吸、眼睛还在欣赏，
So long lives this and this gives life to thee. 这诗就将不朽，令你生命绽放。

Brief Introduction

Sonnet 18 deserves its classic because it is one of the most well-known out of all Shakespeare's 154 sonnets. In the sonnet, the speaker compares his beloved to the summer season, and argues that his beloved is better. He also states that his beloved will live on forever through the words of the poem. There is great use of imagery within the sonnet. The chosen subject matter, describing the theme of love, has created a remarkable longevity for this poem until these days.

Selected Reading

Sonnet 18

Shall I compare thee to a summer's day?
Thou art more lovely and more temperate①:
Rough winds do shake the darling buds of May,
And summer's lease② hath all too short a date:
Sometime too hot the eye of heaven shines,
And often is his gold complexion dimm'd;
And every fair from fair sometime declines③,
By chance or nature's changing course untrimm'd;
But thy eternal summer shall not fade
Nor lose possession of that fair thou owest;

---

①temperate[TOEFL][IELTS]:温和,柔和
②lease[TOEFL][IELTS]:租赁期。这里指夏天延续的时间
③every fair from fair sometime declines:第一个fair指"美貌之人",第二个fair广指"美貌"或"美丽"

Nor shall Death brag thou wander'st in his shade①,

When in eternal lines to time thou growe'st②:

So long as men can breathe or eyes can see,

So long lives this and this③ gives life to thee.

Questions for Discussion

1. Give a brief analysis of *Sonnet 18*.
2. What is the theme of *Sonnet 18*?

Appreciation

Time shall unfold what plighted cunning hides.

Who cover faults, at last shame them derides.

慢慢儿总有一天深藏的奸诈会显出它的原形；罪恶虽然可以掩饰一时，免不了最后出乖露丑。

——《李尔王》，朱生豪译

I yet beseech your Majesty,

If for I want that glib and oily art

To speak and purpose not, since what I well intend,

I'll do't before I speak—that you make known

It is no vicious blot, murther, or foulness,

No unchaste action or dishonoured step,

That hath depriv'd me of your grace and favour;

But even for want of that for which I am richer —

A still-soliciting eye, and such a tongue

As I am glad I have not, though not to have it

Hath lost me in your liking.

---

①Nor shall Death brag thou wander'st in his shade：死亡也无法夸口，无法把你纳入自己的阴影之下

②When in eternal lines to time thou growe'st：lines,诗人的诗行

③this："这",指"诗歌"

凡是我心里想到的事情,我总不愿在没有把它实行以前就放在嘴里宣扬;要是您因此而恼恨我,我必须请求您让世人知道,我所以失去您的欢心的原因,并不是什么丑恶的污点、淫邪的行动,或是不名誉的举止;只是因为我缺少像人家那样一双献媚求恩的眼睛,一条我所认为可耻的善于逢迎的舌头,虽然没有了这些使我不能再接受您的宠爱,可是唯其如此,却使我格外尊重我自己的人格。

——《李尔王》,朱生豪译

Brief Introduction

In this thrilling and hugely influential tragedy, aging King Lear decides to divide his kingdom between his three daughters (Goneril, Regan and Cordelia) according to the love they express for him. He blindly believes the lies of his two scheming older daughters and estranges himself from the one who truly loves him. Cordelia, the third and only daughter who refuses to flatter her father, is banished, but she wins the love of King of France. As the plot develops, not only does the king's own sanity crumble, but the stability of the realm itself is also threatened. Goneril and Regan turn on Lear, leaving him to wander madly in a furious storm.

Meanwhile, the Earl of Gloucester's illegitimate son Edmund turns Gloucester against his legitimate son, Edgar. Gloucester, appalled at the daughters' treatment of Lear, gets news that a French army is coming to help Lear. Edmund betrays Gloucester to Regan and her husband, Cornwall, who puts out Gloucester's eyes and makes Edmund the Earl of Gloucester.

Cordelia and the French army save Lear, but the army is defeated. Edmund imprisons Cordelia and Lear. Edgar then mortally wounds Edmund in a trial by combat. Dying, Edmund confesses that he has ordered the deaths of Cordelia and Lear. Before they can be rescued, Lear brings in Cordelia's body and then he himself dies.

As the honorable and beloved daughter of King Lear, Cordelia ranks among Shakespeare's finest heroines. Although Cordelia's role in the play is minor (appearing on stage only in the first and final act), she is ever-present in the minds of readers as the symbol of virtue and mercy, in stark contrast to her sisters, Goneril and Regan.

Selected Reading

King Lear

ACT I SCENE I

[King Lear's Palace.]

[Enter one bearing a coronet; then LEAR; then the DUKES OF ALBANY and CORNWALL; next, GONERIL, REGAN, CORDELIA, with Followers.]

LEAR. Attend① the lords of France and Burgundy, Gloucester.

EARL OF GlOUCESTER. I shall, my liege②.

[Exeunt Gloucester and Edmund].

LEAR. Meantime we shall express our darker purpose③.
Give me the map here. Know we have divided
In three our kingdom; and 'tis our fast intent④
To shake all cares and business⑤ from our age,
Conferring⑥ them on younger strengths while we
Unburthen'd crawl toward death. Our son of Cornwall,
And you, our no less loving son of Albany,
We have this hour a constant⑦ will to publish
Our daughters' several dowers⑧, that future strife⑨
May be prevented now. The princes, France and Burgundy,
Great rivals⑩ in our youngest daughter's love,

---

①attend：把……请来
②liege：君主,国王
③darker purpose：可以理解为暗中下定的主意或者心里话,undeclared intention
④fast intent：决意
⑤cares and business：琐事,烦恼
⑥confer：把权利或荣誉赠与某人
⑦constant：决意的
⑧several dowers：各自的嫁妆
⑨strife[GRE]：冲突,争斗,不和
⑩rivals[IELTS][TOEFL]：竞争对手

Chapter 2 English Literature in the Renaissance

Long in our court have made their amorous sojourn①,
And here are to be answer'd. Tell me, my daughters,——
Since now we will divest② us both of rule,
Interest③ of territory④, cares of state——
Which of you shall we say doth love us most?
That we our largest bounty may extend
Where nature doth with merit challenge. Goneril,
Our eldest-born, speak first.
GONERIL. Sir, I love you more than words can wield the matter⑤;
Dearer than eyesight, space⑥, and liberty;
Beyond what can be valued, rich or rare;
No less than life, with grace, health, beauty, honour;
As much as child e'er lov'd, or father found⑦;
A love that makes breath poor, and speech unable.
Beyond all manner of so much⑧ I love you.
CORDELIA. [Aside] What shall Cordelia speak? Love, and be silent.
LEAR. Of all these bounds⑨, even from this line to this,
With shadowy⑩ forests and with champains rich'd⑪,
With plenteous⑫ rivers and wide-skirted⑬ meads⑭,

---

①amorous sojourn：为了求婚而留在这里
②divest：剥夺
③interest：文中译为占有，权利
④territory[IELTS][TOEFL]：领土
⑤wield the matter：manage to express 表达
⑥space：the world 世界
⑦found：find 感受到
⑧all manner of so much：我爱你超过上述的一切品质，manner 品质
⑨bounds：疆界
⑩shadowy：浓密的
⑪champains rich'd：肥沃的原野
⑫plenteous：富饶的
⑬wide-skirted：广大的
⑭mead：牧场

We make thee lady. To thine and Albany's issue①

Be this perpetual.② What says our second daughter,

Our dearest Regan, wife to Cornwall? Speak.

REGAN. Sir, I am made Of the selfsame metal that my sister is,

And prize me at her worth③. In my true heart

I find she names my very deed of love;

Only she comes too short,④ that I profess

Myself an enemy to all other joys

Which the most precious square of sense possesses,

And find I am alone felicitate⑤

In your dear Highness' love.

CORDELIA. [Aside] Then poor Cordelia!

And yet not so; since I am sure my love's

More richer than my tongue.

LEAR. To thee and thine hereditary ever

Remain this ample third of our fair kingdom,

No less in space, validity⑥, and pleasure

Than that conferr'd on Goneril. – Now, our joy,

Although the last, not least; to whose young love

The vines⑦ of France and milk of Burgundy

Strive to be interest; what can you say to draw

A third more opulent⑧ than your sisters? Speak.

CORDELIA. Nothing, my lord.

LEAR. Nothing?

---

①issue[IELTS][TOEFL]:出版,发行;重要的议题,这里译为后代

②perpetual[IELTS][TOEFL]:永久的

③prize me at her worth:您凭着她就可以判断我

④only she comes too short:可是她还不能充分说明我的心理

⑤felicitate:使幸福,庆幸

⑥validity:价值

⑦vines:葡萄园

⑧opulent:富饶的

CORDELIA. Nothing.

LEAR. Nothing can come of nothing①. Speak again.

CORDELIA. Unhappy that I am, I cannot heave

My heart into my mouth②. I love your Majesty

According to my bond; no more nor less.

LEAR. How, how, Cordelia? Mend your speech a little,

Lest③ it may mar④ your fortunes.

CORDELIA. Good my lord, You have begot⑤ me, bred⑥ me, lov'd me; I

Return those duties back as are right fit,

Obey you, love you, and most honour you.

Why have my sisters husbands, if they say

They love you all?

Haply⑦, when I shall wed,

That lord whose hand must take my plight shall carry

Half my love with him, half my care and duty.

Sure I shall never marry like my sisters,

To love my father all.

LEAR. But goes thy heart with this?

CORDELIA. Ay, good my lord.

LEAR. So young, and so untender⑧?

CORDELIA. So young, my lord, and true.

---

①Nothing can come of nothing:无中不能生有

②My heart into my mouth:我不会把我的心涌上我的嘴里。这句台词来自:The heart of fools is in their mouth; but the mouth of the wise is in their heart. 愚者想什么说什么,智者先思考后发言

③lest:unless

④mar:损伤

⑤begot:beget 表示作为某人之父

⑥bred:breed 养育

⑦haply:可能

⑧untender:unkind,ungentle 不温柔的

LEAR. Let it be so! thy truth then be thy dower①:

For, by the sacred radiance② of the sun,

The mysteries of Hecate③ and the night;

By all the operation of the orbs④

From whom we do exist and cease to be;

Here I disclaim⑤ all my paternal care⑥,

Propinquity⑦ and property⑧ of blood,

And as a stranger to my heart and me

Hold thee from this for ever. The barbarous Scythian⑨,

Or he that makes his generation messes⑩

To gorge⑪ his appetite⑫, shall to my bosom

Be as well neighbour'd, pitied, and reliev'd⑬,

As thou my sometime daughter.

EARL OF KENT. Good my liege—

LEAR. Peace, Kent!

Come not between the dragon and his wrath⑭.

I lov'd her most, and thought to set my rest⑮

---

①dower:嫁妆

②sacred radiance:神圣的光辉

③Hecate:赫卡特,夜之女神,司魔法和巫术,代表了世界的阴暗面

④operation of the orbs:星球的运行。

⑤disclaim:放弃权利

⑥paternal care:父亲的照顾

⑦propinquity:亲近

⑧Property[IELTS][TOEFL]:财产

⑨Scythian:古代居住在黑海以北平原上的游牧民族

⑩messes:用膳,伙食

⑪gorge:塞饱,狼吞虎咽

⑫appetite[IELTS][TOEFL]:食欲

⑬reliev'd[IELTS][TOEFL]:relieve 抚慰,减轻痛苦

⑭Come not between the dragon and his wrath:不要来批怒龙的逆鳞

⑮set my rest:双关:将其余的土地交付与她;在她的看护之下颐养天年

On her kind nursery. Hence and avoid my sight①!
So be my grave my peace as here I give
Her father's heart from her! Call France! Who stirs②?
Call Burgundy! Cornwall and Albany,
With my two daughters' dowers digest③ this third;
Let pride, which she calls plainness, marry her.
I do invest④ you jointly in my power,
Preeminence⑤, and all the large effects⑥
That troop with⑦ majesty. Ourself, by monthly course⑧,
With reservation of an hundred knights,
By you to be sustain'd, shall our abode
Make with you by due turns. ⑨ Only we still retain
The name, and all th' additions⑩ to a king. The sway⑪,
Revenue⑫, execution⑬ of the rest,
Beloved sons, be yours; which to confirm,
This coronet part betwixt⑭ you.
EARL OF KENT. Royal Lear,

---

①avoid my sight:out of my sight, go away 走开

②Who stirs:Is there no one to move? 群臣都被李尔的狂怒惊呆了,一时竟无人去执行命令

③digest[IELTS][TOEFL]:消化,理解,这里译为接受,合并

④invest[IELTS][TOEFL]:投资,投入,这里译为给予

⑤preeminence:显赫

⑥large effects:君主的尊荣

⑦troop with:伴随着,连带着

⑧by monthly course:按月的

⑨With reservation of an hundred knights, By you to be sustain'd, shall our abode Make with you by due turns:我自己只保留一百名武士,在你们两人的地方按月轮流居住,由你们负责供养。reserve 保留,sustain 供养,维持

⑩additions:国王的名义和尊号

⑪sway:统治

⑫revenue[IELTS][TOEFL]:财政收入

⑬execution[IELTS][TOEFL]:实行,这里指行政

⑭part betwixt:divide between

Whom I have ever honour'd as my king,
Lov'd as my father, as my master follow'd,
As my great patron thought on in my prayers,—
LEAR. The bow is bent and drawn; make from the shaft①.
KENT. Let it fall rather, though the fork invade②
The region of my heart! Be Kent unmannerly
When Lear is mad③. What wouldst thou do④, old man?
Think'st thou that duty shall have dread to speak
When power to flattery bows?⑤ To plainness honour's bound
When majesty falls to folly.⑥ Reverse⑦ thy doom⑧;
And in thy best consideration check
This hideous rashness. Answer my life my judgment⑨,
Thy youngest daughter does not love thee least,
Nor are those empty-hearted whose low sound
Reverbs no hollowness.⑩
LEAR. Kent, on thy life⑪, no more!
EARL OF KENT. My life I never held but as a pawn⑫

---

①make from the shaft:躲开箭。李尔警告肯特不要干涉他的决定

②though the fork invade:即使箭会刺进我的心里。fork 带倒钩的箭头

③Kent unmannerly When Lear is mad:李尔发了疯,肯特也只好不顾礼貌了

④What wouldst thou do:what are you gong to do?

⑤Think'st thou that duty shall have dread to speak When power to flattery bows:你以为有权有位的人像谄媚者低头,尽忠职守的忠臣就不敢说话了吗?

⑥To plainness honour's bound When majesty falls to folly:君王不顾自己的尊严,干了愚蠢的事,在朝的端正人士只好直言进谏

⑦reverse[IELTS][TOEFL]:反转,撤销

⑧doom:判决,定罪

⑨Answer my life my judgment:我用生命为我的判断负责

⑩Nor are those empty-hearted whose low sound Reverbs no hollowness:有些人虽然声音低,发不出多少空空的闹音,但并非没有情义。参看谚语 Empty vessels make the most noise. 满瓶子不响,半瓶子晃荡

⑪on thy life:小心你的性命

⑫pawn:兵卒

Chapter 2　English Literature in the Renaissance

To wage① against thine enemies; nor fear to lose it,

Thy safety being the motive.

LEAR. Out of my sight!

EARL OF KENT. See better, Lear, and let me still remain

The true blank of thine eye②.

LEAR. Now by Apollo③—

EARL OF KENT. Now by Apollo, King,

Thou swear'st thy gods in vain.

LEAR. O vassal! miscreant!④ [Lays his hand on his sword.]

ALBANY & CORNWALL. Dear sir, forbear!

EARL OF KENT. Do;

Kill thy physician, and the fee bestow

Upon the foul disease.⑤ Revoke thy gift⑥,

Or, whilst I can vent clamour⑦ from my throat,

I'll tell thee thou dost evil.

LEAR. Hear me, recreant!

On thine allegiance⑧, hear me!

Since thou hast sought to make us break our vow—

Which we durst never yet⑨,— and with strain'd⑩ pride

---

① wage:发动战争

② let me still remain The true blank of thine eye:还是让我像箭垛上的靶心一样永远站在你的眼前吧。Blank 白色的靶心

③ Apollo:古希腊神话中的太阳神。因为李尔是古代英国国王,当时基督教还没有传到英国,所以莎士比亚让他指着阿波罗发誓。其实古代英国并不信希腊之神,但阿波罗司主管光明和医药,和下文联系,指发誓有讽刺之意

④ vassal! miscreant!:vassal 奴仆 miscreant 恶人

⑤ Kill thy physician, and the fee bestow Upon the foul disease:杀了你的医生,把你的病养得一天比一天厉害吧

⑥ Revoke thy gift:revoke 撤回,废除,宣告无效;gift 指分给 Cordelia 的那部分

⑦ vent clamour:大声疾呼

⑧ On thine allegiance:你给我按照做臣子的规矩来

⑨ durst never yet:我从不食言

⑩ strain'd:过分的

To come between our sentence and our power,—
Which nor our nature nor our place can bear,—
Our potency made good①, take thy reward.
Five days we do allot thee for provision
To shield thee from diseases② of the world;
And on the sixth to turn thy hated back
Upon our kingdom. If, on the tenth day following,
Thy banish'd trunk③ be found in our dominions,
The moment is thy death. Away! By Jupiter,
This shall not be revok'd.
KENT. Fare thee well, King. Since thus thou wilt④ appear,
Freedom lives hence⑤, and banishment is here.
[To Cordelia] The gods to their dear shelter take thee, maid⑥,
That justly think'st and hast most rightly said!
[To Regan and Goneril] And your large speeches may your deeds approve,
That good effects may spring from⑦ words of love.
Thus Kent, O princes, bids you all adieu; He'll shape his old course in a country new. [Exit.]
[Flourish⑧. Enter Gloucester, with France and Burgundy; Attendants.]
EARL OF GLOUCESTER. Here's France and Burgundy, my noble lord.
LEAR. My Lord of Burgundy,
We first address toward you, who with this king
Hath rivall'd for our daughter. What in the least

---

①Our potency made good:为了维护王权的尊严(potency:影响力,支配力)
②diseases:困难,不便
③trunk:身体
④wilt:will 的古体第二人称单数形式
⑤Freedom lives hence:自由不在这里。Hence:away 离开
⑥The gods to their dear shelter take thee, maid:神明庇护你,善良的女郎
⑦spring from[IELTS][TOEFL]:起源,来自
⑧Flourish[IELTS][TOEFL]:繁荣昌盛,这里指喇叭奏花腔(舞台指示)

Chapter 2　English Literature in the Renaissance

Will you require in present dower with her①,

Or cease your quest of love?

BURGUNDY. Most royal Majesty,

I crave no more than hath your Highness offer'd,

Nor will you tender② less.

LEAR. Right noble Burgundy,

When she was dear to us, we did hold her so;

But now her price is fall'n③. Sir, there she stands.

If aught④ within that little seeming substance⑤,

Or all of it, with our displeasure piec'd⑥,

And nothing more, may fitly like your Grace,

She's there, and she is yours.

BURGUNDY. I know no answer.

LEAR. Will you, with those infirmities⑦ she owes⑧,

Unfriended, new adopted to our hate⑨,

Dow'r'd with⑩ our curse, and stranger'd with⑪ our oath,

Take her, or leave her?

BURGUNDY. Pardon me, royal sir.

Election makes not up⑫ on such conditions.

---

①What in the least will you require in present dower with her:你希望她的嫁妆至少要有多少才行?

②tender:给予

③is fall'n:has fallen

④aught:anything

⑤little seeming substance:看上去柔弱的身体

⑥piec'd:增加

⑦infirmities:弱点

⑧owes[IELTS]:拥有,现代英语译为欠债,归因于……

⑨new adopted to our hate:新进遭到我的憎根

⑩Dow'r'd with:以……作嫁妆

⑪stranger'd with: make a stranger to us by 这里莎士比亚临时将 stranger 用作动词

⑫Election makes not up:很难做出决定;election 选择

LEAR. Then leave her, sir; for, by the pow'r that made me①,
I tell you all her wealth. [To France] For you, great King,
I would not from your love make such a stray
To match you where I hate; therefore beseech you
T' avert your liking a more worthier way
Than on a wretch whom nature is asham'd
Almost t' acknowledge hers.
FRANCE. This is most strange,
That she that even but now was your best object,
The argument② of your praise, balm③ of your age,
Most best, most dearest, should in this trice of time
Commit a thing so monstrous to dismantle
So many folds of favour. Sure her offence
Must be of such unnatural degree
That monsters it, or your ore-vouch'd affection
Fall'n into taint; which to believe of her
Must be a faith that reason without miracle
Should never plant in me.
CORDELIA. I yet beseech④ your Majesty,
If for I want that glib⑤ and oily art
To speak and purpose not, since what I well intend,
I'll do't before I speak—that you make known
It is no vicious blot, murther, or foulness,
No unchaste action or dishonoured step,
That hath depriv'd me of your grace and favour;
But even for want of that for which I am richer—

---

①the pow'r that made me:指造物主
②argument[IELTS]:争论辩驳,这里指内容,目标
③balm:安慰物
④beseech:请求
⑤glib:能说善道的

A still-soliciting① eye, and such a tongue

As I am glad I have not, though not to have it

Hath lost me in your liking.

LEAR. Better thou

Hadst not been born than not t' have pleas'd me better.

France. Is it but this-a tardiness in nature

Which often leaves the history unspoke

That it intends to do? My Lord of Burgundy,

What say you to the lady? Love's not love

When it is mingled with regards that stands

Aloof② from th' entire point. Will you have her?

She is herself a dowry.

BURGUNDY. Royal Lear,

Give but that portion which yourself propos'd,

And here I take Cordelia by the hand,

Duchess of Burgundy.

LEAR. Nothing! I have sworn; I am firm.

BURGUNDY. I am sorry then you have so lost a father

That you must lose a husband.

CORDELIA. Peace be with Burgundy!

Since that respects of fortune are his love,

I shall not be his wife.

FRANCE. Fairest Cordelia, that art most rich, being poor;

Most choice, forsaken; and most lov'd, despis'd!

Thee and thy virtues here I seize upon.

Be it lawful I take up what's cast away.

Gods, gods! 'tis strange that from their cold'st neglect

My love should kindle to inflam'd respect③.

---

① still-soliciting: 总是乞求的
② aloof: 远离
③ inflam'd respect: 热烈的敬爱

Thy dow'rless daughter, King, thrown to my chance,
Is queen of us, of ours, and our fair France.
Not all the dukes in wat'rish Burgundy
Can buy this unpriz'd precious maid of me.
Bid them farewell, Cordelia, though unkind.
Thou losest here, a better where to find.
LEAR. Thou hast her, France; let her be thine; for we
Have no such daughter, nor shall ever see
That face of hers again. Therefore be gone
Without our grace, our love, our benison①.
Come, noble Burgundy.
[Flourish. Exeunt Lear, Burgundy, Cornwall, Albany, Gloucester, and Attendants].
FRANCE. Bid farewell to your sisters.
CORDELIA. The jewels of our father, with wash'd eyes
Cordelia leaves you. I know you what you are;
And, like a sister, am most loath② to call
Your faults as they are nam'd. Use well our father.
To your professed bosoms I commit③ him;
But yet, alas, stood I within his grace,
I would prefer him to a better place!
So farewell to you both.
REGAN. Prescribe not us our duties.
GONERIL. Let your study
Be to content your lord, who hath receiv'd you
At fortune's alms④. You have obedience scanted⑤,

---

①benison:祝福
②loath:不情愿
③commit[IELTS][TOEFL]:委托;犯罪
④At fortune's alms:命运的慈悲(alm:施舍救济)
⑤scanted:减少

And well are worth the want that you have wanted. ①

CORDELIA. Time shall unfold what plighted② cunning③ hides.

Who cover faults, at last shame them derides④.

Well may you prosper!

FRANCE. Come, my fair Cordelia. [Exeunt France and Cordelia.]

GONERIL. Sister, it is not little I have to say of what most nearly appertains to⑤ us both. I think our father will hence to-night.

REGAN. That's most certain, and with you; next month with us.

GONERIL. You see how full of changes his age is⑥. The observation we have made of it hath not been little. He always lov'd our sister most, and with what poor judgment he hath now cast her off appears too grossly.⑦

REGAN. 'Tis the infirmity of his age; yet he hath ever but slenderly known himself.

GONERIL. The best and soundest of his time hath been but rash; then must we look to receive from his age, not alone the imperfections of long-ingraffed⑧ condition, but therewithal⑨ the unruly waywardness⑩ that infirm and choleric⑪ years bring with them.

REGAN. Such unconstant starts⑫ are we like to have from him as this of Kent's banishment.

---

①And well are worth the want that you have wanted: 今天空手跟了别人去也是活该

②plighted: plaited 和 pleated 的异体字, 隐藏的

③cunning (GRE): 奸诈的, 狡猾的

④Who cover faults, at last shame them derides: 罪恶虽然可以掩盖一时, 免不了最后出乖露丑

⑤appertains to: 与……相关

⑥full of changes his age is: 上了年纪而行为乖僻

⑦grossly: 明显地, 极其地

⑧ingraffed: 虚弱的, 这里指上了年纪

⑨therewithal: along with it 随之而来的

⑩waywardness: 任性

⑪choleric: 易怒的

⑫unconstant starts: 任性的脾气

GONERIL. There is further compliment① of leave-taking between France and him. Pray you let's hit together. If our father carry authority with such dispositions② as he bears, this last surrender of his will but offend us.

REGAN. We shall further think on't.

GONERIL. We must do something, and i' th' heat③.

[Exeunt.]

Questions for Discussion

1. Analyze the character of Cordelia.
2. What do you think causes Lear's tragedy?

Appreciation

Whence is that knocking?

How is't with me, when every noise appals me?

What hands are here? Ha, they pluck out mine eyes! Will all great Neptune's ocean wash this blood

Clean from my hand? No; this my hand will rather

The multitudinous seas incarnadine,

Making the green one red.

那打门的声音从什么地方来的？究竟怎么一回事，一点点的声音都会吓得我心惊肉跳？这是什么手！嘿！它们要挖出我的眼睛。大洋里所有的水，能够洗净我手上的血迹吗？不，恐怕我这一手的血，倒要把一碧无垠的海水，染成一片殷红呢。

——《麦克白》，朱生豪译

Brief Introduction

Macbeth first appears in the play as a warrior hero, whose fame on the battlefield

---

①compliment[IELTS][TOEFL]：礼节客套；赞扬

②dispositions：脾气

③i' th' heat：趁早

wins him great honor from the king. He receives a prophecy from three witches he encounters that one day he shall be King of Scotland, but the witches also prophesy that future kings will descend from Banquo, a fellow army captain. Prodded by his ambitious wife, Macbeth murders King Duncan and takes the throne for himself.

Because of the prophecy, Macbeth sees Banquo as a threat. He sends mercenaries to kill Banquo and his son. His behavior and the death of Banquo make all the thanes suspicious. They begin to think of Macbeth as a tyrant. Macduff flees to England to support King Duncan' son Malcolm in his effort to raise an army against Macbeth.

When Macbeth visits the three witches to learn more about his fate, they show him three apparitions who warn Macbeth to beware Macduff, but also that no "man born of woman" can defeat him and that he will rule until Birnam Wood marches to Dunsinane (a castle). Macbeth takes it evident that he is invincible. However, his attempts to defy the prophesies fail. The impossible things prophesized are made true. He is finally killed by Macduff, and Malcolm becomes king of Scotland.

Macbeth is one of Shakespeare's most performed and studied tragedies. The play reveals how outward evil stirs up the wickedness in man and destroys him. Consumed by ambition and spurred to action by his wife, Macbeth transforms from a warrior hero into a brutal villain and pays an extraordinary price for committing evil acts. He is an example of the terrible effects that ambition and guilt can have on a man who lacks strength of character. The same prophecy makes Banquo clarify his conscience, while Macbeth unties the knot to his ambition. His character begins at the highest point where features like strength, ambition, power work in a positive mode, but as the plot develops everything good in him subverts further until a declaration of madness is made.

Lady Macbeth is possibly Shakespeare's most famous and vivid female character. She is generally depicted in the popular mind as the epitome of evil. When she gets a message that King Duncan plans to spend the night with them at their castle, it seems to her that their once-in-a-lifetime opportunity has come. she knows that Macbeth is basically too soft—"too full of the milk of human kindness"—to commit murder. When Macbeth hesitates, she holds firm. She argues the case, mocks him, brings his manhood into question and finally prevails. Macbeth kills Duncan in his sleep and from that moment the couple sink into a moral, physical and spiritual collapse.

Selected Reading

Macbeth
ACT II
SCENE II. The Same.

[Enter Lady Macbeth.]
LADY MACBETH. That which hath made them drunk, hath made me bold①;
What hath quench'd② them hath given me fire.
—Hark! —Peace! It was the owl that shriek'd,
The fatal bellman, which gives the stern'st③ good night.
He is about it: the doors are open;
And the surfeited④ grooms⑤ do mock their charge with snores⑥:
I have drugg'd their possets⑦,
That death and nature do contend⑧ about them,
Whether they live or die.
MACBETH. [Within.] Who's there? —what, ho!
LADY MACBETH. Alack! I am afraid they have awak'd,
And 'tis not done: the attempt⑨, and not the deed, Confounds⑩ us. —
Hark! —I laid their daggers⑪ ready;
He could not miss 'em. —Had he not resembled⑫

---

①bold[IELTS][TOEFL]:勇敢的,大胆自信的
②quench[TOEFL]:熄灭
③stern[TOEFL]:严厉的,苛刻的,这里可译为凄厉的
④surfeited:过量的,这里译为醉饱的
⑤grooms:马夫,这里指侍卫
⑥snore:打鼾
⑦possets:牛奶甜酒
⑧contend[CET6][GRE]:竞争,争夺
⑨attempt[IELTS][TOEFL]:企图
⑩confound[GRE]:击败
⑪daggers[TOEFL]:匕首
⑫resemble[IELTS][TOEFL]:相像

My father as he slept, I had done't. —My husband!

[Re-enter Macbeth.]

MACBETH. I have done the deed. —Didst thou not hear a noise?

LADY MACBETH. I heard the owl scream and the crickets cry.

Did not you speak?

MACBETH. When?

LADY MACBETH. Now.

MACBETH. As I descended①?

LADY MACBETH. Ay.

MACBETH. Hark! —Who lies i' the second chamber②?

LADY MACBETH. Donalbain.

MACBETH. This is a sorry sight. [Looks on his hands.]

LADY MACBETH. A foolish thought, to say 'a sorry sight.'

MACBETH. There's one did laugh in 's sleep,

And one cried, 'Murder!' that they did wake each other.

I stood and heard them; but they did say their prayers,

And address'd③ them again to sleep.

LADY MACBETH. There are two lodg'd④ together.

MACBETH. One cried, 'God bless us!' and, 'Amen' the other,

As they had seen me with these hangman⑤'s hands.

Listening their fear, I could not say 'Amen',

When they did say, 'God bless us.'

LADY MACBETH. Consider it not so deeply.

MACBETH. But wherefore could not I pronounce 'Amen'?

I had most need of blessing, and 'Amen'

Stuck in my throat.

LADY MACBETH. These deeds must not be thought

After these ways; so, it will make us mad.

---

①descend[IELTS][TOEFL]:下来
②chamber[IELTS][TOEFL]:房间
③address[IELTS]:向……说话;演讲
④lodge[TOEFL]:借宿,提供住宿
⑤hangman:刽子手

MACBETH. I heard a voice cry, 'Sleep no more!
Macbeth does murder sleep,'—the innocent sleep;
Sleep that knits up the ravell'd sleave of care①,
The death of each day's life, sore② labor's bath,
Balm of hurt minds, great nature's second course,
Chief nourisher③ in life's feast.
LADY MACBETH. What do you mean?
MACBETH. Still it cried, 'Sleep no more!' to all the house: 'Glamis hath
murder'd sleep, and therefore Cawdor
Shall sleep no more,—Macbeth shall sleep no more!'
LADY MACBETH. Who was it that thus cried? Why, worthy Thane,
You do unbend your noble strength to think
So brainsickly④ of things.—Go, get some water,
And wash this filthy⑤ witness⑥ from your hand.
Why did you bring these daggers from the place?
They must lie there: go carry them; and smear
The sleepy grooms with blood.
MACBETH. I'll go no more.
I am afraid to think what I have done;
Look on't again I dare not.
LADY MACBETH. Infirm of purpose!⑦
Give me the daggers: the sleeping and the dead
Are but as pictures; 'tis the eye of childhood
That fears a painted devil. If he do bleed,

---

①Sleep that knits up the ravell'd sleave of care: 译为把忧虑的乱丝编织起来的睡眠（knit 编织; ravell'd 杂乱的; sleave 细丝）
②sore[IELTS]: 疼痛的,酸痛的
③nourisher: 营养,营养剂
④brainsickly: 疯狂的
⑤filthy: 肮脏的
⑥witness[IELTS][TOEFL]: 目击者
⑦Infirm of purpose: 译为意志动摇的人（infirm 病弱的）

I'll gild① the faces of the grooms withal②,

For it must seem their guilt. [Exit. Knocking within.]

MACBETH. Whence is that knocking?

How is't with me, when every noise appals③ me?

What hands are here? Ha, they pluck out mine eyes! Will all great Neptune④'s ocean wash this blood

Clean from my hand? No; this my hand will rather

The multitudinous⑤ seas incarnadine⑥,

Making the green one red.

[Re-enter Lady Macbeth.]

LADY MACBETH. My hands are of your color, but I shame

To wear a heart so white. [Knocking within.] I hear a knocking

At the south entry;—Retire⑦ we to our chamber.

A little water clears us of this deed:

How easy is it then! Your constancy

Hath left you unattended.—[Knocking within.] Hark, more knocking;

Get on your nightgown, lest occasion call us

And show us to be watchers.—Be not lost

So poorly in your thoughts.

MACBETH. To know my deed, twere best not know myself. [Knocking within.]

Wake Duncan with thy knocking! I would thou couldst!

[Exeunt]

---

①gild[GRE]:镀金

②withal:而且,同样

③appal:使惊骇,同 appall

④Neptune:海王星;罗马神话中的海神尼普顿

⑤multitudinous:大量的,众多的

⑥incarnadine:染红

⑦retire[IELTS][TOEFL]:退休;退出(比赛);离开(尤指去僻静处)

ACT III
SCENE II. The Same. Another Room in the Palace.

[Enter Lady Macbeth and a Servant.]

LADY MACBETH. Is Banquo gone from court?

SERVANT. Ay, madam, but returns again tonight.

LADY MACBETH. Say to the King I would attend his leisure

For a few words.

SERVANT. Madam, I will. [Exit.]

LADY MACBETH. Naught's had, all's spent,

Where our desire is got without content①;

'Tis safer to be that which we destroy,

Than, by destruction, dwell in doubtful joy.

[Enter Macbeth.]

How now, my lord? Why do you keep alone,

Of sorriest fancies your companions making;

Using those thoughts which should indeed have died

With them they think on? Things without all remedy

Should be without regard; what's done is done.

MACBETH. We have scotch'd② the snake, not kill'd it;

She'll close, and be herself; whilst our poor malice

Remains in danger of her former tooth.

But let the frame of things disjoint③, both the worlds suffer,

Ere we will eat our meal in fear, and sleep

In the affliction④ of these terrible dreams

That shake us nightly. Better be with the dead,

Whom we, to gain our peace, have sent to peace,

Than on the torture⑤ of the mind to lie

---

①content[IELTS][TOEFL]:满足

②scotch[TOEFL]:阻止,挫败

③disjoint:脱节,解题

④affliction [TOEFL][GRE]:折磨,痛苦

⑤Torture:折磨

Chapter 2 English Literature in the Renaissance

In restless ecstasy①. Duncan is in his grave;
After life's fitful② fever he sleeps well;
Treason has done his worst: nor steel, nor poison,
Malice③ domestic④, foreign levy⑤, nothing,
Can touch him further.
LADY MACBETH. Come on;
Gentle my lord, sleek o'er your rugged looks;
Be bright and jovial⑥ among your guests tonight.
MACBETH. So shall I, love, and so, I pray, be you.
Let your remembrance apply to Banquo;
Present him eminence⑦, both with eye and tongue. Unsafe the while, that we
Must lave our honors in these flattering streams;
And make our faces vizards⑧ to our hearts,
Disguising⑨ what they are.
LADY MACBETH. You must leave this.
MACBETH. O, full of scorpions is my mind, dear wife!
Thou know'st that Banquo, and his Fleance, lives.
LADY MACBETH. But in them nature's copy's not eterne⑩.
MACBETH. There's comfort yet; they are assailable⑪;
Then be thou jocund⑫: Ere⑬ the bat hath flown

---

①ecstasy[GRE]:狂喜,陶醉
②fitful:断断续续的,间歇的,一阵一阵的
③malice:恶意,怨恨
④domestic[IELTS][TOEFL]:国内的,本国的,家庭的
⑤levy[GRE]:征收,征税;税款
⑥jovial[GRE]:快乐的,愉快的,友好的
⑦eminence[TOEFL][GRE]:显赫
⑧vizard:假面
⑨disguise[GRE]:假扮,伪装,掩饰
⑩eterne:永恒的
⑪assailable:可攻击的
⑫jocund:欢乐的,愉快的
⑬Ere:在……之前

His cloister'd① flight; ere to black Hecate's② summons③,
The shard-borne beetle④, with his drowsy⑤ hums,
Hath rung night's yawning⑥ peal⑦, there shall be done
A deed of dreadful note.
LADY MACBETH. What's to be done?
MACBETH. Be innocent⑧ of the knowledge, dearest chuck⑨,
Till thou applaud⑩ the deed.—Come, seeling night⑪,
Scarf up the tender eye of pitiful day;
And with thy bloody and invisible⑫ hand
Cancel and tear to pieces that great bond
Which keeps me pale! —Light thickens; and the crow⑬ Makes wing to the rooky wood;
Good things of day begin to droop⑭ and drowse⑮;
Whiles night's black agents to their preys do rouse.—
Thou marvell'st at my words, but hold thee still;
Things bad begun make strong themselves by ill⑯:
So, pr'ythee, go with me. [Exeunt.]

---

①cloister:修道院或圣堂的禁地
②Hecate:赫卡特,司夜和冥界的女神
③summon[GRE]:召唤
④The shard-borne beetle:振翅而飞的甲虫
⑤drowsy[TOEFL]:昏昏欲睡的
⑥yawn:打哈欠
⑦peal:洪亮的钟声
⑧innocent[IELTS][TOEFL]:无罪的,无辜的,清白的
⑨chuck:亲爱的
⑩applaud[IELTS][TOEFL]:鼓掌
⑪seeling night:使人盲目的黑夜
⑫invisible[IELTS]:看不见的
⑬crow:乌鸦
⑭droop[GRE]:低垂,沮丧
⑮drowse:打瞌睡,昏昏欲睡
⑯Things bad begun make strong themselves by ill:以不义开始的事情,必须用罪恶使他巩固

ACT V
SCENE I. Dunsinane①. A Room in the Castle.

[Enter a Doctor of Physic and a Waiting – Gentlewoman.]

DOCTOR. I have two nights watched with you, but can perceive② no truth in your report. When was it she last walked?

GENTLEWOMAN. Since his Majesty went into the field, I have seen her rise from her bed, throw her nightgown upon her, unlock her closet, take forth paper, fold it, write upon it, read it, afterwards seal it, and again return to bed; yet all this while in a most fast sleep.

DOCTOR. A great perturbation③ in nature,—to receive at once the benefit of sleep, and do the effects of watching! —In this slumbery④ agitation⑤, besides her walking and other actual performances, what, at any time, have you heard her say?

GENTLEWOMAN. That, sir, which I will not report after her.

DOCTOR. You may to me; and 'tis most meet you should.

GENTLEWOMAN. Neither to you nor anyone; having no witness to confirm my speech. Lo you, here she comes!

[Enter Lady Macbeth, with a taper.]

This is her very guise⑥, and, upon my life, fast asleep. Observe her; stand close.

DOCTOR. How came she by that light?

GENTLEWOMAN. Why, it stood by her: She has light by her continually; 'tis her command.

DOCTOR. You see, her eyes are open.

GENTLEWOMAN. Ay, but their sense is shut.

DOCTOR. What is it she does now? Look how she rubs her hands.

---

①Dunsinane:邓西南城堡;苏格兰东部的一座山峰
②perceive[IELTS][TOEFL]:注意到,察觉到
③perturbation:忧虑,不安,烦恼
④slumbery:催眠的,昏昏欲睡的
⑤agitation[TOEFL]:焦虑不安,忧虑,烦乱
⑥guise:伪装

GENTLEWOMAN. It is an accustomed action with her, to seem thus washing her hands. I have known her continue in this a quarter of an hour.

LADY MACBETH. Yet here's a spot.

DOCTOR. Hark, she speaks! I will set down what comes from her, to satisfy my remembrance the more strongly.

LADY MACBETH. Out, damned spot! Out, I say! —One; two; why then 'tis time to do't;—Hell is murky①! —Fie, my lord, fie! A soldier, and afeard? What need we fear who knows it, when none can call our power to account? —Yet who would have thought the old man to have had so much blood in him?

DOCTOR. Do you mark that?

LADY MACBETH. The Thane of Fife had a wife; where is she now? —What, will these hands ne'er be clean? —No more o' that, my lord, no more o' that: You mar all with this starting.

DOCTOR. Go to, go to; you have known what you should not.

GENTLEWOMAN. She has spoke what she should not, I am sure of that; heaven knows what she has known.

LADY MACBETH. Here's the smell of the blood still. All the perfumes② of Arabia will not sweeten this little hand. Oh, oh, oh!

DOCTOR. What a sigh is there! The heart is sorely charged.

GENTLEWOMAN. I would not have such a heart in my bosom for the dignity③ of the whole body.

DOCTOR. Well, well, well—

GENTLEWOMAN. Pray God it be, sir.

DOCTOR. This disease is beyond my practice; yet I have known those which have walked in their sleep who have died holily in their beds.

LADY MACBETH. Wash your hands, put on your nightgown; look not so pale. —I tell you yet again, Banquo's buried; he cannot come out on's grave. DOCTOR. Even so?

LADY MACBETH. To bed, to bed; there's knocking at the gate. Come,

---

①murky:污浊的,昏暗的
②perfumes:香水
③dignity:尊严,尊贵,高尚

come, come, come, give me your hand. What's done cannot be undone. To bed, to bed, to bed. [Exit.]

DOCTOR. Will she go now to bed?

GENTLEWOMAN. Directly.

DOCTOR. Foul whisperings are abroad; Unnatural deeds

Do breed unnatural troubles; infected① minds

To their deaf pillows will discharge their secrets.

More needs she the divine than the physician②.

God, God, forgive us all! —Look after her;

Remove from her the means of all annoyance③,

And still keep eyes upon her. —So good-night.

My mind she has mated, and amazed my sight.

I think, but dare not speak.

GENTLEWOMAN. Good-night, good doctor.

[Exeunt.]

Questions for Discussion

1. Describe Macbeth and Lady Macbeth's characters.
2. Analyze the following lines.

"Will all great Neptune's ocean wash this blood

Clean from my hand? No; this my hand will rather

The multitudinous seas incarnadine,

Making the green one red."

Appreciation

All the world's a stage,

And all the men and women merely players;

They have their exits and their entrances,

---

①infected:感染的

②physician[IELTS]:医生

③annoyance:烦恼

And one man in his time plays many parts,
His acts being seven ages.
全世界就是一个舞台,
男男女女不过是一些演员；
他们都有下场的时候,也都有上场的时候,
一个人在一生中扮演着很多角色,
他的表演可以分为七个时期。

———《皆大欢喜》,朱生豪译

Brief Introduction

"All the world's a stage" is the phrase that begins a monologue from William Shakespeare's *As You Like It*. The speech compares the world to a stage and life to a play and catalogues a man's life into seven stages, which is sometimes referred to as the seven ages of man: infant, schoolboy, lover, soldier, justice, pantaloon, and old age. It is one of Shakespeare's most frequently quoted passages. Shakespeare reduces the life of human beings to a stage performance. During the entire life span, everyone plays their roles at different ages.

Selected Reading

As You Like It
Act II, Scene VII

All the world's a stage①,
And all the men and women merely players;
They have their exits② and their entrances③,
And one man in his time plays many parts,
His acts being seven ages. At first, the infant④,

---

①stage[IELTS]:舞台
②exit[TOEFL]:出口
③entrance[GRE]:入口
④infant[GRE]:婴儿

Chapter 2 English Literature in the Renaissance

Mewling① and puking② in the nurse's arms.
Then the whining③ schoolboy, with his satchel④
And shining morning face, creeping like snail⑤
Unwillingly⑥ to school. And then the lover,
Sighing⑦ like furnace⑧, with a woeful⑨ ballad⑩
Made to his mistress' eyebrow. Then a soldier,
Full of strange oaths⑪ and bearded like the pard⑫,
Jealous⑬ in honour, sudden and quick in quarrel,
Seeking the bubble⑭ reputation⑮
Even in the cannon's⑯ mouth. And then the justice⑰,
In fair round belly with good capon⑱ lined,
With eyes severe⑲ and beard of formal cut,
Full of wise saws⑳格言 and modern instances㉑;

---

①mewl:呜咽;啜泣
②puke:呕吐
③whine:哭哭啼啼;哀嚎
④satchel:旧时书包
⑤snail[CET6]:蜗牛
⑥unwillingly:不情愿地;勉强地
⑦sigh[CET4]:叹气
⑧furnace[IELTS]:熔炉;火炉
⑨woeful:忧伤的
⑩ballad:民谣,民歌
⑪oath[TOEFL]:誓言
⑫pard:豹子
⑬jealous[IELTS]:珍爱的,珍惜的;嫉妒的
⑭bubble[TOEFL][IELTS]:气泡
⑮reputation[IELTS]:名誉
⑯cannon[IELTS]:大炮
⑰justice[TOEFL][IELTS]:法官;公平,公正
⑱capon:阉鸡(育肥以供食用)
⑲severe[IELTS]:严肃的,严峻的,严重的
⑳saw:格言;锯
㉑instance:实例

And so he plays his part. The sixth age shifts
Into the lean and slippered① pantaloon②,
With spectacles③ on nose and pouch④ on side;
His youthful hose⑤, well saved, a world too wide
For his shrunk⑥ shank⑦, and his big manly voice,
Turning again toward childish treble⑧ pipes
And whistles in his sound. Last scene of all,
That ends this strange eventful⑨ history,
Is second childishness⑩ and mere oblivion⑪,
Sans⑫ teeth, sans eyes, sans taste, sans everything.

Questions for Discussion

1. How does Shakespeare divide a man's life?
2. Describe the characteristics of people in each stage.

Terms

1. Renaissance
2. Spenserian stanza and sonnet
3. Soliloquy

---

①slippered：穿拖鞋的
②pantaloons：傻老头
③spectacles：[复数]眼镜
④pouch：荷包，小袋子
⑤hose：水管；旧式紧身男裤
⑥shrunk：shrink 的过去式和过去分词，收缩
⑦shank：小腿
⑧treble：高音
⑨eventful[TOEFL]：多事的，多变故的
⑩childishness：幼稚，孩子气
⑪oblivion：沉睡，遗忘
⑫sans：无，没有

Chapter 2 English Literature in the Renaissance

4. Stanza
5. Meter
6. Sonnet

Chapter 3

Literature of the English Revolution and Restoration

I. Historical Background

The earlier 17th century, and especially the period of the English Revolution (1640 – 1660), was a time of intense ferment in all areas of life—religion, science, politics, domestic relations, and culture.

1. The House of Stuart

After the death of Elizabeth in 1603, James VI of Scotland succeeded the throne known as James I. With the belief of "Divine Right of Kings", James I never allowed the Parliament to interfere in his rule. His succession brought a temporary union of England and Scotland, but his reign was troubled by religious controversy.

The Puritans became very powerful in the Parliament. They demanded further religious reformation away with the elaborate ceremonies, calling a purer form of worship, and demanded a simple religious belief. The refusal of their proposals in purifying the Church, and the pro-Spanish foreign policy made many Puritans flee England for Holland. The most famous sailing was made by 102 puritans in 1620, which landed America from Plymouth with a ship named Mayflower.

2. The Civil War

King Charles I succeeded the throne after his father James I's death. Without enough money, Charles I was not capable to handle the severe religious dispute and the clash between the king and the parliament, and dissolved the parliament for not granting import duties for life. His efforts to obtain money without the aid of the Parliament by all kinds of extraordinary levies became notorious. Conflicts between the King and the Parliament finally brought about a civil war in 1642.

❀ Chapter 3 Literature of the English Revolution and Restoration ❀

The various classes in England soon split up into two camps. The parliament was supported by the merchants, the workers and the peasants; while the king was supported by the conservative gentry, the big landlords and the monopolists. The king's men were called "Cavaliers" because they were skillful at riding and shooting, and the soldiers of the parliament were called "Roundheads" because they wore their hair short. At last, the royalists were defeated by the parliament army led by Oliver Cromwell. In 1649 Charles Ⅰ was sentenced to death, and England was declared to be a commonwealth 君主立宪制 and Cromwell became the Lord Protector.

In 1658, Cromwell died and his son Richard succeeded him as the new Lord Protector, who was too weak-minded. In 1660, Charles Ⅱ was welcomed back and became the new king. That was known as the Restoration. Charles Ⅱ carried on reprisals on the revolutionaries and persecuted the puritans.

3. The Glorious Revolution

A white terror was introduced to the country during the reign of Charles Ⅱ and James Ⅱ, brother of Charles Ⅱ. In 1688, James Ⅱ was forced to flee to France. His Protestant daughter Mary Stuart and her husband William, Duke of Orange, were invited to come and rule over England. This was the so-called "Glorious Revolution"— "glorious" because it was bloodless and there was no revival of the revolutionary demands. After a century of disputes and battles, modern England was firmly established and capitalism would develop freely within the state structure of modern England constitutional monarchy. In 1688, William signed "The Bill of Rights" presented to him by the Parliament, which greatly restricted the power of the English king and henceforth England has become a country of constitutional monarchy.

The Revolution of 1688 meant three things: the supremacy of Parliament, the beginning of modern England, and the final triumph of the principle of political liberty for which the Puritan had fought and suffered hardship for a hundred years.

II. Literary Background

The 17th century literature is closely related to politics. English literature of the revolution and restoration was very much concerned with the tremendous social upheavals of the time. Literature in the 17th century mainly includes baroque literature, puritan literature and classicist literature, roughly according to the sequence of time. John Milton and John Bunyan stood firmly with the English Revolution. The Cavalier poets sided with the king. The Metaphysical poets wrote in their unique way, paying more attention to religion than politics.

Literature 4 Johns: John Milton, John Bunyan—two representatives of the puritan writers; John Donne, the greatest metaphysical poet; John Dryden, noted for his literary criticism and forerunner of the English classicism.

1. Baroque literature

It is the transition from Renaissance to classicism. Classicism is the main literary school in Europe esp. in France in 17th century and a little later in England, which praises the leadership of the king and combines closely literature with reality and politics and demands the restraint of personal wishes and expresses the subjects that emotion is submissive to responsibility and individual to the country.

2. Puritan literature

Puritanism was the religious doctrine of the revolutionary bourgeoisie during this period which preached thrift, sobriety 清醒, hard work, but with very little extravagant enjoyment of the fruits of labor. Worldly pleasures were condemned as harmful. The Puritans believed in simplicity of life. In the triumph of Puritanism under Cromwell, severe laws were passed, many simple pleasures were forbidden and an austere standard of living was forced upon unwilling people. The London theaters were closed in 1642. *The Bible* became the one book of the people.

The Revolution Period was one of confusion in literature due to the breaking up of the old ideals. Puritanism disapproved of the sonnets and the love poetry written in the previous period. Literature was as divided in spirit as were the struggling parties.

The Revolution period produced one of the most important poets in English literature, John Milton, whose work would glorify any age and people, and in his work the indomitable revolutionary spirit found its noblest expression. This period is also called the Age of Milton. The main literary form of the period was poetry. In the field of prose writing of the Puritan Age, John Bunyan occupies the most important position. They both represented the extremes of English life in the 17th century and wrote the two remarkable works that have imbued with the mighty Puritan spirit.

3. Metaphysical Poets—Neo-Platonism

The early 17th century was an age of transition, of conscious change. In literature, there is also a tendency to investigate novelties, just as in the spirit of science. The term "metaphysical poetry" is commonly used to designate the works of the 17th century writers under the influence of John Donne, the founder of this school. The metaphysical

Chapter 3 Literature of the English Revolution and Restoration

works are characterized by mysticism in content and fantasticality in form.

They tended to logically reason the things, esp. emotions; psychologically analyze the emotions of love and religion; love the novelty and the shocking; use the metaphysical conceits, and ignore the conventional devices. In literature, a conceit is an extended metaphor with a complex logic that governs a poetic passage or entire poem.

The group was to have a significant influence on 20th century poetry, especially through T. S. Eliot, whose essay *The Metaphysical Poets* (1921) helped bring their poetry back into favor with audience. T. S. Eliot is an example of modern poets who have been mostly affected by the metaphysical influence.

"*When the evening is spread out against the sky*

 Like a patient etherized upon a table" (*T. S. Eliot*)

4. Cavalier Poets

Another school of poets prevailing in the period was the Cavalier Poets. Most of these poets were courtiers and soldiers who sided with the king to fight against the revolution. They mostly wrote short songs on the flitting joys of the day, but underneath their light-heartedness lies some forbidding and impending doom. Their poetry expresses the spirit of pessimism. The representatives of this school are Sir John Suckling (1609 – 1642), Richard Lovelace (1618 – 1657), Thomas Carew (1595 – 1639) and Robert Herrick (1591 – 1674). Cavalier poets wrote some best known poems in English literary history, though they were conservative in politics. A case in point is Herrick's "Gather Your Rose Buds While You May".

Unit 1 John Milton

Appreciation

What though the field be lost? 我们损失了什么?
All is not lost; the unconquerable Will, 并不是一无所剩;
And study of revenge, immortal hate, 坚定的意志、热切的复仇心、不灭的憎恨;
And courage never to submit or yield, 以及永不屈服、永不退让的勇气,
And what is else not to be overcome? 难道还有比这些更难战胜的吗?

Author

John Milton was born in London in December 1608. In 1625, Milton went to Christ's College, Cambridge University and spent seven years there, earning his B. A. and M. A. then retired to the family homes in London and Horton, for years of private study and literary composition. He began his traveling around Europe, mostly in Italy, and then returned to England in 1639.

The phases of Milton's life parallel the major historical and political divisions in Stuart Britain. Under the rule of Charles I and its breakdown, he launched a career as pamphleteer and publicist. Under the Commonwealth of England, he acted as an official spokesman in certain of his publications. During the Restoration of 1660, Milton, now completely blind, completed most of his major works of poetry. Three great poems: *Paradise Lost* 失乐园, *Paradise Regained* 复乐园, *Samson Agonistes* 力士参孙。

William Hayley's 1796 biography called Milton the "greatest English author" and he remains generally regarded as "one of the preeminent writers in the English language". Samuel Johnson praised *Paradise Lost* as "a poem which... with respect to design may claim the first place, and with respect to performance, the second, among the productions of the human mind". His book *Paradise Lost* is called Three Western poetry with *Homer* 荷马史诗 and *The Divine Comedy* 神曲.

Brief Introduction

Paradise Lost is Milton's masterpiece. Before its composition, he had had the subject in his mind for a quarter of a century, and made some drafts about the characters and plot. It is a long epic, published first in 1667 in 12 books, written in blank verse, which is written in regular metrical but unrhymed lines, almost always iambic pentameters. It is also a quintessential epic poem, following the conventions originating from the works of Homer and Virgil and the Anglo-Saxon epic *Beowulf*.

The poem concerns the Judeo-Christian story of the Fall of Man: the temptation of Adam and Eve by Satan and their expulsion from the Garden of Eden. The story of the epic goes as follows: Satan and his followers rose against God, but they were defeated and cast out of Heaven into Hell before Adam and Eve were created. Even in Hell, Satan and his adherents are planning another plot. Having managed to escape from Hell, Satan goes to the newly created world to corrupt man. Satan chooses for his battlefield the most perfect of spots ever created by God—the Garden of Eden, where live the first man and woman, Adam and Eve, who are allowed by God to enjoy the superme beauties of Paradise. Having over-heard the secret of the Tree of Knowledge of Good and Evil in the Garden of Eden, Satan enters the body of the serpent and convinces Eve that he has eaten the fruit of the *Tree of Knowledge* and gained wisdom and speech. She eats the fruit from the forbidden tree, and then persuades Adam to eat the fruit too. God sees all this and both Adam and Eve are deprived of immortality. They are expelled from the Paradise to live an earthly life of hardships and suffering. Satan is punished by God and turned into a serpent.

Selected Reading

Paradise Lost

Book Ⅰ

What though the field① be lost?
All is not lost②; the unconquerable Will,
And study③ of revenge, immortal hate,
And courage never to submit or yield,
And what is else not to be overcome④?
That Glory⑤ never shall his wrath or might
Extort⑥ from me. To bow and sue for grace⑦
With suppliant knee, and deifie his power,

---

①field: the battle 战役;斗争
②all is not lost: not all is lost 并非所有的方面都失败了
③study: earnest intention 强烈的愿望
④what is else not to be overcome: what else is not to be overcome? 还有什么是比这更难以战胜的吗?
⑤that glory: the glory of not being overcome
⑥extort[IELTS]:obtain 侵占, 强求
⑦sue for grace: beg for mercy 乞求怜悯

Who① from the terrour② of this Arm so late
Doubted his Empire③, that were low indeed,
That were an ignominy④ and shame beneath⑤
This downfall⑥; since by Fate⑦ the strength of Gods⑧
And this Empyreal substance⑨ cannot fail⑩,
Since through experience of this great event⑪
In Arms not worse, in foresight much advanc't,
We may with more successful hope resolve
To wage by force or guile eternal Warr
Irreconcileable, to our grand Foe⑫,
Who now triumphs, and in th'excess of joy
Sole reigning holds the Tyranny of Heav'n⑬.
So spake⑭ th'Apostate Angel⑮, though in pain,

---

①Who: the God 此处指上帝

②terrour: terror

③Who from the terrour of this Arm so late/ Doubted his Empire: God, fearing the strength of our power which he lately confronted became uncertain of his authority and rule. Arm: battle 战争; so late: lately; Empire: imperium (Lat.), power 权威统治

④ignominy: dishonor 耻辱

⑤beneath[TOEFL]: worse than 有过之而无不及

⑥this downfall: the defeat of Satan 撒旦的失败

⑦by fate: 命中注定

⑧Gods: gods (Satan still believes himself gods.) 神

⑨Empyreal substance: heavenly being, angels 天使

⑩fail: perish 毁灭

⑪this great event: the rebellion of Satan from God and the battle against God

⑫our grand Foe: God 上帝

⑬Who now triumphs, and in th'excess of joy/ Sole reigning holds the Tyranny of Heav'n: who (God) now wins and in too much of joy holds the merciless control of heaven with monopoly. 他现在正沉湎于成功，得意忘形，独揽大权，在天上掌握暴政呢

⑭spake: speak 的过去式

⑮th'Apostate Angel: here refers to Satan 变节的天使，撒旦

Vaunting① aloud, but rackt② with deep despare:

And him thus answer'd soon his bold Compeer③.

O Prince, O Chief of many Throned Powers,

That led th'imbattelld④ Seraphim to Warr

Under thy conduct⑤, and in dreadful deeds

Fearless, endanger'd Heav'ns perpetual King;

And put to proof his high Supremacy,

Whether upheld by strength, or Chance, or Fate,

Too well I see and rue⑥ the dire⑦ event,

That with sad overthrow and foul⑧ defeat

Hath lost us Heav'n, and all this mighty Host⑨

In horrible destruction laid thus low,

As far as⑩ Gods and Heav'nly Essences⑪

Can perish: for the mind and spirit remains

Invincible, and vigour soon returns,

Though all our Glory extinct, and happy state

Here swallow'd up in endless misery.

But what if he our Conquerour, (whom I now

Of force⑫ believe Almighty, since no less

---

①vaunt:boast 吹嘘

②rackt:racked 被折磨

③his bold Compeer:Beelzebub。Beelzebub（比尔泽布）又名 Baal-Zebul、Baal-Zebub,"豪宅之主""苍蝇王"。在希腊神话中也有这个魔王的痕迹,因为万神之父,Zeus 又名"避讳苍蝇者"。（失乐园中的）堕落天使

④imbattled:embattled 严阵以待的

⑤conduct[TOEFL][IELTS]:command 指挥

⑥rue:regret 后悔

⑦dire:dreadful or terrible 可怕的

⑧foul[TOEFL][IELTS]:shameful 可耻的

⑨mighty Host:strong army, the rebel angels 反对派的天使

⑩As far as:与前文的 thus 相搭配,意为"如此……以至于"

⑪Heav'nly Essences:the angels; essence: being

⑫of force:necessarily 必定地

Than such could have orepow'rd such force as ours)
Have left us this our spirit and strength intire①
Strongly to suffer and support② our pains,
That we may so suffice③ his vengeful ire④,
Or do him mightier service as his thralls
By right of⑤ Warr, what e're his business be
Here in the heart of Hell to work in Fire,
Or do his Errands in the gloomy Deep;
What can it then avail though yet we feel
Strength undiminisht, or eternal being
To undergo eternal punishment?⑥
Whereto with speedy words th'Arch-fiend⑦ reply'd.

Fall'n Cherube, to be weak is miserable
Doing or Suffering⑧: but of this be sure,
To do aught⑨ good never will be our task,
But ever to do ill our sole delight,
As being the contrary to his high will
Whom we resist. If then his Providence
Out of our evil seek to bring forth good,
Our labour⑩ must be to pervert that end,

---

① intire: entire 完整的
② support: endure 忍受
③ suffice: satisfy 满足
④ ire: anger 愤怒
⑤ by right of: through 通过……的方式
⑥ or eternal being / To undergo eternal punishment?: or being eternal, so as to undergo eternal punishment?
⑦ Arch-fiend: Satan 大恶魔
⑧ Doing or Suffering: Taking action or enduring 无论是采取行动还是在这里忍耐
⑨ aught: anything 任何东西
⑩ labour: effort 努力

Chapter 3　Literature of the English Revolution and Restoration

And out of good still① to find means of evil;
Which oft times may succeed, so as perhaps
Shall grieve him, if I fail not, and disturb
His inmost counsels from thir② destind aim.
But see the angry Victor hath recall'd
His Ministers③ of vengeance and pursuit
Back to the Gates of Heav'n: The Sulphurous Hail
Shot after us in storm, oreblown④ hath laid
The fiery Surge, that from the Precipice
Of Heav'n receiv'd us falling, and the Thunder,
Wing'd with red Lightning and impetuous rage,
Perhaps hath spent his shafts, and ceases now
To bellow through the vast and boundless Deep.
Let us not slip⑤ th'occasion, whether scorn,
Or satiate⑥ fury yield it from our Foe.
Seest thou yon⑦ dreary Plain, forlorn⑧ and wilde⑨,
The seat of desolation⑩, voyd of light⑪,
Save⑫ what the glimmering of these livid flames
Casts pale and dreadful? Thither⑬ let us tend
From off the tossing of these fiery waves,

---

①still: always 总是；常常
②thir: their
③His Ministers: the cherubs(天使＜cherub 复数＞) at God's disposal
④oreblown: blown over 被吹倒
⑤slip[TOEFL][IELTS]: miss 错过
⑥satiate: satiated, satisfied 满足了的
⑦yon: distant 远方的
⑧forlorn: desolate 人迹罕至的
⑨wilde: wild 荒凉的
⑩desolation: wilderness 荒芜
⑪voyd of light: void of light 没有光
⑫save: except 除了
⑬thither: to there 向那边

There rest, if any rest can harbour① there,
And reassembling our afflicted Powers,
Consult how we may henceforth most offend②
Our Enemy, our own loss how repair③,
How overcome this dire Calamity,
What reinforcement we may gain from Hope,
If not what resolution from despare④.

Questions for Discussion

1. Briefly summarize this excerpt.
2. Analyze Satan in *Paradise Lost*.

Unit 2   John Bunyan

Appreciation

So the men were brought to examination; and they that sat upon them asked them whence they came, whither they went, and what they did there in such an unusual Garb? The men told them that they were Pilgrims and Strangers in the World, and that they were going to their own Country, which was the Heavenly Jerusalem; and that they had given no occasion to the men of the Town, nor yet to the Merchandizers, thus to abuse them, and to let them in their Journey, except it was for that, when one asked them what they would buy, they said they would buy the Truth.

于是那两个人被带去受审讯;审问他们的人问他们,从哪儿来,往哪儿去,穿着这种稀奇古

---

①harbour[IELTS]: dwell 存在于

②offend[IELTS]: hurt 冒犯

③our own loss how repair: how we may repair our loss 我们如何修复我们的损失

④what resolution from despare: what resolution we may gain from despair 我们可能从绝望中获得什么决策

Chapter 3 Literature of the English Revolution and Restoration

怪的衣服在那儿干什么。那两个人说,他们是旅客,在世上是寄居的,他们到自己的家乡去,也就是到天上的耶路撒冷去;而且还说他们认为市民和商人没有理由这样辱骂他们,妨碍他们路,除非当有个人问他们要买什么时,他们说要买真理这件事可以算作一个理由。

Author

John Bunyan was born in 1628 to Thomas and Margaret Bunyan in Bunyan's End in the parish of Elstow, Bedfordshire, England. Although he is regarded as a literary genius today, he had little formal education. His varied spiritual experience furnished his sensitive imagination with profound impression and vivid images. He wrote them down. The result is his book, *The Pilgrim's Progress*.

Brief Introduction

The Pilgrim's Progress, published in 1678, was written in the old fashioned medieval form of allegory and dream. It is a Christian allegory, which is regarded as one of the most significant works of English literature, and has been translated into more than 200 languages. Protestant missionaries commonly translated it as the first thing after the Bible. It tells of the spiritual pilgrimage of Christian.

The Pilgrim's Progress tells of a religious man's search for salvation, and gives a truthful picture of English society. The basis of the allegorical narrative is the idea of a journey. The traveler's name is Christian, and he represents every Christian in human world. The figures and places he encounters on his journey stand for the various experiences every Christian must go through in the quest for salvation.

The whole book falls into two parts. Part 1 tells of the religious conversion of Christian and his religious life in this world. Part 2 describes the subsequent conversion of his wife and their children. Christian, with a book in his hand and a burden on his back, flees from the City of Destruction and meets the perils and temptations of the Slough of Despond, Vanity Fair, and Doubting Castle. He faces and overcomes the demon Appollyon, journeys through the Interpreter's House, the Palace Beautiful, the Valley of the Shadow of Death, and the Delectable Mountains and finally reaches the Celestial City. The "pioneer pilgrims"—Christian and his associates—belong to the

Puritan sect, who was undergoing persecution in the reign of Charles II, especially during the earlier years of Restoration. Bunyan uses simple, strong, masculine and direct style and language of the common people, which all readers can understand. He links the religious allegory with realistic character sketches.

One of the most remarkable passages is Vanity Fair in which the persecution of Christian and his friend Faithful are described. Christian, the hero, and his companion, Faithful, are passing through a town called Vanity during the season of the local fair. On the Vanity Fair, honors, titles, kingdoms, lusts, pleasures and lives can be sold or bought, and cheating, roguery, murder and adultery are normal phenomena. In the descriptions of the Vanity Fair, Bunyan not only gives us a symbolic picture of London at the time of the Restoration but of the whole bourgeois society.

"Vanity Fair" is a remarkable passage. It is an epitome 缩影 of the English society after the Restoration.

Selected Reading

The Pilgrim's Progress
Vanity Fair

Then I saw in my Dream, that when they① were got② out of the Wilderness, they presently saw a Town before them, and the name of that Town is Vanity; and at the Town there is a Fair kept, called Vanity Fair: it is kept all the year long; it beareth③ the name of Vanity Fair, because the Town where 'tis④ kept is lighter than Vanity; and also because all that is there sold, or that cometh thither, is Vanity. As is the saying of the wise, all that cometh is Vanity.

This Fair is no new-erected business, but a thing of ancient standing; I will

---

①they: Christian and Faithful
②were got: had got
③beareth: bears 承受
④tis: it is

Chapter 3 Literature of the English Revolution and Restoration

shew you the original① of it.

Almost five thousand years agone②, there were Pilgrims walking to the Celestial City, as these two honest persons are; and Beelzebub, Apollyon, and Legion, with their Companions, perceiving by the path that the Pilgrims made, that their way to the City lay through this Town of Vanity, they contrived here to set up a Fair; a Fair wherein should be sold all sorts of Vanity, and that it should last all the year long: therefore at this Fair are all such Merchandize sold, as Houses, Lands, Trades, Places, Honours, Preferments③, Titles, Countries, Kingdoms, Lusts, Pleasures, and Delights of all sorts, as Whores, Bawds, Wives, Husbands, Children, Masters, Servants, Lives, Blood, Bodies, Souls, Silver, Gold, Pearls, Precious Stones, and what not④?

And moreover, at this Fair there is at all times to be seen Jugglings, Cheats, Games, Plays, Fools, Apes, Knaves, and Rogues, and that of every kind.

Here are to be seen too, and that for nothing, Thefts, Murders, Adulteries, false-swearers, and that of a blood-red colour.

And as in other Fairs of less moment⑤, there are the several Rows and Streets under their proper⑥ names, where such and such Wares are vended; so here likewise you have the proper places, Rows, Streets, (viz.⑦ Countries and Kingdoms) where the Wares of this Fair are soonest to be found: Here is the Britain Row, the French Row, the Italian Row, the Spanish Row, the German Row, where several sorts of Vanities are to be sold. But as in other Fairs, some one commodity is as the chief of all the Fair, so the ware of Rome and her Merchandize is greatly promoted in this Fair; only our English nation, with some

---

①original: origin 原点

②agone: ago

③Preferments: appointments and promotions to political or ecclesiastical positions 美差，肥缺

④and what not: and so on

⑤moment: importance 重要，契机

⑥proper[TOEFL]: own 本身的

⑦viz.: videlicet, namely

others, have taken a dislike① thereat②.

Now, as I said, the way to the Celestial City lies just through this Town where this lusty③ Fair is kept; and he that will go to City, and yet not go through this Town, must needs go out of the world. The Prince of Princes④ himself, when here, went through this Town to his own Country, and that upon a Fair-day too; yea, and as I think, it was Beelzebub, the chief Lord of this Fair, that invited him to buy of his Vanities: yea, would have made him Lord of the Fair, would he but⑤ have done him reverence as he went through the Town. Yea, because he was such a person of honour, Beelzebub had him from Street to Street, and shewed him all the Kingdoms of the World in a little time, that he might, (if possible) allure that Blessed One⑥ to cheapen⑦ and buy some of his Vanities; but he had no mind to the Merchandize, and therefore left the Town, without laying out so much as one Farthing upon these Vanities. This Fair therefore is an antient thing, of long standing, and a very great Fair.

Now these Pilgrims, as I said, must needs go through this Fair. Well, so they did; but behold, even as they entered into the Fair, all the people in the Fair were moved, and the Town itself as it were in a hubbub about them; and that for several reasons:

Firstly, the Pilgrims were clothed with such kind of Raiment as was diverse from the Raiment of any that traded in that Fair. The people therefore of the Fair made a great gazing upon them: some said they were Fools, some they were Bedlams, and some they are Outlandish men.

Secondly, and as they wondered at their Apparel, so they did likewise at their Speech; for few could understand what they said: they naturally spoke the language of Canaan, but they that kept the Fair were the men of this World; so

---

①dislike: disapproval 反感
②thereat: at it, at Rome
③lusty: merry, cheerful 精力充沛的
④Prince of Princes: Christ
⑤would he but: if only he would
⑥that Blessed One: Christ
⑦cheapen: barter for, to trade for, 贬低

that, from one end of the Fair to the other, they seemed Barbarians① each to the other.

Thirdly, but that which did not a little amuse② the Merchandizers was, that these Pilgrims set very light by all their Wares, they cared not so much as to look upon them; and if they called upon them to buy, they would put their fingers in their ears, and cry, turn away mine eyes from beholding Vanity, and look upwards, signifying that their trade and traffic③ was in Heaven.

One chanced mockingly, beholding the carriages④ of the men, to say unto them, What will ye buy? But they, looking gravely upon him, answered, We buy the Truth. At that there was an occasion taken to despise the men the more; some mocking, some taunting, some speaking reproachfully, and some calling upon others to smite them. At last things came to a hubbub and great stir in the Fair, insomuch that all order was confounded. Now was word presently brought to the Great One of the Fair, who quickly came down and deputed some of his most trusty friends to take those men into examination, about whom the Fair was almost overturned. So the men were brought to examination; and they that sat upon them asked them whence they came, whither they went, and what they did there in such an unusual Garb? The men told them that they were Pilgrims and Strangers in the World, and that they were going to their own Country, which was the Heavenly Jerusalem; and that they had given no occasion to the men of the Town, nor yet to the Merchandizers, thus to abuse them, and to let⑤ them in their Journey, except it was for that, when one asked them what they would buy, they said they would buy the Truth. But they that were appointed to examine them did not believe them to be any other than Bedlams and Mad, or else such as came to put all things into a confusion in the Fair. Therefore they took them and beat them, and besmeared them with dirt,

---

①Barbarians: foreigners, 外国人, 外来人
②amuse [IELTS]: cause to gaze in astonishment, wonder, 消遣
③trade and traffic: business 贸易和交通
④carriage: behaviour 举止
⑤let: hinder, 障碍

and then put them into the Cage, that they might be made a spectacle to all the men of the Fair.

Questions for Discussion

1. How is satire used in *Vanity Fair*?
2. What does Bunyan want to express in *The Pilgrim's Progress*?

Unit 3   John Donne

Appreciation

  Such wilt thou be to me, who must, 这就是你和我的关系, 我必须,
  Like the other foot, obliquely run; 像另一只脚, 斜走侧踮,
  Thy firmness makes my circle just, 你的坚定能使我的圆圈圆得完美,
  And makes me end where I begun. 让我的游离结束在我开始的地点。

Author

  John Donne was born in 1572 in London, England. Born into a Roman Catholic family, Donne's personal relationship with religion can be seen in his poetry. John Donne is known as the founder of the Metaphysical Poets, a term created by Samuel Johnson, an eighteenth-century English essayist, poet, and philosopher. Donne reached beyond the rational and hierarchical structures of the seventeenth century with his exacting and ingenious conceits, advancing the exploratory spirit of his time.

Brief Introduction

  In *A Valediction: Forbidding Mourning*, the speaker explains that he is forced to spend time apart from his lover, but before he leaves, he tells her that their farewell should not be the occasion for mourning and sorrow. In the same way that virtuous men die mildly and without complaint, they should leave without "tear-flood" and "sigh-tempests", for to publicly announce their feelings in such a way would profane their love. The speaker says that when the earth moves, it brings "harm and fears", but when the spheres experience "trepidation", though the impact is greater, it is also innocent. The lover of "dull sublunary lovers" cannot survive separation, but it removes that which constitutes the love itself; but the love he shares with his beloved is so refined and "inter-assured of the mind" that they need not worry about missing "eyes, lips and hands".

Though he must go, their souls are still one, and therefore, they are not enduring a breach, they are experiencing an "expansion"; in the same way that gold can be stretched by beating it "to airy thinness", the soul they share will simply stretch to take in all the space between them. If their souls are separate, he says, they are like the feet of a compass: His lover's soul is the fixed foot in the center, and his is the foot that moves around it. The firmness of the center foot makes the circle that the outer foot draws perfect.

Selected Reading

A Valediction: Forbidding Mourning[①]

As virtuous men pass mildly away[②],
And whisper to their souls to go[③],
Whilst some of their sad friends do say,
"The breath goes now," and some say, "No,"

So let us melt[④], and make no noise,

---

① A Valediction: Forbidding Mourning: A farewell. Don't grieve over my leaving. 再见，节哀
② pass mildly away: die peacefully 安祥地去世
③ Whisper to their souls to go: 向他们的灵魂说走
④ So let us melt: 让我们融化，合二为一

No tear-floods, nor sigh-tempests move①;
'Twere profanation of our joys
To tell the laity our love.②

Moving of the earth③ brings harms and fears,
Men reckon what it did and meant;④
But trepidation of the spheres⑤,
Though greater far, is innocent.⑥

Dull sublunary lovers' love⑦
(Whose soul is sense⑧) cannot admit⑨
Absence⑩, because it doth⑪ remove
Those things which elemented it.

---

①No tear-floods, nor sigh-tempests move：不再叹如风暴，泪如洪波。诗人把泪水比作洪水，把叹息比作风暴。move: stir up 激起，搅起

②'Twere profanation of our joys / To tell the laity our love：如果向俗人诉说我们的爱情，就是对我们欢乐的亵渎。'Twere: It were, 诗人在这里使用了虚拟语气，说明事实上他不可能把自己的爱情向俗人诉说。profanation: blasphemy 亵渎

③Moving of the earth：earthquake 地震

④Men reckon what it did and meant：人们猜测着，它（地震）的运动和意图

⑤trepidation of the spheres：trembling of the spheres 诸天体的震荡。根据托勒密的天文学（地心说），trepidation 指的是天体运行轨道中的第九重天（水晶圈）或第八重天（众恒星的轨道）的震荡或移动

⑥Though greater far, is innocent：尽管诸天体震荡（与地震相比）更为巨大，然而，这种震荡却是无害的。innocent: harmless. 根据托勒密的学说，诸天体运动有序和谐，虽然更加强烈巨大，却不会对人们构成伤害。然而，地震却能引起人们的恐慌。这里，诗人把爱人的别离比作巨大的天体运动，高尚而神秘，因此不能为凡人所理解

⑦Dull sublunary lovers' love：乏味的凡夫俗子的爱情

⑧Whose soul is sense：他们所注重的是感官。凡夫俗子的爱情重视感官上的满足，而不是精神上的追求。这和多恩本人所持的柏拉图式的爱情观形成鲜明的对照

⑨admit[TOEFL]：suffer, stand 可容纳

⑩absence[TOEFL]：being away 没有

⑪doth：does

Chapter 3 Literature of the English Revolution and Restoration

But we, by a love so much refined①
That our selves know not what it is,
Inter-assured of the mind,
Careless, eyes, lips, and hands to miss.

Our two souls therefore, which are one,
Though I must go, endure not yet
A breach, but an expansion.
Like gold to airy thinness beat.

If they be two, they are two so
As stiff twin compasses are two②:
Thy soul, the fixed foot, makes no show
To move, but doth, if the other do;

And though it in the center sit,
Yet when the other far doth roam,
It leans, and hearkens after it③,
And grows erect, as that comes home.

Such wilt thou be to me, who must,
Like the other foot, obliquely run;④
Thy firmness makes my circle just,⑤
And makes me end where I begun.

---

①refined[TOEFL]: purified 精练的
②As stiff twin compasses are two: as stiff as the two legs of compass 如同圆规的双脚那样坚定
③It leans, and hearkens after it: 它(圆周角)也随之倾斜,并且侧耳倾听。hearken: listen to
④who must / like the other foot, obliquely run: (我)必将像那另一只脚,即动脚,倾斜着身子转圈。这里诗人着意指他即将启程的欧洲之旅。obliquely: slantingly 斜的
⑤Thy firmness makes my circle just: 你的坚定使我把圆画得完整

Questions for Discussion

1. What are the writing features of *A Valediction*: *Forbidding Mourning*?
2. How is conceit used in *A Valediction*: *Forbidding Mourning*?

Unit 4　Henry Fielding

Appreciation

Tom Jones has two purposes—positive and negative aspects of the same purpose, really: (1) "to show the simple beauty of morality, and to urge men to yearn for it." (2) "In order to show that "those who snatches unjustly are often unworthy, the means used are not only mean, but also untrustworthy and always unworthy.

——Henry Fielding

汤姆心地善良,近乎中国孔子所讲的仁道。菲尔丁在书中多次发表关于善行的谈话,都像是从中文翻译过来的。汤姆很像中国小说中的英雄人物,整个小说如果把背景改换一下,很可能成为一部中国小说。

——美国《星期六评论》

Author

Henry Fielding was a novelist and playwright during the English Restoration as well as one of the founders of London's first police force, the Bow Street Runners. His fame is established chiefly upon his success as a novelist. His most successful novels were *Joseph Andrews* and *Tom Jones*. Henry Fielding wrote 4 novels in his life. He is regarded as "Founder of the English realistic novel", of all the eighteenth-century novelists he was the first to set out, both in theory and practice.

Chapter 3　Literature of the English Revolution and Restoration

Brief Introduction

Tom Jones is a masterpiece of Henry Fielding on the subject of human nature. It is a Bildungsroman and a picaresque novel. Mr. Allworthy, a kind and wealthy widower, lives in Somerset with his ill-humored unmarried sister Bridget. Late one evening, Allworthy finds a baby lying on his bed. He names it Tom, adding the surnames Jones on the assumptions that the mother is Jenny Jones. Meanwhile Bridget marries the Captain Blifil and they have a son, Master Blifil, who is brought up with Tom. Blifil tries to discredit Tom whenever he can. Tom becomes a vigorous, kind-hearted youth. Mr. Allworthy has a neighbor, Squire Western, who has a lovely young daughter, Sophia, his heiress. During his recuperation at Western's house, he and Sophia fall in love. Meanwhile, due to Blifil's machinations, Tom is disinherited and evicted from Mr. Allworthy's house. Tom then embarks upon a series of adventures at a number of roadside inns while on his way to London. Finally, Blifil is disinherited, Tom is revealed as Allworthy's nephew, and he gets engaged to his beloved Sophia.

It is generally regarded as Fielding's greatest book and as an influential English book.

Selected Reading

Tom Jones

BOOK XVIII Chapter 10

When Allworthy returned to his lodgings①, he heard Mr Jones was just arrived before him. He hurried therefore instantly into an empty chamber, whither he ordered Mr Jones to be brought to him alone.

It is impossible to conceive a more tender or moving scene than the meeting between the uncle and nephew (for Mrs Waters, as the reader may well suppose, had at her last visit discovered to him the secret of his birth). The first

---
①lodging[TOEFL]:寓所;暂住;寄宿

agonies of joy which were felt on both sides are indeed beyond my power to describe: I shall not therefore attempt it. After Allworthy had raised Jones from his feet, where he had prostrated① himself, and received him into his arms, "O my child!" he cried, "how have I been to blame! how have I injured you! What amends② can I ever make you for those unkind, those unjust suspicions which I have entertained, and for all the sufferings they have occasioned to you?" "Am I not now made amends?" cries Jones. "Would not my sufferings, if they had been ten times greater, have been now richly repaid? O my dear uncle, this goodness, this tenderness overpowers, unmans③, destroys me. I cannot bear the transports which flow so fast upon me. To be again restored to your presence, to your favour; to be once more thus kindly received by my great, my noble, my generous benefactor."—"Indeed, child," cries Allworthy, "I have used you cruelly."——He then explained to him all the treachery④ of Blifil, and again repeated expressions of the utmost concern, for having been induced by that treachery to use him so ill. "O, talk not so!" answered Jones; "indeed, sir, you have used me nobly. The wisest man might be deceived as you were; and, under such a deception⑤, the best must have acted just as you did. Your goodness displayed itself in the midst of your anger, just as it then seemed. I owe everything to that goodness, of which I have been most unworthy. Do not put me on self-accusation, by carrying your generous sentiments too far. Alas! sir, I have not been punished more than I have deserved; and it shall be the whole business of my future life to deserve that happiness you now bestow⑥ on me; for, believe me, my dear uncle, my punishment hath not been thrown away upon me: though I have been a great, I am not a hardened sinner; I thank Heaven, I have had time to reflect on my past life, where, though I cannot

---

①prostrate: 俯伏;趴着
②amend[TOEFL]: 弥补;修正;修订
③unman: 征服
④treachery:背叛;背信弃义
⑤deception[IELTS][TOEFL]: 蒙骗;欺骗
⑥bestow[TOEFL]:授予;献给

charge myself with any gross villainy①, yet I can discern follies and vices more than enough to repent and to be ashamed of; follies which have been attended with dreadful consequences to myself, and have brought me to the brink of destruction." "I am rejoiced, my dear child," answered Allworthy, "to hear you talk thus sensibly; for as I am convinced hypocrisy (good Heaven! how have I been imposed on by it in others!) was never among your faults, so I can readily believe all you say. You now see, Tom, to what dangers imprudence alone may subject virtue (for virtue, I am now convinced, you love in a great degree). Prudence is indeed the duty which we owe to ourselves; and if we will be so much our own enemies as to neglect it, we are not to wonder if the world is deficient② in discharging their duty to us; for when a man lays the foundation of his own ruin, others will, I am afraid, be too apt to build upon it. You say; however, you have seen your errors, and will reform them. I firmly believe you, my dear child; and therefore, from this moment, you shall never be reminded of them by me. Remember them only yourself so far as for the future to teach you the better to avoid them; but still remember, for your comfort, that there is this great difference between those faults which candor may construe into imprudence, and those which can be deduced from villainy only. The former, perhaps, are even more apt to subject a man to ruin; but if he reform, his character will, at length, be totally retrieved③; the world, though not immediately, will in time be reconciled to him; and he may reflect, not without some mixture of pleasure, on the dangers he hath escaped; but villainy, my boy, when once discovered is irretrievable; the stains which this leaves behind, no time will wash away. The censures of mankind will pursue the wretch, their scorn will abash him in public; and if shame drives him into retirement, he will go to it with all those terrors with which a weary child, who is afraid of hobgoblins④, retreats from company to go to bed alone. Here his

---

①villainy：罪恶；恶行
②deficient[TOEFL]：缺乏的；缺少的
③retrieve[TOEFL]：挽救；取回；索回
④hobgoblin：鬼；妖怪

murdered conscience will haunt him. Repose, like a false friend, will fly from him. Wherever he turns his eyes, horror presents itself; if he looks backward, unavailable repentance treads on his heels; if forward, incurable despair stares him in the face, till, like a condemned prisoner confined in a dungeon①, he detests his present condition, and yet dreads the consequence of that hour which is to relieve him from it. Comfort yourself, I say, my child, that this is not your case; and rejoice with thankfulness to him who hath suffered you to see your errors, before they have brought on you that destruction to which a persistence in even those errors must have led you. You have deserted them; and the prospect now before you are such, that happiness seems in your own power."
At these words Jones fetched a deep sigh; upon which, when Allworthy remonstrated, he said, "Sir, I will conceal nothing from you: I fear there is one consequence of my vices I shall never be able to retrieve. O, my dear uncle! I have lost a treasure." "You need say no more," answered Allworthy; "I will be explicit with you; I know what you lament; I have seen the young lady, and have discoursed with her concerning you. This I must insist on, as an earnest of your sincerity in all you have said, and of the steadfastness of your resolution, that you obey me in one instance. To abide entirely by the determination of the young lady, whether it shall be in your favour or no. She hath already suffered enough from solicitations which I hate to think of; she shall owe no further constraint② to my family: I know her father will be as ready to torment③ her now on your account as he hath formerly been on another's; but I am determined she shall suffer no more confinement, no more violence, no more uneasy hours."
"O, my dear uncle!" answered Jones, "lay, I beseech you, some command on me, in which I shall have some merit in obedience. Believe me, sir, the only instance in which I could disobey you would be to give an uneasy moment to my Sophia. No, sir, if I am so miserable to have incurred④ her displeasure beyond

---

①dungeon:地牢

②constraint[TOEFL]:逼迫;限制;约束

③torment[IELTS]:(精神上的)折磨;痛苦

④incur[IELTS]:引起;招致

all hope of forgiveness, that alone, with the dreadful reflection of causing her misery, will be sufficient to overpower me. To call Sophia mine is the greatest, and now the only additional blessing which heaven can bestow; but it is a blessing which I must owe to her alone." "I will not flatter you, child," cries Allworthy; "I fear your case is desperate: I never saw stronger marks of an unalterable resolution in any person than appeared in her vehement① declarations against receiving your addresses; for which, perhaps, you can account better than myself." "Oh, sir! I can account too well," answered Jones; "I have sinned against her beyond all hope of pardon; and guilty as I am, my guilt unfortunately appears to her in ten times blacker than the real colors. O, my dear uncle! I find my follies are irretrievable; and all your goodness cannot save me from perdition."

Chapter 11

Mrs Miller then asked what was to be done with Blifil? "for indeed," says she, "I cannot be easy while such a villain is in my house."—Allworthy answered, "He was as uneasy as herself on the same account." "Oh!" cries she, "if that be the case, leave the matter to me, I'll soon show him the outside out of my doors, I warrant you. Here are two or three lusty fellows below-stairs." "There will be no need of any violence," cries Allworthy; "if you will carry him a message from me, he will, I am convinced, depart of his own accord." "Will I?" said Mrs Miller; "I never did anything in my life with a better will." Here Jones interfered, and said, "He had considered the matter better, and would, if Mr Allworthy pleased, be himself the messenger. I know," says he, "already enough of your pleasure, sir, and I beg leave to acquaint him with it by my own words. Let me beseech② beseech: you, sir," added he, "to reflect on the dreadful consequences of driving him to violent and sudden despair. How unfit, alas! is this poor man to die in his present situation." This suggestion had not the least effect on Mrs Miller. She left the

---

① vehement: (感情) 强烈的
② beseech: 恳求; 哀求

room, crying, "You are too good, Mr Jones, infinitely too good to live in this world." But it made a deeper impression on Allworthy. "My good child," said he, "I am equally astonished at the goodness of your heart, and the quickness of your understanding. Heaven indeed forbid that this wretch should be deprived of any means or time for repentance! That would be a shocking consideration indeed. Go to him, therefore, and use your own discretion; yet do not flatter him with any hopes of my forgiveness; for I shall never forgive villainy farther than my religion obliges① me, and that extends not either to our bounty or our conversation."

Jones went up to Blifil's room, whom he found in a situation which moved his pity, though it would have raised a less amiable passion in many beholders. He cast himself on his bed, where he lay abandoning himself to despair, and drowned in tears; not in such tears as flow from contrition, and wash away guilt from minds which have been seduced② or surprised into it unawares, against the bent of their natural dispositions, as will sometimes happen from human frailty, even to the good; no, these tears were such as the freighted thief sheds in his cart, and are indeed the effects of that concern which the most savage natures are seldom deficient in feeling for themselves.

It would be unpleasant and tedious to paint this scene in full length. Let it suffice③ to say, that the behavior of Jones was kind to excess. He omitted nothing which his invention could supply, to raise and comfort the drooping④ spirits of Blifil, before he communicated to him the resolution of his uncle that he must quit the house that evening. He offered to furnish him with any money he wanted, assured him of his hearty forgiveness of all he had done against him, that he would endeavor to live with him hereafter as a brother, and would leave nothing unattempted to effectuate a reconciliation with his uncle.

Blifil was at first sullen and silent, balancing in his mind whether he should

---

①oblige[TOEFL]:规定;强迫;迫使
②seduce[IELTS][TOEFL]:唆使;诱骗
③suffice[IELTS]:足够;足以
④drooping:消沉;垂头丧气

Chapter 3 Literature of the English Revolution and Restoration

yet deny all; but, finding at last the evidence too strong against him, he betook himself at last to confession. He then asked pardon of his brother in the most vehement manner, prostrated himself on the ground, and kissed his feet; in short he was now as remarkably mean as he had been before remarkably wicked.

Jones could not so far check his disdain①, but that it a little discovered itself in his countenance at this extreme servility. He raised his brother the moment he could from the ground, and advised him to bear his afflictions more like a man; repeating, at the same time, his promises, that he would do all in his power to lessen them; for which Blifil, making many professions of his unworthiness, poured forth a profusion of thanks; and then, he having declared he would immediately depart to another lodging, Jones returned to his uncle.

Among other matters, Allworthy now acquainted Jones with the discovery which he had made concerning the £500 bank-notes. "I have," said he, "already consulted② a lawyer, who tells me, to my great astonishment, that there is no punishment for a fraud of this kind. Indeed, when I consider the black ingratitude of this fellow toward you, I think a highwayman, compared to him, is an innocent person."

"Good Heaven!" says Jones, "is it possible? —I am shocked beyond measure at this news. I thought there was not an honest fellow in the world. The temptation of such a sum was too great for him to withstand; for smaller matters have come safe to me through his hand. Indeed, my dear uncle, you must suffer me to call it weakness rather than ingratitude; for I am convinced the poor fellow loves me, and hath done me some kindnesses, which I can never forget; nay, I believe he hath repented of this very act; for it is not above a day or two ago, when my affairs seemed in the most desperate situation, that he visited me in my confinement③, and offered me any money I wanted. Consider, sir, what a temptation to a man who hath tasted such bitter distress, it must be, to have a

---

① disdain[IELTS]:鄙夷;鄙视
② consult[IELTS][TOEFL]:咨询;请教
③ confinement[TOEFL]:监禁;禁闭

sum in his possession which must put him and his family beyond any future possibility of suffering the like."

"Child," cries Allworthy, "you carry this forgiving temper too far. Such mistaken mercy is not only weakness, but borders on injustice, and is very pernicious① to society, as it encourages vice. The dishonesty of this fellow I might, perhaps, have pardoned, but never his ingratitude. And give me leave to say, when we suffer any temptation to atone for dishonesty itself, we are as candid and merciful as we ought to be; and so far I confess I have gone; for I have often pitied the fate of a highwayman, when I have been on the grand jury; and have more than once applied to the judge on the behalf of such as have had any mitigating circumstances in their case; but when dishonesty is attended with any blacker crime, such as cruelty, murder, ingratitude, or the like, compassion and forgiveness then become faults. I am convinced the fellow is a villain, and he shall be punished; at least as far as I can punish him."

Questions for Discussion

1. Why is *Tom Jones* a successful novel?
2. Classical epics typically rely on the use of Divine Intervention, or the supernatural, in order to shape the outcome of events. Does Tom Jones follow or deviate from this aspect of classical epics in its plot?

Terms

1. Allegory
2. Blank Verse
3. Conceit
4. Metaphysical poets
5. Cavalier poets

---

① pernicious: 有害的

Chapter 3 Literature of the English Revolution and Restoration

Chapter 4

18th-Century English Literature

I. Historical Background

1. The Augustan Age

After the tempestuous 17th century, England entered a period of comparatively peace and unity. In the middle of the 18th century, England had become the first powerful capitalist country in the world. The Tory and the Whig joined hands against tyranny and restoration of Catholicism, establishing a constitutional monarchy. The Puritan spirit of wisdom, diligence, honesty, and thriftiness contributed greatly to the development of the country.

Abroad, a vast expansion of British colonies in Asia, Africa and North America, and a continuous increase of colonial wealth and trade provided England with a market for which the small-scale, manual production methods of the home industry were hardly adequate. Besides, there were large-scale and long-drawn-out wars by professional armies and the station of large regiments in the colonies. The peaceful change of occupants of the throne entitled this period with the name Augustan Age or the Golden Age, chosen by those neoclassicists because of their admiration for the ancient culture of Roman Emperor Augustus Caesar (27BC – 14AD) and the belief that the greatest height of all proceeding civilizations had now found a worthy and comparable successor in the 18th century England.

2. The Industrial Revolution

The 18th century England witnessed unprecedented technical innovations which equipped industry with stream, the new moving force, and new tool, and rapid growth of industry and commerce, which influenced the way of social life as a whole. This is called the Industrial Revolution.

The Industrial Revolution widely developed in Britain and the English bourgeoisie accumulated more wealth and money and their social status was raised. The Enclosure Movement forced the peasants to seek new employment for their daily bread with a cheap price. The Industrial Revolution in Britain first began in the textile industry. And with the invention of large machines, new power had to be found. The increased production and trade promoted the transportation revolution. As a result, "workshop of the world" became another name for Britain by 1830.

With the fast development of industry in Britain, many big cities turned into "Black Country" with countless chimneys. More and more impoverished people herded into labour market and tended to work more time with less payment.

3. Great Changes in Social Life

The Industrial Revolution simplified class structure of Britain. The noble class could no longer compete with the middle class both in political influence and social influence. The biggest social problem in Britain at that time was the contradiction between the capitalist class and the proletariat class. The former was composed of the industrial and commercial classes and their appendices, and the latter was composed of expropriated small peasantry, victimized small craftsmen and small traders.

4. The Enlightenment

The 18th century marked the beginning of an intellectual movement, known as the Enlightenment, an expression of struggle of bourgeoisie against feudalism. The Enlightenment was a furtherance of the Renaissance of the 15th and 16th centuries.

The English enlighteners were bourgeois democratic thinkers. The purpose was to enlighten the whole world with the light of modern philosophical and artistic ideas. They celebrated reason or rationality, equality and science and advocated universal education. They stressed the importance of knowledge and reason, and they longed for a country of freedom, equality and love.

People were encouraged to cultivate a sound sense of rationality and a witty intellectuality. More schools were set up. Besides the popular forms of poetry, novel and drama, the period also saw the appearance of such popular press as pamphlets, newspapers and periodicals.

In the meantime of the Industrial Revolution, social life developed rapidly. Coffeehouses became the most striking feature of London life because people from many different walks of life could have enjoyable social lives and discuss intriguing and thought-provoking matters, especially those regarding philosophy to politics in a unique environment. The first English coffeehouse opened in Oxford in 1650. Nearly all writers frequented the coffeehouses and thus such manners as politics and fashion became subjects of literature.

II. Literary Background

In the later part of the 18th century, people began to feel discontented with the rigidity of rationality. A demand for a release of one's spontaneous feeling, a relaxation from the cold and rigid logic of rationality and an escape from the inhuman Industrial Revolution gradually took shape in the form of sentimental and pre-romantic novel and poetry. Novel, sentimental and pre-romantic poetry and fiction appeared in the last few decades of the 18th century.

1. Neoclassicism

In the early decades of the 18th century, the Enlightenment Movement brought about a revival of interest in the old classical works. This tendency is known as neoclassicism.

In England, neoclassicism was initiated by John Dryden, culminated in Alexander Pope and continued by Samuel Johnson. It was a reaction against the fire of passions that blazed in the late Renaissance, whose literary artistic model was the classical literature of ancient Greek and Latin authors, such as Homer, Virgil, Horace. They believed that the artistic ideals should be order, logic, restrained emotion and accuracy, and that literature should be judged in terms of its service to humanity. Neoclassicism made a rapid growth and prevailed in the 18th century. In drama, they follow the Three Unities closely which were called respectively unity of action, unity of place, and unity of time.

Alexander Pope (1688 – 1744) is the early representative poet of neoclassical school, best known for his satirical verse and for his translation of Homer, who introduced Enlightenment and popularized the neoclassical literary tradition from France. Pope was a master in the art of poetry whose style also depended upon his great patience in elaborating his art. By frequently writing in the form of heroic couplet, he became so perfect that no one has been able to approach him. He was singularly direct and compact. He represented the highest glory and authority in matters of literary art and made great contributions to the theory and practice of prosody 诗学. His Major Works: *An Essay on Criticism* (a manifesto of English neo-classicism)论批评, *Essay on Man* 人论, *The Dunciad* 愚人志, *The Rape of the Lock* 卷发遭劫记.

He was a great satirist and a literary critic who occupied a prominent place in his time. The early period of the 18th century has often been named after him as "The Age of Pope".

2. The Rise of the Novel

The novel emerged in England at the beginning of the 18th century in the form of a fictional imitation of the diaries, autobiographies, travelers' tales and biographies of criminals. The rise and growth of the realistic novel is the most prominent achievement. Realism plays a leading role in the 18th century literature, readers of novel were enlarging, and novel writing became colorful.

The summit of 18th century English literature is the novel. Excellent novelists emerged and told about ordinary people's thoughts, feelings and struggles. By combining the allegorical tradition of the moral fables with the picaresque 流浪汉的 tradition of the lower-caste stories, they achieved in their works both realism and moral teaching. The realist novelists of the 18th century are Daniel Defoe, Jonathan Swift, Henry Fielding and Tobias George Smollett.

3. Sentimentalism

One of the significant and popular trends in the second half of the 18th century is sentimentalism, which is a mild kind of protest against the social crisis. It could be defined to be overindulgence in one's emotion for the sake of his overwhelming discontent towards the social reality, and pessimistic belief and emphasis upon the virtues of man. Along with a new vision of love, sentimentalism presented a new view of human nature which prized feeling over thinking, passion over reason, and personal instincts of "pity, tenderness and benevolence" over social duties. Literary work of the sentimentalism marked by a sincere sympathy for the poverty-stricken, expropriated 征用 peasants, wrote the "simple annals of the poor". Sentimentalists appealed to sentiment, to the human heart and turned to the countryside for its material.

Thomas Gray, Oliver Goldsmith, Laurence Sterne, Samuel Richardson are representatives of Sentimentalism who criticized the viciousness of the social reality, and dreamed in vain for the return of the patriarchal mode of life. The obvious hopelessness of their dream brought about a pessimistic outlook. They blamed reason and the Industrial Revolution for the miseries and injustices in the aristocratic-bourgeois society and indulged in sentiment. Generally speaking, sentimentalism found fine expression in poetry and novel. They attacked the progressive aspect of this great social change in order to eliminate it and sighed for the return of the patriarchal times which they idealized. Writing still in a classical style, sentimentalism marks the midway in the transition from neoclassicism to its opposite, Romanticism in English poetry.

4. Pre-Romanticism

Pre-Romanticism originated among the conservative groups of men and letters as a reaction against the Enlightenment. In the second half of the 18th century, a new literary movement arose in Europe, called the Romantic Revival. It was marked by a strong protest against Classicism, by a recognition of the claims of passion and emotion, and by a renewed interest in medieval literature. In England, this movement showed itself in the trend of Pre-Romanticism in poetry. William Blake and Robert Burns are the representatives. Their writings provide a new code of social morality for the rising bourgeoisie and give a true picture of the social life of England in the 18th century.

Unit 1 Daniel Defoe

Appreciation

It might be truly said, that now I worked for my bread. I believe few people have thought much upon the strange multitude of little things necessary in the providing, producing, curing, dressing, making, and finishing this one article of bread.

人们常说"为面包而工作",其意思是"为生存而工作"。为了制成面包这样小小的不起眼的东西,你首先得做好播种准备,生产出粮食,再要经过晒、筛、制、烤等种种奇怪而繁杂的必不可少的过程，真不能不令人惊叹。我也想，很少人会想到，我们天天吃的面包要真的自己动手从头做起是多么不容易啊！

Author

The son of a London butcher, and educated at a Dissenters' academy, Defoe was typical of the new kind of man reaching prominence in England in the 18th century.

Defoe has been called the father of modern journalism; during his lifetime he was associated with 26 periodicals. In 1719 he published his famous *Life and Strange Surprising Adventures of Robinson Crusoe*, followed by two less engrossing sequels. Based in part on the experiences of Alexander Selkirk, *Robinson Crusoe* is considered by some critics to be the first true novel in English. From 1719 to 1724, Defoe published the novels for which he is famous.

Daniel Defoe died on April 24, 1731, probably while in hiding from his creditors. He was interred in Bunhill Fields, London, where his grave can still be visited.

Brief Introduction

At the head of Defoe's works stands his most important work *The Life and Strange Surprising Adventures of Robinson Crusoe* and held its popularity for more than two centuries.

The story was based upon the experiences of a Scotch sailor called Alexander Selkirk, who had been marooned on a desert island off the coast of Chile and lived there in solitude for four or five years. After his return to Europe in 1709, his experiences became known. Defoe got inspiration from this real story and with many incidents of his own imagination, he successfully produced the famous novel *Robinson Crusoe*.

The story is told in the first person singular as if it was told by some sailor-adventurer himself. In this novel, Defoe created the image of a true empire-builder, a colonizer and a foreign trader, who has the courage and will to face hardships and the determination to preserve himself and improve his livelihood by struggling against nature. Crusoe represents the English bourgeoisie at the earlier stage of its development. Being a bourgeois writer, Defoe glorifies the hero and defends the policy of colonialism of British government.

Selected Reading

Robinson Crusoe

Chapter 3

I was now, in the months of November and December, expecting my crop of barley and rice. The ground I had manured and dug up for them was not great; for, as I observed, my seed of each was not above the quantity of half a peck, for I had lost one whole crop by sowing in the dry season. But now my crop promised very well, when on a sudden I found I was in danger of losing it all again by enemies of several sorts, which it was scarcely possible to keep from it; as, first, the goats, and wild creatures which I called hares, who, tasting the sweetness of the blade, lay in it night and day, as soon as it came up, and eat it so close, that it could get no time to shoot up into stalk.

This I saw no remedy for but by making an enclosure about it with a hedge; which I did with a great deal of toil, and the more, because it required speed. However, as my arable land was but small, suited to my crop, I got it totally well fenced in about three weeks'time; and shooting some of the creatures in the daytime, I set my dog to guard it in the night, tying him up to a stake at the gate, where he would stand and bark all night long; so in a little time the enemies forsook the place, and the corn grew very strong and well, and began to ripen apace.

But as the beasts ruined me before, while my corn was in the blade, so the birds were as likely to ruin me now, when it was in the ear; for, going along by the place to see how it throve, I saw my little crop surrounded with fowls, of I know not how many sorts, who stood, as it were, watching till I should be gone. I immediately let fly among them, for I always had my gun with me. I had no sooner shot, but there rose up a little cloud of fowls, which I had not seen at all, from among the corn itself.

This touched me sensibly, for I foresaw that in a few days they would devour all my hopes; that I should be starved, and never be able to raise a crop at all; and what to do I could not tell; however, I resolved not to lose my corn, if possible, though I should watch it night and day. In the first place, I went among it to see what damage was already done, and found they had spoiled a good deal of it; but that as it was yet too green for them, the loss was not so great but that the remainder was likely to be a good crop if it could be saved.

I stayed by it to load my gun, and then coming away, I could easily see the thieves sitting upon all the trees about me, as if they only waited till I was gone away, and the event proved it to be so; for as I walked off, as if I was gone, I was no sooner out of their sight than they dropped down one by one into the corn again. I was so provoked, that I could not have patience to stay till more came on, knowing that every grain that they ate now was, as it might be said, a peck-loaf to me in the consequence; but coming up to the hedge, I fired again, and killed three of them. This was what I wished for; so I took them up, and served them as we serve notorious① thieves in England-hanged them in chains, for a terror to of them. It is impossible to imagine that this should have such an effect as it had, for the fowls② would not only not come at the corn, but, in short, they forsook all that part of the island, and I could never see a bird near the place as long as my scarecrows③ hung there.

This I was very glad of, you may be sure, and about the latter end of December, which was our second harvest of the year, I reaped my corn.

I was sadly put to it for a scythe or sickle to cut it down, and all I could do was to make one, as well as I could, out of one of the broadswords④, or cutlasses⑤, which I saved among the arms out of the ship. However, as my first crop was but small, I had no great difficulty to cut it down; in short, I reaped it in my way, for I cut nothing off but the ears, and carried it away in a great

---

①notorious[TOEFL][IELTS]:声名狼藉的
②fowl:家禽
③scarecrow:稻草人,威吓物
④broadsword:大刀;腰刀
⑤cutlass:弯刀;短剑

basket which I had made, and so rubbed it out with my hands; and at the end of all my harvesting, I found that out of my half-peck① of seed I had near two bushels of rice, and about two bushels② and a half of barley; that is to say, by my guess, for I had no measure at that time.

However, this was a great encouragement to me, and I foresaw that, in time, it would please God to supply me with bread. And yet here I was perplexed again, for I neither knew how to grind or make meal of my corn, or indeed how to clean it and part it; nor, if made into meal, how to make bread of it; and if how to make it, yet I knew not how to bake it. These things being added to my desire of having a good quantity for store, and to secure a constant supply, I resolved not to taste any of this crop but to preserve it all for seed against the next season; and in the meantime to employ all my study and hours of working to accomplish this great work of providing myself with corn and bread.

It might be truly said, that now I worked for my bread. I believe few people have thought much upon the strange multitude of little things necessary in the providing, producing, curing, dressing, making, and finishing this one article of bread.

I, that was reduced to a mere state of nature, found this to my daily discouragement; and was made more sensible of it every hour, even after I had got the first handful of seed-corn, which, as I have said, came up unexpectedly, and indeed to a surprise.

First, I had no plough to turn up the earth—no spade or shovel to dig it. Well, this I conquered by making me a wooden spade, as I observed before; but this did my work but in a wooden manner③; and though it cost me a great many days to make it, yet, for want of iron, it not only wore out soon, but made my work the harder, and made it be performed much worse.

However, this I bore with, and was content to work it out with patience,

---

①half-peck:半配克,4 夸脱

②bushel:蒲式耳

③but in a wooden manner: but in a clumsy manner 但用一个笨拙的方式

and bear with the badness of the performance. When the corn was sown, I had no harrow, but was forced to go over it myself, and drag a great heavy bough of a tree over it, to scratch it, as it may be called, rather than rake① or harrow② it.

When it was growing, and grown, I have observed already how many things I wanted to fence it, secure it, mow or reap it, cure and carry it home, thrash, part it from the chaff③, and save it. Then I wanted a mill to grind it sieves to dress it, yeast④ and salt to make it into bread, and an oven to bake it; but all these things I did without, as shall be observed; and yet the corn was an inestimable⑤ comfort and advantage to me too. All this, as I said, made everything laborious and tedious to me; but that there was no help for. Neither was my time so much loss to me, because, as I had divided it, a certain part of it was every day appointed to these works; and as I had resolved to use none of the corn for bread till I had a greater quantity by me, I had the next six months to apply myself wholly, by labour and invention, to furnish myself with utensils proper for the performing all the operations necessary for making the corn, when I had it, fit for my use.

But first I was to prepare more land, for I had now seed enough to sow above an acre of ground. Before I did this, I had a week's work at least to make me a spade, which, when it was done, was but a sorry one indeed, and very heavy, and required double labour to work with it. However, I got through that, and sowed my seed in two large flat pieces of ground, as near my house as I could find them to my mind⑥, and fenced them in with a good hedge, the stakes⑦ of which were all cut off that wood which I had set before, and knew it would grow; so that, in a year's time, I knew I should have a quick or living hedge, that would want but little repair. This work did not take me up less than

---

①rake：耙子
②harrow：耙地
③chaff：糠；谷壳
④yeast：酵母
⑤inestimable[IELTS]：无价的；难以估计的
⑥to my mind：to my liking 中人的意
⑦stake[IELTS]：桩，棍子

three months, because a great part of that time was the wet season, when I could not go abroad.

Within doors, that is when it rained and I could not go out, I found employment in the following occupations—always observing, that all the while I was at work I diverted① myself with talking to my parrot, and teaching him to speak; and I quickly taught him to know his own name, and at last to speak it out pretty loud, "Poll", which was the first word I ever heard spoken in the island by any mouth but my own. This, therefore, was not my work, but an assistance to my work; for now, as I said, I had a great employment upon my hands, as follows: I had long studied to make, by some means or other, some earthen vessels, which, indeed, I wanted sorely, but knew not where to come at them. However, considering the heat of the climate, I did not doubt but if I could find out any clay, I might make some pots that might, being dried in the sun, be hard enough and strong enough to bear handling, and to hold anything that was dry, and required to be kept so; and as this was necessary in the preparing corn, meal, which was the thing I was doing, I resolved to make some as large as I could, and fit only to stand like jars, to hold what should be put into them.

It would make the reader pity me, or rather laugh at me, to tell how many awkward ways I took to raise this paste; what odd, misshapen, ugly things I made; how many of them fell in and how many fell out, the clay not being stiff enough to bear its own weight; how many cracked by the over-violent heat of the sun, being set out too hastily; and how many fell in pieces with only removing, as well before as after they were dried; and, in a word, how, after having laboured hard to find the clay—to dig it, to temper it, to bring it home, and work it—I could not make above two large earthen ugly things (I cannot call them jars) in about two months' labour.

However, as the sun baked these two very dry and hard, I lifted them very gently up, and set them down again in two great wicker② baskets, which I had

---

①divert[TOEFL][IELTS]:转移

②wicker:柳条

made on purpose for them, that they might not break; and as between the pot and the basket there was a little room to spare, I stuffed it full of the rice and barley straw; and these two pots being to stand always dry I thought would hold my dry corn, and perhaps the meal, when the corn was bruised.

Though I miscarried so much in my design for large pots, yet I made several smaller things with better success; such as little round pots, flat dishes, pitchers, and pipkins, and any things my hand turned to; and the heat of the sun baked them quite hard.

But all this would not answer my end, which was to get an earthen pot to hold what was liquid, and bear the fire, which none of these could do. It happened after some time, making a pretty large fire for cooking my meat, when I went to put it out after I had done with it, I found a broken piece of one of my earthenware vessels in the fire, burnt as hard as a stone, and red as a tile. I was agreeably surprised to see it, and said to myself, that certainly they might be made to burn whole, if they would burn broken.

This set me to study how to order my fire, so as to make it burn some pots. I had no notion of a kiln, such as the potters burn in, or of glazing them with lead, though I had some lead to do it with; but I placed three large pipkins① and two or three pots in a pile, one upon another, and placed my firewood all round it, with a great heap of embers② under them. I plied the fire with fresh fuel round the outside and upon the top, till I saw the pots in the inside red-hot③ quite through, and observed that they did not crack at all. When I saw them clear④ red, I let them stand in that heat about five or six hours, till I found one of them, though it did not crack, did melt or run; for the sand which was mixed with the clay melted by the violence of the heat, and would have run into glass if I had gone on; so I slacked my fire gradually till the pots began to abate of the red colour; and watching them all night, that I might not let the fire abate too

---

① pipkin: 小瓦罐；小汲桶
② embers: 余烬
③ red-hot: 热狗
④ clear: completely 完全地

fast, in the morning I had three very good (I will not say handsome) pipkins, and two other earthen pots, as hard burnt as could be desired, and one of them perfectly glazed with the running of the sand.

After this experiment, I need not say that I wanted no sort of earthenware for my use; but I must needs say as to the shapes of them, they were very indifferent①, as any one may suppose, when I had no way of making them but as the children make dirt pies, or as a woman would make pies that never learned to raise paste.

No joy at a thing of so mean a nature was ever equal to mine, when I found I had made an earthen pot that would bear the fire; and I had hardly patience to stay till they were cold before I set one on the fire again with some water in it to boil me some meat, which it did admirably well; and with a piece of a kid I made some very good broth, though I wanted oatmeal, and several other ingredients requisite to make it as good as I would have had it been.

My next concern was to get me a stone mortar to stamp or beat some corn in; for as to the mill, there was no thought of arriving at that perfection of art with one pair of hands. To supply this want, I was at a great loss; for, of all the trades in the world, I was as perfectly unqualified for a stone-cutter as for any whatever; neither had I any tools to go about it with. I spent many a day to find out a great stone big enough to cut hollow, and make fit for a mortar, and could find none at all, except what was in the solid rock, and which I had no way to dig or cut out; nor indeed were the rocks in the island of hardness sufficient, but were all of a sandy, crumbling② stone, which neither would bear the weight of a heavy pestle, nor would break the corn without filling it with sand. So, after a great deal of time lost in searching for a stone, I gave it over, and resolved to look out for a great block of hard wood, which I found, indeed, much easier; and getting one as big as I had strength to stir, I rounded it, and formed it on the outside with my axe and hatchet, and then with the help of fire and infinite labour, made a hollow place in it, as the Indians in Brazil make their canoes.

---

①they were very indifferent: they were not very good 他们不是很好
②crumble[TOEFL][IELTS]: 破碎, 粉碎

After this, I made a great heavy pestle or beater of the wood called the ironwood; and this I prepared and laid by against I had my next crop of corn, which I proposed to myself to grind, or rather pound into meal to make bread.

My next difficulty was to make a sieve or searce, to dress my meal, and to part it from the bran and the husk; without which I did not see it possible I could have any bread. This was a most difficult thing even to think on, for to be sure I had nothing like the necessary thing to make it—I mean fine thin canvas or stuff to searce the meal through. And here I was at a full stop for many months; nor did I really know what to do. Linen I had none left but what was mere rags; I had goat's hair, but neither knew how to weave it or spin it; and had I known how, here were no tools to work it with. All the remedy that I found for this was, that at last I did remember I had, among the seamen's clothes which were saved out of the ship, some neckcloths of calico or muslin①; and with some pieces of these I made three small sieves proper enough for the work; and thus I made shift for some years: how I did afterwards, I shall show in its place.

The baking part was the next thing to be considered, and how I should make bread when I came to have corn; for first, I had no yeast. As to that part, there was no supplying the want, so I did not concern myself much about it. But for an oven I was indeed in great pain. At length I found out an experiment for that also, which was this: I made some earthen-vessels very broad but not deep, that is to say, about two feet diameter, and not above nine inches deep. These I burned in the fire, as I had done the other, and laid them by; and when I wanted to bake, I made a great fire upon my hearth, which I had paved with some square tiles of my own baking and burning also; but I should not call them square.

When the firewood was burned pretty much into embers or live coals, I drew them forward upon this hearth, so as to cover it all over, and there I let them lie till the hearth was very hot. Then sweeping away all the embers, I set down my loaf or loaves, and whelming down the earthen pot upon them, drew the embers all round the outside of the pot, to keep in and add to the heat; and

---

①neckcloths of calico or muslin: 白布或棉布领带

thus as well as in the best oven in the world, I baked my barley-loaves, and became in little time a good pastrycook[①] into the bargain; for I made myself several cakes and puddings of the rice; but I made no pies, neither had I anything to put into them supposing I had, except the flesh either of fowls or goats.

It need not be wondered at if all these things took me up most part of the third year of my abode here; for it is to be observed that in the intervals of these things I had my new harvest and husbandry to manage; for I reaped my corn in its season, and carried it home as well as I could, and laid it up in the ear, in my large baskets, till I had time to rub it out, for I had no floor to thrash it on, or instrument to thrash[②] it with.

And now, indeed, my stock of corn increasing, I really wanted to build my barns bigger; I wanted a place to lay it up in, for the increase of the corn now yielded me so much, that I had of the barley about twenty bushels, and of the rice as much or more; insomuch that now I resolved to begin to use it freely; for my bread had been quite gone a great while; also I resolved to see what quantity would be sufficient for me a whole year, and to sow but once a year.

Upon the whole, I found that the forty bushels of barley and rice were much more than I could consume in a year; so I resolved to sow just the same quantity every year that I sowed the last, in hopes that such a quantity would fully provide me with bread.

Question for Discussion

Discuss Crusoe as an embodiment of the rising middle-class virtues in the mid-18th century England.

---

①pastrycook:做西点、面包的人
②thrash:打谷;逆风浪行

Unit 2 Jonathan Swift

Appreciation

The other project was, a scheme for entirely abolishing all words whatsoever; and this was urged as a great advantage in point of health, as well as brevity. For it is plain, that every word we speak is, in some degree, a diminution of our lunge by corrosion, and consequently, contributes to the shortening of our lives. An expedient was therefore offered, "that since words are only names for things, it would be more convenient for all men to carry about them such things as were necessary to express a particular business they are to discourse on."

另一项计划则是,无论什么词汇,一概废除。他们坚决主张,不论从健康的角度考虑,还是从简练的角度考虑,这一计划都大有好处,因为大家都清楚,我们每说一个词,或多或少会对肺部有所侵蚀,这样也就缩短了我们的寿命。因此他们就想出了一个补救的办法:既然词只是事物的名称,那么,大家在谈到具体事情的时候,把表示那具体事情所需的东西带在身边,不是来得更方便吗?

Author

Jonathan Swift was born in Dublin, Ireland. And he is probably the foremost prose satirist in the English language, and is less well known for his poetry. He is also known for two styles of satire: the Horatian and Juvenalian styles.

Swift's family had several interesting literary connections: His grandmother, Elizabeth (Dryden) Swift, was the niece of Sir Erasmus Dryden, grandfather of the poet John Dryden. The same grandmother's aunt, Katherine (Throckmorton) Dryden, was the first cousin of Elizabeth, wife of Sir Walter Raleigh. His great-great grandmother, Margaret (Godwin) Swift, was the sister of Francis Godwin, author of *The Man in the Moone* which influenced parts of Swift's *Gulliver's Travels*. His uncle, Thomas Swift, married a daughter of the poet and playwright Sir William Davenant, a godson of William Shakespeare.

Brief Introduction

Gulliver's Travels contains four parts; each of them deals with one particular voyage of the hero and his extraordinary adventures on some remote island.

The third part, which is often considered to be the least interesting, deals with a series of the hero's adventures at several places. The first place that Gulliver gets to is the floating island of Laputa. Gulliver finds out here the king and the noble persons are a group of absent-minded philosophers and astronomers who care for nothing but mathematics and music and who speak always in mathematical terms of lines and circles. They often do useless research work, for example a scientist makes researches on how to get sunlight from cucumbers. Another scientist is studying how to construct a house by first building the room and then laying the base. Through these descriptions, Swift satirizes the scientists who keep themselves aloof from practical life.

Selected Reading

Gulliver's Travels

Part III. A VOYAGE TO LAPUTA, BALNIBARBI, LUGGNAGG, GLUBBDUBDRIB, AND JAPAN.

Chapter 5

The author permitted to see the grand academy of Lagado[①]. The academy largely described. The arts where in the professors employ themselves.

This academy is not an entire single building, but a continuation of several houses on both sides of a street, which growing waste, was purchased and applied to that use.

I was received very kindly by the warden, and went for many days to the academy. Every room has in it one or more projectors; and I believe I could not

---

①Lagado: Lagado is the capital of the nation Balnibarbi, which is ruled by a tyrannical king from a flying island called Laputa. Lagado is on the ground below Laputa, and also has access to Laputa at any given time to proceed in an attack or defense

be in fewer than five hundred rooms.

The first man I saw was of a meagre aspect, with sooty hands and face, his hair and beard long, ragged, and singed in several places. His clothes, shirt, and skin, were all of the same colour. He has been eight years upon a project for extracting sunbeams out of cucumbers, which were to be put in phials hermetically sealed①, and let out to warm the air in raw inclement summers. He told me, he did not doubt, that, in eight years more, he should be able to supply the governor's gardens with sunshine, at a reasonable rate: but he complained that his stock was low, and entreated me "to give him something as an encouragement to ingenuity, especially since this had been a very dear season for cucumbers." I made him a small present, for my lord had furnished me with money on purpose, because he knew their practice of begging from all who go to see them.

I went into another chamber, but was ready to hasten back, being almost overcome with a horrible stink. My conductor pressed me forward, conjuring me in a whisper "to give no offence, which would be highly resented;" and therefore I durst not so much as stop my nose. The projector of this cell was the most ancient student of the academy; his face and beard were of a pale yellow; his hands and clothes daubed over with filth. When I was presented to him, he gave me a close embrace, a compliment I could well have excused. His employment, from his first coming into the academy, was an operation to reduce human excrement to its original food, by separating the several parts, removing the tincture which it receives from the gall②, making the odour③ exhale, and scumming off the saliva. He had a weekly allowance, from the society, of a vessel filled with human ordure, about the bigness of a Bristol barrel.

I saw another at work to calcine④ ice into gunpowder; who likewise showed

---

①hermetically sealed: completely sealed, especially against the escape or entry of air 密封的
②gall: 胆汁
③odour[IELTS]:气味
④calcine: 煅烧

me a treatise he had written concerning the malleability① of fire, which he intended to publish.

There was a most ingenious architect, who had contrived a new method for building houses, by beginning at the roof, and working downward to the foundation; which he justified to me, by the like practice of those two prudent insects, the bee and the spider.

There was a man born blind, who had several apprentices in his own condition: their employment was to mix colours for painters, which their master taught them to distinguish by feeling and smelling. It was indeed my misfortune to find them at that time not very perfect in their lessons, and the professor himself happened to be generally mistaken. This artist is much encouraged and esteemed by the whole fraternity.

In another apartment I was highly pleased with a projector who had found a device of ploughing the ground with hogs, to save the charges of ploughs, cattle, and labour. The method is this: in an acre of ground you bury, at six inches distance and eight deep, a quantity of acorns, dates, chestnuts, and other mast or vegetables, whereof these animals are fondest; then you drive six hundred or more of them into the field, where, in a few days, they will root up the whole ground in search of their food, and make it fit for sowing, at the same time manuring it with their dung: it is true, upon experiment, they found the charge and trouble very great, and they had little or no crop. However it is not doubted, that this invention may be capable of great improvement.

I went into another room, where the walls and ceiling were all hung round with cobwebs, except a narrow passage for the artist to go in and out. At my entrance, he called aloud to me, "not to disturb his webs." He lamented "the fatal mistake the world had been so long in, of using silkworms, while we had such plenty of domestic insects who infinitely excelled the former, because they understood how to weave, as well as spin." And he proposed further, "that by employing spiders, the charge of dyeing silks should be wholly saved;" whereof I was fully convinced, when he showed me a vast number of flies most

---

①malleability[TOEFL]: 可塑性

beautifully coloured, wherewith he fed his spiders, assuring us "that the webs would take a tincture from them; and as he had them of all hues, he hoped to fit everybody's fancy, as soon as he could find proper food for the flies, of certain gums, oils, and other glutinous① matter, to give a strength and consistence to the threads."

There was an astronomer, who had undertaken to place a sun-dial upon the great weathercock on the town-house, by adjusting the annual and diurnal motions of the earth and sun, so as to answer and coincide with all accidental turnings of the wind.

I was complaining of a small fit of the colic, upon which my conductor led me into a room where a great physician resided, who was famous for curing that disease, by contrary operations from the same instrument. He had a large pair of bellows②, with a long slender muzzle of ivory; this he conveyed eight inches up the anus, and drawing in the wind, he affirmed he could make the guts as lank as a dried bladder. But when the disease was more stubborn and violent, he let in the muzzle while the bellows were full of wind, which he discharged into the body of the patient; then withdrew the instrument to replenish it, clapping his thumb strongly against the orifice③ of then fundament; and this being repeated three or four times, the adventitious④ wind would rush out, bringing the noxious⑤ along with it, (like water put into a pump) and the patient recovered. I saw him try both experiments upon a dog, but could not discern any effect from the former. After the latter the animal was ready to burst, and made so violent a discharge as was very offensive to me and my companion. The dog died on the spot, and we left the doctor endeavouring to recover him, by the same operation.

I visited many other apartments, but shall not trouble my reader with all the

---

①glutinous [IELTS]：有黏性的
②bellows[TOEFL]：风箱
③orifice：口、孔
④adventitious：偶然的
⑤noxious[TOEFL][IELTS]：毒

curiosities I observed, being studious of brevity.

I had hitherto seen only one side of the academy, the other being appropriated to the advancers of speculative learning, of whom I shall say something, when I have mentioned one illustrious person more, who is called among them "the universal artist". He told us, "he had been thirty years employing his thoughts for the improvement of human life." He had two large rooms full of wonderful curiosities, and fifty men at work. Some were condensing air into a dry tangible substance, by extracting the nitre①, and letting the aqueous② or fluid particles percolate③; others softening marble, for pillows and pin-cushions; others petrifying the hoofs of a living horse, to preserve them from foundering. The artist himself was at that time busy upon two great designs; the first, to sow land with chaff④, wherein he affirmed the true seminal virtue to be contained, as he demonstrated by several experiments, which I was not skilful enough to comprehend. The other was, by a certain composition of gums, minerals, and vegetables, outwardly applied, to prevent the growth of wool upon two young lambs; and he hoped, in a reasonable time to propagate the breed of naked sheep, all over the kingdom.

We crossed a walk to the other part of the academy, where, as I have already said, the projectors in speculative learning resided.

The first professor I saw, was in a very large room, with forty pupils about him. After salutation, observing me to look earnestly upon a frame, which took up the greatest part of both the length and breadth of the room, he said, "Perhaps I might wonder to see him employed in a project for improving speculative knowledge, by practical and mechanical operations. But the world would soon be sensible of its usefulness; and he flattered himself, that a more noble, exalted thought never sprang in any other man's head. Every one knew

---

①nitre: 硝
②aqueous: 水
③percolate[TOEFL]: 过滤
④chaff: 糠

how laborious① the usual method is of attaining to arts and sciences; whereas, by his contrivance, the most ignorant person, at a reasonable charge, and with a little bodily labour, might write books in philosophy, poetry, politics, laws, mathematics, and theology, without the least assistance from genius or study." He then led me to the frame, about the sides, whereof all his pupils stood in ranks. It was twenty feet square, placed in the middle of the room. The superfices was composed of several bits of wood, about the bigness of a die, but some larger than others. They were all linked together by slender wires. These bits of wood were covered, on every square, with paper pasted on them; and on these papers were written all the words of their language, in their several moods, tenses, and declensions; but without any order. The professor then desired me, "to observe; for he was going to set his engine at work." The pupils, at his command, took each of them hold of an iron handle, whereof there were forty fixed round the edges of the frame; and giving them a sudden turn, the whole disposition of the words was entirely changed. He then commanded six-and-thirty of the lads, to read the several lines softly, as they appeared upon the frame; and where they found three or four words together that might make part of a sentence, they dictated to the four remaining boys, who were scribes. This work was repeated three or four times, and at every turn, the engine was so contrived, that the words shifted into new places, as the square bits of wood moved upside down.

Six hours a day the young students were employed in this labour; and the professor showed me several volumes in large folio, already collected, of broken sentences, which he intended to piece together, and out of those rich materials, to give the world a complete body of all arts and sciences; which, however, might be still improved, and much expedited, if the public would raise a fund for making and employing five hundred such frames in Lagado, and oblige the managers to contribute in common their several collections.

He assured me "that this invention had employed all his thoughts from his youth; that he had emptied the whole vocabulary into his frame, and made the

---

①laborious[TOEFL][IELTS]：费力的

strictest computation of the general proportion there is in books between the numbers of particles, nouns, and verbs, and other parts of speech."

I made my humblest acknowledgment to this illustrious person, for his great communicativeness; and promised, "if ever I had the good fortune to return to my native country, that I would do him justice, as the sole inventor of this wonderful machine;" the form and contrivance of which I desired leave to delineate on paper, as in the figure here annexed. I told him, "although it were the custom of our learned in Europe to steal inventions from each other, who had thereby at least this advantage, that it became a controversy which was the right owner; yet I would take such caution, that he should have the honour entire, without a rival."

We next went to the school of languages, where three professors sat in consultation upon improving that of their own country.

The first project was, to shorten discourse, by cutting polysyllables[①] into one, and leaving out verbs and participles, because, in reality, all things imaginable are but norms.

The other project was, a scheme for entirely abolishing all words whatsoever; and this was urged as a great advantage in point of health, as well as brevity. For it is plain, that every word we speak is, in some degree, a diminution of our lunge by corrosion, and, consequently, contributes to the shortening of our lives. An expedient was therefore offered, "that since words are only names for things, it would be more convenient for all men to carry about them such things as were necessary to express a particular business they are to discourse on." And this invention would certainly have taken place, to the great ease as well as health of the subject, if the women, in conjunction with the vulgar and illiterate, had not threatened to raise a rebellion unless they might be allowed the liberty to speak with their tongues, after the manner of their forefathers; such constant irreconcilable enemies to science are the common people. However, many of the most learned and wise adhere to the new scheme of expressing themselves by things; which has only this

---

① polysyllables：多音节词

inconvenience attending it, that if a man's business be very great, and of various kinds, he must be obliged, in proportion, to carry a greater bundle of things upon his back, unless he can afford one or two strong servants to attend him. I have often beheld two of those sages almost sinking under the weight of their packs, like pedlars① among us, who, when they met in the street, would lay down their loads, open their sacks, and hold conversation for an hour together; then put up their implements, help each other to resume their burdens, and take their leave.

But for short conversations, a man may carry implements in his pockets, and under his arms, enough to supply him; and in his house, he cannot be at a loss. Therefore the room where company meet who practise this art, is full of all things, ready at hand, requisite to furnish matter for this kind of artificial converse.

Another great advantage proposed by this invention was, that it would serve as a universal language, to be understood in all civilised nations, whose goods and utensils are generally of the same kind, or nearly resembling, so that their uses might easily be comprehended. And thus ambassadors would be qualified to treat with foreign princes, or ministers of state, to whose tongues they were utter strangers.

I was at the mathematical school, where the master taught his pupils after a method scarce imaginable to us in Europe. The proposition, and demonstration, were fairly written on a thin wafer, with ink composed of a cephalic② tincture③. This, the student was to swallow upon a fasting stomach, and for three days following, eat nothing but bread and water. As the wafer digested, the tincture mounted to his brain, bearing the proposition along with it. But the success has not hitherto been answerable, partly by some error in the quantum or composition, and partly by the perverseness of lads, to whom this bolus④ is so nauseous, that they generally steal aside, and discharge it upwards, before it can operate; neither have they been yet persuaded to use so long an abstinence,

---

①pedlars：商贩
②cephalic：头
③tincture：浸染、药酒
④bolus：药丸、小球

as the prescription requires.

Question for Discussion

Analyze *Gulliver's Travels* to illustrate the use of satire in the third part.

Unit 3　William Blake

Appreciation

To see a World in a Grain of Sand，一沙一世界，
And a Heaven in a Wild Flower，一花一天堂。
Hold Infinity in the palm of your hand，无限掌中置，
And Eternity in an hour. 刹那成永恒。

Auguries of Innocence
Songs of Innocence

Author

William Blake was a Pre-Romanticist or forerunner of the romantic poetry of the 19th century, the most extraordinary literary genius of his age.

Blake was the son of a London tradesman. In his childhood, he was a strange and imaginative child. He never went to school but learned to read and write at home. He was poet, painter, and engraver, who created a unique form of illustrated verse; his poetry, inspired by mystical vision, is among the most original, lyric, and prophetic in the language.

Blake was the most independent and the most original of all the romantic poets of the 18th century, showing contempt for the rule of reason, and treasuring the individual's imagination. His lyrics display all the characteristics of the romantic spirit (natural sentiment and individual originality). Blake's most popular poems have always been *Songs of Innocence* (1789). These lyrics—fresh, direct observations—are notable for their eloquence. In 1794, disillusioned with the possibility of human perfection, Blake issued *Songs of Experience*, employing the same lyric style and much of the same subject matter as in *Songs of Innocence*. Blake wrote his poem *The Tiger* in plain and direct language.

His poems often carry the lyric beauty with immense compression of meaning. He tends to present his view in visual images rather that abstract ideas. Symbolism in wide range is also a distinctive feature of his poetry. His poems were full of romantic spirit, imagery symbolism and revolutionary spirit. He influenced the Romantic poets with recurring themes of good and evil, heaven and hell, knowledge and innocence, and external reality versus inner imagination. He paved the way for the romantic movement of the 19th century. He was not really understood by his peers, but the 20th century readers appreciate the greatness he achieved in his varied fields of interest.

Brief Introduction

After the French Revolution broke out, the English government felt so alarmed as to strengthen the suppression of democratic activities in England. London, the English capital appeared quite different from before. It was filled with gloom, terror and misery.

The speaker wanders through the streets of London and comments on his observations. He sees despair in the faces of the people he meets and hears fear and repression in their voices. The woeful cry of the chimney sweeper stands as a chastisement to the Church, and the blood of a soldier stains the outer walls of the monarch's residence. The nighttime holds nothing more promising: the cursing of prostitutes corrupts the newborn infant and sullies the "Marriage hearse".

William Blake's *London* is a poem about a society that is troubled by the mistakes of the generation before. Blake uses the rhetorical components of imagery, alliteration, and word choice to illustrate the meaning of the poem. Blake creates complexity by using his rhetorical skills, which in turn opens up the poem for personal interpretation. The rhythm pattern is iambic tetrameter, trochaic tetrameter and the rhyme scheme is abab, cdcd, efef, dgdg. Repetition is Anvil music.

Selected Reading

London

I wander thro'[①] each charter'd street,

---

①thro': through

Near where the charter'd① Thames does flow.
And mark in every face I meet
Marks of weakness, marks of woe.

In every cry of every Man,
In every Infant's cry of fear,
In every voice: in every ban②,
The mind-forg'd manacles I hear

How the Chimney-sweeper's cry③
Every blackening Church appalls,
And the hapless Soldier's sigh④
Runs in blood down Palace walls.

But most thro' midnight streets I hear
How the youthful Harlot's curse
Blasts the new-born Infant's tear⑤

---

①charter'd: given liberty of freedom, but also taken over as private property 被霸占的街道, 当时伦敦的街道均被有钱人所霸占

②ban[TOEFL][IELTS]: a prohibition, also possibly a marriage ban-notice of intended matrimony 本节中诗人连用5个every 以强调伦敦城中无论男女老幼, 都不能幸免被踩躏的命运

③How the Chimney-sweeper's cry/Every blackening Church appalls: How the chimney sweepers' cry appalls every blackening Church. Chimney-sweeper's cry: 扫烟囱孩子的哭声, 当时, 有许多穷孩子以扫烟囱为生。blackening Church: 被熏黑的教堂。这里诗人采用了借代的手法, 意指黑心的僧人

④the hapless Soldier's sigh/ Runs in blood down Palace walls: Palace 指的是政府所在的宫殿。In blood: in the form of blood。18世纪的英国政府派遣成千上万的士兵到国外为扩张英国势力而战, 许多伤兵回国后沦为乞丐, 流落街头。他们的哀号仿佛在以鲜血和生命向政府抗议

⑤tear: the harlot infects the parents with venereal disease, and thus the infant is inflicted with prenatal blindness 新生儿的父母感染疾病, 垂直遗传给婴儿, 导致他生下来就失明

And blights with plagues the Marriage hearse①.

Questions for Discussion

1. What is the theme of *London*?
2. Analyze the following words in *London*: mark, five every, blackning Church, Palace, marriage hearse. How do these words help the writer to strengthen the theme?
3. What is the most striking formal feature of *London*? What role does it play?
4. How do you understand "Chartered Street" and "Chartered Thames"? What does the speaker see when he wanders? What is the atmosphere in London? Pay attention to the repetition of the word. What role does it serve?
5. What kind of figures of speech are used in this quatrain? Analyze "Chimney-sweeper's cry appalls every blackning Church" and "the hapless Soldier's sigh runs down Palace walls in blood".

Appreciation

Tyger! Tyger! burning bright
In the forests of the night,
What immortal hand or eye
Could frame thy fearful symmetry?

老虎！老虎！黑夜的森林中
燃烧着的煌煌的火光，
是怎样的神手或天眼
造出了你这样的威武堂堂？

——《老虎》，郭沫若译

---

①hearse: the marriage coach becomes a funeral hearse. 诗人把 marriage 和 hearse 连在一起，使人想起妇女由于生活所迫沦为妓女的悲惨命运。对于这些备受凌辱的妇女来说，婚姻对于她们毫无幸福可言。因此，婚车一如灵柩

Brief Introduction

As a forerunner of British Romanticism, Blake's poems are concerned with creation and full of romantic elements. Among his works, *Songs of Innocence* and *Songs of Experience* are two famous ones.

The Tyger is one of William Blake's best-loved and most-quoted poems, which is collected in *Songs of Experience*. The short poem is of regular form and meter, reminiscent of a children's nursery rhyme. It is six quatrains (four-line stanzas) rhymed AABB. Some readers see the tyger as an emblem of evil and darkness, and some critics have interpreted the poem as an allegory of the French Revolution. Others believe Blake is describing the artist's creative process. The interpretations are abound. What is certain is that, being part of Blake's *Songs of Experience*, *The Tyger* represents one of two "contrary states of the human soul." Here, "experience" is perhaps used in the sense of disillusionment being contrary to "innocence" or the naiveté of a child. Blake seeks for balance and harmony in this unbalanced world. His poems express the dialectic unity of the beautiful and the ugly, the good and the evil, the white and the black in the world.

The famed literary critic Alfred Kazin called *The Tyger* "a hymn to pure being" and "what gives it its power is Blake's ability to fuse two aspects of the same human drama: the movement with which a great thing is created, and the joy and wonderment with which we join ourselves to it."

Selected Reading

The Tyger①

Tyger Tyger, burning bright,
In the forests of the night;
What immortal② hand or eye,

---

①Tyger: tiger 的古体
②immortal: 不朽的

Could frame① thy② fearful symmetry③?

In what distant deeps or skies
Burnt the fire of thine④ eyes!
On what wings dare he aspire⑤?
What the hand, dare seize the fire?

And what shoulder, &⑥ what art,
Could twist⑦ the sinews⑧ of thy heart?
And when thy heart began to beat,
What dread hand? & what dread feet?

What the hammer? what the chain,
In what furnace⑨ was thy brain?
What the anvil⑩? what dread grasp,
Dare its deadly terrors clasp⑪?

When the stars threw down their spears⑫
And water'd⑬ heaven with their tears:

---

①frame[IELTS][TOEFL]:n. 框架;v. 制作框架
②thy: your 的古体,用作第二人称单数所有格形式
③symmetry[TOEFL]:对称
④thine: your 的古体,两种用法:(第二人称单数的物主代词)你的(所有物);(第二人称所有格单数 thy 的另一种形式,用于元音或 h 前)你的
⑤aspire[GRE]:渴望(成就)
⑥what shoulder, & what art:原文如此(下文带 & 的句子亦是)
⑦twist[IELTS][TOEFL]:扭,拧
⑧sinew[IELTS]:肌腱;力量的来源;关键环节;要害之处
⑨furnace[IELTS]:熔炉
⑩anvil[GRE]:铁砧
⑪clasp[GRE]:紧握
⑫spear[GRE]:矛;标枪
⑬water'd:即 watered

Did he smile his work to see?
Did he who made the Lamb① make thee②?

Tyger, Tyger burning bright,
In the forests of the night:
What immortal hand or eye,
Dare frame thy fearful symmetry?

Questions for Discussion

1. How symbolism is used in this poem?
2. Compare *Songs of Innocence* and *Songs of Experience*.

Unit 4 Robert Burns

Appreciation

Till a' the seas gang dry, my dear, 纵使大海干涸水流尽,
And the rocks melt wi' the sun; 太阳将岩石烧作灰尘,
I will luve thee still, my dear, 亲爱的, 我永远爱你,
While the sands o' life shall run. 只要我一息犹存。

Author

Born on January 25, 1759, in Alloway, Scotland, to William and Agnes Brown Burnes, Robert Burns followed his father's example by becoming a tenant farmer. As a poet he recorded and celebrated aspects of farm life, regional experience, traditional culture, class

---

① the Lamb:《羔羊》, 布莱克的另一首代表作, 出自诗集《天真之歌》, 往往与《经验之歌》中的名篇《老虎》形成对比
② thee: you 的古体, 第二人称单数宾格

culture and distinctions, and religious practice and belief in such a way as to transcend the particularities of his inspiration, becoming finally the national poet of Scotland.

Brief Introduction

A Red, Red Rose has been regarded as one of the best love poems. It is a ballad and also a popular love song in reality. The poem contains about 100 words merely. It is very short and brief, but it has presented a pure-hearted and impressive love story for us. It is about a couple of lovers: the hero is going to leave his lover for a while, and the content is the oath he wants to express to his lover. The writer uses many precise and simple words to speak out his true and unchangeable love to his lover. It can make readers feel the deep and strong affection.

Selected Reading

A Red, Red Rose

O, my Luve's① like a red, red rose
That's newly sprung in June;
O, my Luve's like the melodie②,
That's sweetly play'd③ in tune.

As fair art④ thou⑤, my bonnie⑥ lass⑦,

---

① Luve: 苏格兰方言 = ove, 注意大写 L, 表达了"重要"和"唯一"的内涵
② melodie: 来自法语, 是19、20世纪法国从德国的抒情歌曲学来的, 它是带伴奏的艺术歌曲。19世纪的 melodie 一般用严肃抒情诗做歌词, 由钢琴伴奏的独唱演员演唱。Melodie 的特点是诗歌与音乐的完美统一。因此, melodie 准确来说不是"乐曲""曲调", 而是"歌曲"
③ play'd: played, 诗歌用字
④ art: are, 古英语, 第二人称系动词
⑤ thou: you, 古英语, 第二人称主格
⑥ bonnie: 苏格兰方言, 健康的, 美丽的, 可爱的, 可人的
⑦ lass: 年轻未婚女子, 姑娘;多数用于非正式对少女的称呼;因与 lassie 有关, 所以也有女性恋人的意思

So deep in luve am I;
And I will luve thee still, my dear,
Till a'① the seas gang dry.

Till a' the seas gang② dry, my dear,
And the rocks melt wi'③ the sun;
I will luve thee④ still, my dear,
While the sands o'⑤ life shall run.

And fare-thee-weel⑥, my only Luve!
And fare-thee-weel, a while!
And I will come again, my Luve,
Tho'⑦ 'twere⑧ ten thousand mile!

Question for Discussion

A Valediction: *Forbidding Mourning* and *A Red, Red Rose* are two love poems, but they are completely different. Choose your favorite one and make an analysis on it.

Appreciation

My heart's in the Highlands, my heart is not here,
My heart's in the Highlands a-chasing the deer.

---

①a': all, 诗歌语言
②gang: go, 苏格兰方言
③wi': with, 诗歌语言
④thee: you, 古英语，第二人称宾格
⑤o': of, 诗歌语言
⑥fare-thee-weel: (bid)farewell(to)thee, 诗歌语言
⑦tho': though, 诗歌语言
⑧'twere: it were（起到省略一个音节的作用），诗歌语言

A-chasing the wild deer, and following the roe;
My heart's in the Highlands, wherever I go.

我的心呀在高原,这儿没有我的心

我的心呀在高原,追赶着鹿群,

追赶着野鹿,跟踪着小鹿,

我的心呀在高原,别处没有我的心!

——《我的心呀在高原》,王佐良译

Brief Introduction

My Heart's in the Highlands is one of the best-known poems written by Robert Burns in which he expressed his unshakable love for his homeland. As a traveler far away from home, the poet calls to mind the unforgettable beautiful scenery and the past happy days in the highlands. He keenly expresses his love for his homeland, and declares that wherever he goes his heart will be forever in it.

Selected Reading

My Heart's in the Highlands①

My heart's in the Highlands, my heart is not here;
My heart's in the Highlands a-chasing② the deer③;
A – chasing the wild deer, and following the roe④,
My heart's in the Highlands, wherever I go.

Farewell⑤ to the Highlands, farewell to the North,
The birth place of Valour⑥, the country of Worth,

---

①highlands[IELTS]:高地,高原地区,山岳地带。诗中指苏格兰高地。
②chase[IELTS]:追赶,追逐
③deer:鹿(单复数同形)
④roe:the deer [OE] 来自古英语 raha,狍,小鹿;Fish eggs 鱼子
⑤farewell[IELTS]:再会,再见。较正式的用词,离别时常用的告别语
⑥valour: = valor(美)英勇,勇气;勇士

Wherever I wander, wherever I rove①,
The hills of the Highlands for ever I love.

Farewell to the mountains high cover'd with snow;
Farewell to the straths② and green valleys below;
Farewell to the forests and wild-hanging woods;
Farewell to the torrents③ and loud-pouring floods.

My heart's in the Highlands, my heart is not here,
My heart's in the Highlands a-chasing the deer
Chasing the wild deer, and following the roe;
My heart's in the Highlands, wherever I go.

Questions for Discussion

1. What kind of feeling does the author express in the poem?
2. Can you name poems with the same theme in Chinese culture? What do you think make the poems touching and evocative?

Appreciation

Should auld acquaintance be forgot,
And never brought to mind?
Should auld acquaintance be forgot,
And auld lang syne?

怎能忘记旧日朋友,
心中能不怀想。
旧日朋友岂能相忘,
友谊地久天长。

——《友谊地久天长》,邓映锡译

---

①rove:漫游,流浪
②straths:平底河谷
③torrents[IELTS][TOEFL]:急流,激流

Chapter 4 18th-Century English Literature

Brief Introduction

Although *Auld Lang Syne* is globally recognized, it is frequently sung with slight variations from Burns' original lyrics. Burns' English writing often included Scottish dialects. He was a charismatic pioneer of the Romantics literary movement. *Auld Lang Syne* is sung in many countries at the stroke of Midnight on New Year's Eve to help usher in the new year. Burns claims to have transcribed the folk song from an old man who had had the song passed on to him.

Burns' version builds on earlier works. Poems and songs with somewhat similar text have been found dating back as far as anonymous ballad in the Bannatyne Manuscript of 1568. Another version, the first that contains a form of the 'auld lang syne' phrase, is attributed to the courtly poet Sir Robert Ayton (1570 – 1638). The song's Scots title may be translated into English literally as "old long since", or "long long ago", "days gone by" or "old times". Consequently "For auld lang syne", as it appears in the first line of the chorus, might be loosely translated as "for (the sake of) old times". The poem is a reminder to remember and cherish old friendships, good deeds and toast health and good will for the year ahead.

Selected Reading

Auld Lang Syne[①]

Should auld acquaintance[②] be forgot,
And never brought to mind[③]?
Should auld acquaintance be forgot,
And auld lang syne?

For auld lang syne, my jo[④],
For auld lang syne,

---

① Auld lang syne: old long since 或 days gone by, 译为昔日时光, 又译为友谊地久天长
② acquaintance [IELTS] [TOEFL]: 熟人
③ brought to mind: remembered 想起
④ Jo: (苏格兰语) 亲爱的

We'll tak a cup o' kindness yet[1],
For auld lang syne.

And surely ye'll be your pint-stowp[2]!
And surely I'll be mine!
And we'll tak a cup o' kindness yet,
For auld lang syne.

We twa hae run about the braes[3],
And pu'd the gowans fine[4];
But we've wander'd mony a weary foot[5],
Sin auld lang syne.

We twa hae paidl'd i' the burn[6],
Frae morning sun till dine[7];
But seas between us braid hae roar'd[8]
Sin auld lang syne.

And there's a hand, my trusty fiere[9]!
And gie's a hand o' thine[10]!

---

[1] We'll tak a cup o' kindness yet: We'll take another cup of friendship 让我们再共饮一杯美酒
[2] And surely ye'll be your pint-stowp: And surely you'll drink your fill (a pint = half a quart; stowp = a drinking vessel 苏格兰酒壶,大杯子),译为干了你这杯酒
[3] We twa hae run about the braes: We two have run about the hills (braes = hills)我们俩在山间游荡
[4] pu'd the gowans fine: pulled the fine gowans (pou'd = pulled; gowans = yellow or white field flower 春白菊) 采摘野花
[5] wander'd mony a weary foot: wandered many a weary foot (weary 疲惫的)长途跋涉
[6] paidl'd i' the burn: paddled in the brook(paddle 桨;用桨划船)泛舟湖上
[7] Frae morning sun till dine: from morning sun till dinner time 从早到晚
[8] seas between us braid hae roar'd: broad seas between us have roared (braid = broad; roar 咆哮)
[9] fiere: comrade
[10] gie's a hand o' thine: give us a hand of yours 伸出你的手

And we'll tak a right gude-willy waught,
For auld lang syne.

And surely ye'll be your pint-stowp !
And surely I'll be mine !
And we'll tak a cup o' kindness yet,
For auld lang syne.

Question for Discussion

1. What's the meaning of the phrase 'Auld lang syne'?

Terms

1. Satire
2. Neoclassicism
3. Fiction
4. Sentimentalism

---

① tak a right gude-willy waught: gude-willy = good will; waught = a deep draught, 即 take a right good-will draught 干了这杯美酒

Chapter 5

Romanticism in English Literature

I. Historical Background

1. The French Revolution

The French Revolution was a period of far-reaching social and political upheaval in France that lasted from 1789 until 1799, and was partially carried forward by Napoleon during the later expansion of the French Empire. The conflict between the old and the new class and the anger and desire brought by enlightenment catalyzed this Revolution. On July 14, 1789, the Parisian people stormed the Bastille, which marked the outbreak of the French Revolution and its influence soon swept all over Europe. Inspired by liberal and radical ideas, the Revolution profoundly altered the course of modern history, triggering the global decline of absolute monarchies while replacing them with republics and liberal democracies.

2. The Impact of the French Revolution

The French Revolution had a major impact on Europe and the New World, which gave a great stimulus to the growth of modern nationalism, and all social contradictions in England sharpened, too. People of the lower classes and the progressive intellectuals hoped to realize "liberty, equality and fraternity" in England. Britain saw minority support but the majority, and especially the elite, strongly opposed the French Revolution.

II. Literary Background

1. The Romanticism Age

Romanticism rose and grew under the impetus of the Industrial Revolution and

French Revolution which was an especially important influence on the political thinking of many of the Romantic poets. Though Romanticism was a revolt against aristocratic social and political norms of the Age of Enlightenment, it as well was a reaction against the scientific rationalization of nature.

At the turn of the 18th and 19th century romanticism appeared in England as a new trend in literature. The Romantic period was one of major social change in England because of the depopulation of the countryside and the rapid development of overcrowded industrial cities. In 1798 William Wordsworth and Samuel Taylor Coleridge published *Lyrical Ballads* which marked the beginning of the Romantic Age. It is an age of romantic enthusiasm, an age of poetry and an age for women novelists. In 1832, the last romantic writer Walter Scott died, so in that year, the Romantic Age came to an end.

Romanticism is an international artistic literary, intellectual and philosophical movement originated in Europe toward the end of the 18th century and in most areas was at its peak in the approximate period from 1800 to 1850.

2. Contrast With Neoclassicism

The Romanticists paid great attention to the spiritual and emotional life of man. The stylistic keynote of Romanticism is intensity, and its watchword is "imagination": remembered childhood, unrequited love, and the exiled hero were constant themes. Romantics had a new intuition for the primal power of the wild landscape, the spiritual correspondence between Man and Nature, and the aesthetic principle of "organic" form. Characteristics of Romanticism Imagination were worship of nature, symbolism and myth, simplicity and humanity, spontaneity.

Romanticism constitutes a change of direction from attention to the outer world of social civilization to the inner world of the human spirit. In essence it designates a literary and philosophical theory which tends to see the individual as the very center of all life and all experience. It also places the individual at the center of art, making literature most valuable as an expression of this or her unique feelings, particular attitudes and valuing its accuracy in portraying the individual's experiences.

3. Two Schools of Romantic Poets

Lake Poets

The elder generation represented by Wordsworth, Coleridge and Southey were known as Lake Poets because they lived and knew one another in the last few years of the 18th century in the district of the great lakes in Northwestern England. The former two published *The Lyrical Ballads* together in 1798, while all three of them had radical inclinations in their youth but later turned conservative and received pensions and poet laureateships from the aristocracy. They sang the beautiful nature and their poems were simple, pure and fresh.

Active romanticists

Younger generation represented by Byron, Shelley and Keats, firm supporters of the French Revolution, expressed the aspiration of the labouring classes and set themselves against the bourgeois society and the ruling class, as they bore a deep hatred for the wicked exploiters and oppressors and had an intensive love for liberty. They are referred to as Satanic Poets by Robert Southey for their violent imagination and rebellious spirit. Their poems were full of fighting spirit and political consciousness.

4. Types of Poetry

In terms of content

Lyrical Poems: Songs 韵文   Odes 颂诗   Elegy 挽诗
Narrative Poems: Epics (heroic poems) 史诗   Ballads 民谣
Dramatic Poems: usu. in dialogue; in blank verse

In terms of meter

Metrical Poems 格律诗: regular rhyme; regular rhythm; definite number of lines
Free Verse 自由诗: irregular rhyme and rhythm; irregular number of lines
Blank Verse 无韵诗: without rhyme; with rhythm

Unit 1　William Wordsworth

Appreciation

并不是由于决心才正确，应该由于习惯而正确。不仅能做正确的事，而且养成不是正确的事就做不了的习惯。

威廉·华兹华斯

※ Chapter 5　Romanticism in English Literature ※

荣誉之所以伟大,就因为得之不易。

威廉·华兹华斯

Author

On April 7, 1770, William Wordsworth was born in Cockermouth, Cumbria, England. Equally important in the poetic life of Wordsworth was his 1795 meeting with the poet, Samuel Taylor Coleridge. It was with Coleridge that Wordsworth published the famous *Lyrical Ballads* in 1798. And the poems themselves are some of the most influential in Western literature.

Wordsworth's most famous work, *The Prelude* (1850), is considered by many to be the crowning achievement of English romanticism. The poem, revised numerous times, chronicles the spiritual life of the poet and marks the birth of a new genre of poetry.

Brief Introduction

Writing Bachground: A visit to Ullswate(阿尔斯沃特湖畔) by Dorothy Wordsworth, from The Grasmere Journal—Thursday 15 April, 1802.

I Wandered Lonely as a Cloud is a poem about nature. The poem can be divided into two parts: the scenery and lyrical. With his pure and poetic language, Wordsworth brings us into a beautiful world where there are daffodils, trees and breeze. We follow the poet at every turn of his feelings. We share his sadness when he *wandered lonely as a cloud* and his delight the moment his heart "with pleasure fills". We come to realize the great power of nature that may influence our life deeply as revealed in the poem.

Through describing a scene of joyful daffodils recollected in memory, the poet hopes to illustrate his theory of poetic inspiration—"spontaneous overflow of powerful feelings, which originates in emotion recollected in tranquility". *I Wandered Lonely as a Cloud* becomes one of the best examples of the Romantic idea of nature.

Selected Reading

I Wandered Lonely as a Cloud

I wandered lonely as a cloud

That floats on high① o'er vales② and hills,
When all at once I saw a crowd,
A host, of golden daffodils③;
Beside the lake, beneath the trees,
Fluttering④ and dancing in the breeze.

Continuous as the stars that shine
And twinkle on the milky way,
They stretched in never-ending line
Along the margin of a bay:
Ten thousand saw I at a glance,
Tossing⑤ their heads in sprightly⑥ dance.

The waves beside them danced; but they
Out-did the sparkling⑦ waves in glee⑧:
A poet could not but be gay,
In such a jocund⑨ company:
I gazed—and gazed—but little thought
What wealth the show to me had brought:

For oft⑩, when on my couch I lie

---

①on high: in the sky, 在空中
②vales: 谷;溪谷
③daffodils: 水仙花
④Fluttering: 飘动
⑤Tossing: 使……上下摇动
⑥sprightly: 活泼的;愉快的
⑦sparkling: 闪闪发光的
⑧glee: 快乐
⑨jocund: 高兴的, 快乐的
⑩oft: 时常

In vacant① or in pensive② mood,
They flash upon that inward eye③
Which is the bliss④ of solitude⑤;
And then my heart with pleasure fills,
And dances with the daffodils.

Questions for Discussion

1. Try to interpret the meaning of the title *I Wandered Lonely as a Cloud* and the theme.
2. Analyze the figure of speech in *I Wandered Lonely as a Cloud*.

Unit 2 Samuel Taylor Coleridge

Appreciation

There is no gap between the living and the lifeless, between nature and men, or between matter and the mind, for all these modes of being consist of diverse and inter-correspondent levels of organization of the same to elemental powers and their respective polar forces.

——Samuel Taylor Coleridge

Author

Samuel Taylor Coleridge, a leader of the British Romantic movement, was born on

---

①vacant[IELTS][TOEFL]：空虚的;空的
②pensive[TOEFL]：沉思的，忧郁的
③inward eye：the soul, 指心灵
④bliss：极乐;天赐的福
⑤solitude[TOEFL]：孤独;隐居

October 21, 1772, in Devonshire, England. In 1798 Coleridge and Wordsworth collaborated on a joint volume of poetry entitled *Lyrical Ballads*. The collection is considered the first great work of the Romantic school of poetry and contains Coleridge's famous poem, *The Rime of the Ancient Mariner*.

Brief Introduction

An Ancient Mariner, unnaturally old and skinny, with deeply-tanned skin and a "glittering eye", stops a Wedding Guest who is on his way to a wedding reception with two companions. He tries to resist the Ancient Mariner, who compels him to sit and listen to his woeful tale. The Ancient Mariner tells his tale, largely interrupted save for the sounds from the wedding reception and the Wedding Guest's fearsome interjections.

The Ancient Mariner tells the Wedding Guest that he wanders from country to country, and has a special instinct that tells him to whom he must tell his story. After he tells it, he is temporarily relieved of his agony. The Ancient Mariner tells the Wedding Guest that better than any merriment is the company of others in prayer. He says that the best way to become close with God is to respect all of his creatures, because he loves them all. Then he vanishes. Instead of joining the wedding reception, the Wedding Guest walks home, stunned. We are told that he awakes the next day "sadder and wiser" for having heard the Ancient Mariner's tale.

Selected Reading

The Rime of the Ancient Mariner

Argument
How a ship having passed the line was driven by storms to the cold country towards the South Pole; and how from thence she made her course to the tropical Latitude of the Great Pacific Ocean; and of the strange things that befell; and in what manner the Ancient Mariner came back to his own country.

PART I

It is an ancient Mariner,

And he stoppeth one of three.
"By thy long grey beard and glittering① eye,
Now wherefore stopp'st thou me?

The Bridegroom's doors are opened wide,
And I am next of kin;
The guests are met, the feast is set:
May'st hear the merry din."

He holds him with his skinny hand,
"There was a ship," quoth he.
"Hold off! unhand me, grey-beard loon!"
Eftsoons② his hand dropt he.

He holds him with his glittering eye—
The Wedding-Guest stood still,
And listens like a three years' child:
The Mariner hath his will③.

The Wedding-Guest sat on a stone:
He cannot choose but hear;
And thus spake④ on that ancient man,
The bright-eyed Mariner.

"The ship was cheered, the harbour cleared,
Merrily did we drop

---

①glittering[IELTS]:闪烁, 闪耀
②eftsoons: at once, 立刻
③The Mariner hath his will: the Mariner has gained the control of the will of the Wedding Guest by "his glittering eye"
④spake:说(speak 的过去式)

Below the kirk①, below the hill,
Below the lighthouse top.

The Sun came up upon the left,
Out of the sea came he!
And he shone bright, and on the right
Went down into the sea.

Higher and higher every day,
Till over the mast at noon②—"
The Wedding-Guest here beat his breast,
For he heard the loud bassoon.③

The bride hath paced into the hall,
Red as a rose is she;
Nodding their heads before her goes
The merry minstrelsy④.

The Wedding-Guest he beat his breast,
Yet he cannot choose but hear;
And thus spake on that ancient man,
The bright-eyed Mariner.

And now the STORM-BLAST came, and he
Was tyrannous⑤ and strong:
He struck with his o'ertaking wings,

---

①kirk: church, 教堂
②Till over the mast at noon: the ship had reached the equator (the "Line"), 他的船已经到达赤道
③bassoon: 巴松管(一种吹奏乐器)
④minstrelsy: 吟游技艺
⑤tyrannous: 暴虐的

Chapter 5 Romanticism in English Literature

And chased us south along.

With sloping masts and dipping prow①,
As who pursued with yell and blow
Still treads the shadow of his foe②,
And forward bends his head,
The ship drove fast, loud roared the blast③,
And southward aye we fled.

And now there came both mist and snow,
And it grew wondrous cold:
And ice, mast-high, came floating by,
As green as emerald④.

And through the drifts the snowy clifts
Did send a dismal⑤ sheen⑥:
Nor shapes of men nor beasts we ken—
The ice was all between.

The ice was here, the ice was there,
The ice was all around:
It cracked and growled⑦, and roared and howled,
Like noises in a swound⑧!

---

①prow:船首;机头
②foe[TOEFL]：敌人
③blast[TOEFL][IELTS]：爆破
④emerald:绿宝石
⑤dismal:凄凉的，忧郁的
⑥sheen：光辉
⑦growled:低声吼叫
⑧swound：swoon, 昏晕;狂喜

At length did cross an Albatross①

Thorough the fog it came;

As if it had been a Christian soul,

We hailed it in God's name.

It ate the food it ne'er had eat,

And round and round it flew.

The ice did split with a thunder-fit;

The helmsman② steered us through!

And a good south wind sprung up behind;

The Albatross did follow,

And every day, for food or play,

Came to the mariner's hollo!

In mist or cloud, on mast or shroud③,

It perched④ for vespers⑤ nine;

Whiles all the night, through fog-smoke white,

Glimmered the white Moon-shine.

"God save thee, ancient Mariner!

From the fiends, that plague thee thus! —

Why look'st thou so?"—With my cross-bow⑥

I shot the ALBATROSS.

---

①albatross:信天翁

②helmsman:舵手

③shroud: the rope supporting the mast 支持桅杆的绳子

④perch[TOEFL]:栖息;就位

⑤vesper:晚祷

⑥cross-bow:弩

Question for Discussion

Analyze *The Rime of the Ancient Mariner* written by Samuel Taylor Coleridge.

Unit 3　George Gordon Byron

Appreciation

他在 1824 年 4 月 19 日死于希腊西部的迈索隆吉翁,当时他正在英勇战斗,企图为希腊夺回他往日的自由与光荣。

——姐姐奥古斯塔为他写的墓志铭

他是贵族、诗人、美男子、英雄,是多重性质的象征,真挚磅礴的热情,独立不羁的精神,是我对拜伦最心仪的。

——木心《文学回忆录》

Author

George Gordon Byron was born on January 22, 1788 in Aberdeen, Scotland, and inherited his family's English title at the age of ten, becoming Baron Byron of Rochdale.

He was commonly known simply as Lord Byron, was an English poet and a leading figure in the Romantic Movement. He travelled widely across Europe, especially in Italy where he lived for seven years. Later in life, Byron joined the Greek War of Independence fighting the Ottoman Empire, for which many Greeks revere him as a national hero. He died in 1824 at the young age of 36 from a fever contracted while in Missolonghi. Due to his outspoken trait in political affairs and his rocky personal life, Byron was forced to flee England and settled in Italy and began writing his masterpiece, *Don Juan*, an epic-satire novel-in-verse loosely based on a legendary hero. When he died on April 19, 1824, at the age of 36, *Don Juan* was yet to be finished, though 17 cantos had been written.

His major works include, *Childe Harold's Pilgrimage* (1812), *Prometheus*

(1816), *The Lament of Tasso* (1817), *Heaven and Earth* (1821), *The Prophecy of Dante* (1819), *The Age of Bronze* (1823).

Today, Byron's *Don Juan* is considered one of the great long poems in English written since Milton's *Paradise Lost*. Modern critics generally consider it to be Byron's masterpiece. The Byronic hero, characterized by passion, talent, and rebellion, pervades Byron's work and greatly influenced the work of later Romantic poets. Byron was a British poet and a leading figure in Romanticism, and was regarded as one of the greatest European poets.

Brief Introduction

Don Juan is a satiric poem by Lord Byron, based on the legend of Don Juan. Byron himself called it an "Epic Satire". Don Juan was of noble origin, and he was amiable and charming to ladies. He loved a married woman Julia, after the affair was discovered, he was compelled to go abroad. Because of a shipwreck, Juan fell into the sea, finally reached the seashore of a Greek Isles. There Juan fell in love with Haidee, the beautiful daughter of a pirate. But her father returned and forced them to part resulting in her heart-broken death, and Juan was sold as a slave to Constantinople, but managed to escape and joined the Russian Army. Then Juan was sent back to England to perform a political mission.

The poem is in eight line iambic pentameter with the rhyme scheme ab ab ab cc—often the last rhyming couplet is used for a humor comic line or humorous bathos. This rhyme scheme is known as ottava rima, a rhyming stanza form of Italian origin, used for long poems on heroic themes which effect of ottava rima in English is often comic. The language is colloquial and conversational.

"The Isles of Greece" is the important episode of the poem, taken from Canto III of *Don Juan*. Don Juan and his adventures form the structure of the poem. In the early 19th century, Greece was under the rule of the Turks. By contrasting the freedom of ancient Greece and the present enslavement, the poet appealed to the people to fight for liberty.

Byron's true intention is to dipict a panoramic view of different types of society and employs his rich knowledge of the world and the wisdom to represent in Byronic hero attributes like rebelling, suffering exile and etc. This technique is used in the shipwreck scene with different elements, such as tragic heroism, selfishness and complete virtual comedy, which is fully justified in the love story between Juan and Haidee. The different emotions of love, enjoyment, suffering, hatred and fear build into the brilliant pictures of life. The combination of the real and ideal Don Juan form a whole story, with an immediate reponse shown in a stabilizing voic.

Selected Reading

The Isles of Greece

1

THE isles of Greece! the isles of Greece!
Where burning Sappho① loved and sung,
Where grew the arts of war and peace②,
Where Delos③ rose and Phoebus④ sprung!
Eternal summer gilds them yet,
But all, except their sun, is set.

2

The Scian and the Teian muse⑤,
The hero's harp, the lover's lute⑥,

---

①burning Sappho: 热情的萨福, 是公元前7世纪末至6世纪初古希腊勒斯波斯 Lesbos 杰出的女抒情诗人, 善于写情诗, 其作品热情奔放, 极负盛名
②the arts of war and peace: 文治武功; 战争与和平的艺术 arts of war: 军事学
③Delos: 爱琴海中的得洛斯岛, 位于爱琴海西南部的希腊; 相传太阳神阿波罗 Apollo 生在得洛斯, 阿波罗神殿也在这里
④Phoebus: Apoll, 希腊神话中的太阳神
⑤The Scian and the Teian Muse: the Scian Muse, 指荷马史诗《伊利亚特》Illiad 和《奥德修纪》Odyssey 的作者; the Teian Muse, 指古希腊诗人阿那克里翁; Muse, 希腊神话中掌管文艺、音乐等的九位女神, 专指诗神
⑥The hero's harp, the lover's lute: 前者指荷马, 也指荷马的史诗, 抒情诗人阿那克里翁以大型乐器竖琴这里比喻创作英雄史诗作者荷马, 小巧的琵琶比喻写爱情诗的阿那克里昂。英雄史诗是在比较大型的乐器竖琴 harp 伴奏下演唱的; 后者是在比较小型的乐器 lute 伴奏下演唱的。爱情诗一般是比较甜美的, 这里指阿那克里翁, 也指他的爱情诗

Have found the fame your shores refuse①;
Their place of birth alone is mute
To sounds which echo further west
Than your sires' "Islands of the Blest②".

3

The mountains look on Marathon—
And Marathon looks on the sea;
And musing there an hour alone,
I dream'd that Greece might yet be free
For, standing on the Persians' grave③,
I could not deem myself a slave.

4

A king sat on the rocky brow④
Which looks on sea-born Salamis⑤;
And ships, by thousands, lay below,
And men in nations⑥;—all were his!
He counted them at break of day—
And when the sun set, where were they?

---

①Have found the fame your shores refuse: 荷马和阿那克里翁被希腊故土忘却了，但他们在其他地方却深受崇敬

②your sires' "Islands of the Blest": blest, blessed, 极乐岛，你们祖先的宝岛。根据希腊神话，为众神所宠爱的人们死后，他们的灵魂都前往遥远的西部海域的极乐岛居住。古希腊诗人以此称现代的佛得角群岛 Cape Verde 或加那利群岛 the Canaries，在今塞内加尔以西，或加那利群岛 the Canaries 在今摩洛哥以西。宙斯(Zeus)让他所宠爱的人住在大地边缘的忘忧之岛，无人生之苦。这说明荷马和阿那克里翁的名声远扬，超出了古希腊人当时所知道的历史范围

③Persians' grave: 指入侵的波斯军在马拉松战役中战死士兵葬身的坟墓

④A king sate on the rocky brow: rocky brow, 悬崖。薛西斯一世率领强大的波斯舰队在希腊沿海萨拉米斯(Salamis)岛旁的海战，原以为强大的波舰队有1,200艘舰，小艇3,000艘必胜，不料被希腊海军仅300艘舰只一举全歼。据埃斯库罗斯 Aeschylus 悲剧《波斯人》，实际当时薛西斯 480 年 9 月 9 日坐在埃嘉勒山上 Aegaleos 目睹舰队一日内化为乌有

⑤Salamis: 萨拉米斯，位于爱琴海萨罗尼克湾内，希腊阿帝卡州岛屿

⑥men in nations: men, soldiers, 指波斯军队中从被波斯征服的亚非国家里招募的士兵

Chapter 5　Romanticism in English Literature

5

And where are they? and where art thou,
My country[①]? On thy voiceless shore
The heroic lay[②] is tuneless now—
The heroic bosom beats no more!
And must thy lyre, so long divine,
Degenerate into hands like mine[③]?

6

'Tis something, in the dearth of fame[④],
Though link'd among a fetter'd race[⑤],
To feel at least a patriot's shame,
Even as I sing, suffuse[⑥] my face;
For what is left the poet here?
For Greeks a blush—for Greece a tear[⑦].

7

Must we but weep o'er days more blest?
Must we but blush? —Our fathers bled[⑧].

---

①And where are they? And where art thou...country：拜伦假托一位希腊人怀古讽今：由上一行的过去时态（were）变成现在时态（are），诗人从古到今的时间转折旨在调转笔锋，将听众的注意力引向当前希腊人民遭受土耳其人奴役这一现实，从古代波斯人的败绩转到被奴役的希腊

②The heroic lay：lay-song，英雄之歌

③And must thy lyre, so long divine...mine：lyre，七弦琴，古希腊人作为伴唱诗歌的乐器，此处指诗歌

④in the dearth of fame：dearth，lack，在这屈辱的时候缺少伟大人物和英雄壮举

⑤link'd among a fetter'd race：被锁在一个被奴役的民族之内，指希腊从1453 到1829 年在土耳其的统治之下

⑥suffuse：overspread with colour，redden 血

⑦For Greeks a blush—for Greece a tear：希腊的不幸催人泪下，希腊当为之羞愧

⑧Must we but blush? —Our fathers bled：拜伦模仿头韵体诗以but、blush、bled 押头韵，句中略作停顿，造成强烈的效果

Earth! render back from out thy breast①
A remnant of our Spartan dead②!
Of the three hundred grant but three,
To make a new Thermopylae③.

8

What, silent still, and silent all?
Ah! no; the voices of the dead
Sound like a distant torrent's fall,
And answer, "Let one living head,
But one arise,—we come, we come!"
'Tis but the living who are dumb.

9

In vain—in vain: strike other chords④;
Fill high the cup of Samian wine⑤!
Leave battles to the Turkish hordes,
And shed the blood of Scio's vine⑥!
Hark! rising to the ignoble call⑦—

---

① Earth! Render back from out thy breast. —Thermopylae：公元前 480 年，波斯军队入侵希腊，斯巴达王莱奥尼达斯率领 300 名斯巴达勇士，在通往希腊东部的关隘温泉关据险固守 3 天，和薛西斯一世率领的波斯侵略军血战，后因希腊奸细给波斯人指路，腹背受敌，全部阵亡

② Spartan dead：指在温泉关战役中阵亡的 300 名斯巴达士兵。古希腊的斯巴达人以作战骁勇著称。温泉关是希腊北部和中部交界处的险要关隘，位于高山和海岸之间

③ Thermopylae：得摩比利或温泉关；此处指著名的温泉关战役，因附近有两个硫黄温泉而得名

④ strike other chords：弹奏别的曲调吧，即歌唱与抗争无关的其他主题

⑤ Samian wine：萨摩斯岛 Samos 所产的酒；萨摩斯是爱琴海中距小亚细亚大陆最近的希腊岛屿，盛产葡萄，以葡萄酒闻名

⑥ Leave battles to the Turkish hordes, vine：hordes 游牧部落。Scio's vine 希奥(意)以出产葡萄、橙子和柠檬著称。当时希腊人受"蛮人"hordes 的奴役，只饮葡萄之血即葡萄酒。诗人讽刺土耳其蛮人，旨在刺激希腊人起来斗争

⑦ the ignoble call：ignoble, dishonourable, 不光彩的号召

How answers each bold bacchanal①!

10

You have the Pyrrhic dance② as yet,
Where is the Pyrrhic phalanx③ gone?
Of two such lessons, why forget
The nobler and the manlier one?
You have the letters Cadmus④ gave—
Think ye he meant them for a slave?

11

Fill high the bowl with Samian wine!
We will not think of themes like these!
It made Anacreon's song divine⑤;
He served—but served Polycrates⑥—
A tyrant; but our masters then
Were still, at least, our countrymen.

---

①bold Bacchanal：勇敢的酒徒，酒神巴克斯的崇拜者，意含讽刺；Bacchanal 来源于 Bacchus，希腊神话中的酒神

②Pyrrhic dance：在希腊的节日里流行这种舞蹈，以急速的笛子伴奏，舞者做各种进攻和防守状。是古希腊伊庇鲁斯国王皮瑞克发明并以其名字命名的模拟战斗的一种战舞，舞步轻快，源出于塞萨利南部多里斯 Doris，斯巴达士兵的部分训练内容，舞者身穿盔甲。这种风俗一直流传至罗马时代的后期

③Pyrrhic phalanx：古希腊军队的步兵方阵，一般是前后八人，由手持长矛和短剑的步兵组成。据传说这种舞蹈是以希腊西北部伊庇鲁斯（Epirus）国王皮瑞克（Pyrrhicus，公元前319－公元前272）的名字命名的，这种方阵多次击败罗马军队

④Cadmus：卡德摩斯，希腊传说中的人物，腓尼基国王阿革诺尔 Agenor 之子，建立了底比斯城 Thebes，将腓尼基字母传入希腊

⑤It made Anacreon's song divine：它使阿那克里昂的诗歌成为天上之曲。阿那克里昂 Anacreon 是公元前 6 世纪的希腊诗人，歌颂醇酒和爱情，诗风壮丽，可谓神化所主，不似人间来者。It 指 Samian wine

⑥Polycrates：波利克拉特斯，公元前 6 世纪希腊萨摩斯岛的僭主，在东爱琴海上建立霸权，他崇尚文艺，诗人阿那克里翁在波斯人入侵俄斯期间，曾在萨摩斯岛避居波利克拉特斯宫廷。后被波斯人钉死在十字架上

12

The tyrant of the Chersonese[①]
Was freedom's best and bravest friend;
That tyrant was Miltiades[②]!
Oh! that the present hour would lend
Another despot of the kind[③]!
Such chains as his were sure to bind[④].

13

Fill high the bowl with Samian wine!
On Suli's rock, and Parga's shore[⑤],
Exists the remnant of a line
Such as the Doric mothers bore[⑥];
And there, perhaps, some seed is sown,

① the Chersonese:Tyrant,按古希腊语,指拥有绝对权利的统治者。指米太亚德(Miltiades,公元前540-公元前489),雅典统帅,公元前490年决定性的马拉松战役中以11,000兵力击败了波斯的10万大军,后来成为半岛 Chersonese 僭主:源自希腊文 Chersonesos 半岛。(poetic)半岛,此处大写,特指格拉里珀黎 Grallipoli,位于达达尼尔海峡 Dardanelles 北面

② Miltiades:米太亚德,公元前480年,波斯人全面入侵阿提卡,他被任命为十大元帅之一,他鼓动希腊人奋起御敌,并在马拉松战役中击败波斯侵略军。公元前5世纪初,成为色雷斯半岛 Thracian Chersonese 今达达尼亚半岛的君主。他曾和波斯王大流士一起和锡西厄人 Scythians 作战,后脱离波斯人,逃到雅典。虽曾招致专制罪指控,但获开释

③ Oh! that the present hour would lend...kind:Oh, I wish (that)。为但愿现在能有 Miltiades 这样一位君主鼓动人们起来斗争

④ Such chains as his were sure to bind:such chains,锁链一定能把希腊人团结起来;用 chains 一词,说明 miltiades 既是独裁者,又有团结人民的组织才干。Bind, to unite (the Greeks)

⑤ On Suli's rock, and Parga's shore:苏里;希腊伊庇鲁斯,今希腊西部和阿尔巴尼亚南部的山区。拜伦在《恰尔德·哈罗尔德游记》Childe Harold 中说,当地的人民正在抗击土耳其侵略军,他认为爱好自由的希腊人的后代当在那里作战。拜伦在希腊时招募500名苏里壮士参加独立军,自己出钱支付他们的军饷

⑥ Such as the Doric mothers bore:Doric mothers,多利安人即斯巴达人的母亲们;多利安母亲所生的人,指斯巴达勇士。Doric of Dorians,多利安人的,指古希腊最早的居民多利安人,是古希腊人的一支,进入埃夫罗塔斯河谷,建立了斯巴达城邦,因此多利安人指斯巴达人

Chapter 5　Romanticism in English Literature

The Heracleidan① blood might own.

14

Trust not for freedom to the Franks②—
They have a king who buys and sells③:
In native swords and native ranks④,
The only hope of courage dwells:
But Turkish force and Latin fraud⑤
Would break your shield, however broad.

15

Fill high the bowl with Samian wine!
Our virgins dance beneath the shade—
I see their glorious black eyes shine;
But, gazing on each glowing maid,
My own the burning tear-drop laves⑥,
To think such breasts must suckle slaves.

16

Place me on Sunium's marble steep⑦—
Where nothing, save⑧ the waves and I,
May hear our mutual murmurs⑨ sweep:

---

①The Heracleidan: of Hercules,传说希腊神话中的大力神赫丘利 Hercues 的后裔,此处指斯巴达人。Blood,古希腊人的血统

②Franks:法兰克人,一般指法国人或拉丁族人;此处泛指西欧人。地中海东部诸国和岛屿,包括叙利亚、黎巴嫩等在内的自希腊至埃及的地区的人们对西欧人的总称

③They have a king who buys and sells:指他们(the Franks)的国王为自己的利益而拿其他民族的利益做交易。诗人劝告希腊人不要依赖外国人为他们争得自由

④In native swords and native ranks:依靠自己的武装,依靠自己的队伍

⑤Latin fraud:指西欧人的欺诈。拜伦认为希腊人要获得自由,只能依靠自己

⑥My own the burning tear-drop laves: laves, washes,正常的语序是 the burning tear-drop laves my own: laves, washes, fills. My own: my own eyes

⑦Sunium's marbled steep: Sunium 现称 Cape Colennam,位于希腊的阿提卡南部森纽 Sunium,指雅典保护神雅典娜 Athena 之庙,位于雅典东南约 50 千米,即今天的开普柯罗尼(Cape Coloni)

⑧save[TOEFL]:except

⑨our mutual murmurs:指诗人的哀叹和海浪的涛声似乎在相互低声对答

· 155 ·

> There, swan-like, let me sing and die①;
> A land of slaves shall ne'er be mine—
> Dash down yon cup of Samian wine②!

Questions for Discussion

1. Who is "Sappho" in line 2?
   Who is "Phoebus" in line 4?
   Whom does the "Scia Jian muse" refer to?
2. What is the whole section *The Isles of Greece* about?
3. What is the theme of *The Isles of Greece*?

Unit 4　John Keats

Appreciation

自然是人类快乐的源泉。

——**Harcourt Brace Jovanovich**

"拜伦使浪漫主义的影响遍及全世界,雪莱透过浪漫主义前瞻大同世界,但他们在吸收前人精华和影响后人诗艺上,作用都不及济慈。"

——王佐良

Author

English Romantic poet John Keats was born on October 31, 1795, in London. Having no formal education or literary training, Keats read well in Greek and Elizabethan literature, and had Homer, Spenser, Shakespeare and Milton among his

---

① swan-like, let me sing and die：传说天鹅总在死前歌唱。诗人被比作天鹅,如以 the Swan of Avon 喻莎士比亚,以 the Mantuan swan 喻维吉尔

② Dash down yon cup of Samian wine：yon（古）,yongder, that. 摔碎那个盛萨摩斯美酒的杯子! 传说天鹅将死时会唱起悲歌,这里暗示诗人决心像天鹅那样唱一首英勇战斗的歌

literary passions. To seek a warm climate, later in life he went to Italy to improve his health. He died there on February 23, 1821, at the age of 25, and was buried in the Protestant cemetery.

Keats was known as a sensuous poet whose poetry describes the beauty of the natural world and art as the vehicle for his poetic imagination. His skill with poetic imagery and sound reproduces this sensuous experience for his readers. His poetry evolves from this love of nature and art into a deep compassion for humanity. He was one of the main figures of the second generation of Romantic poets along with Lord Byron and Percy Bysshe Shelley.

His artistic aim is to create a beautiful world of imagination as opposed to the miserable reality of truth. As the principal poets of the English Romantic movement, Keats is mainly known for such poems as *Ode on a Grecian Urn* 希腊古瓮颂, *On the Grasshopper and the Cricket* 蛐蛐与蟋蟀, *Bright Star* 闪亮的星星, *When I have Fear* 当我害怕的时候, *To Autumn* 秋颂, *On Melancholy* 忧郁颂.

His five long poems: *Endymion* 恩底弥翁, *Isabella* 伊莎贝拉, *The Pot of Basil* 芳香的草本植物, *The Eve of St. Agnes* 圣·爱格尼斯节前夕, *Lamia* 莱米亚, *Hyperion* 赫坡里昂. He is, like Shakespeare, Milton and Wordsworth, one of the indisputable great English poets. And his mighty poems will no doubt have a lasting place in the history of English literature.

Brief Introduction

A nightingale had built its nest near the house of a friend of the Keats in Hampstead in the spring of 1819. In the deep of night, under the thick branches, Clarion in bird song, the poet wrote the first 8 stanzas in one breath multiple lines of *Ode to a Nightingale*. Inspired by the bird's song, Keats composed the poem in one day.

Ode to a Nightingale describes a series of conflicts between reality and the Romantic ideal of uniting with nature. Here Keats not only expresses his rapture upon hearing the beautiful songs of the nightingale and his desire to go to the ethereal world of beauty together with the bird, but also shows his deep sympathy for and his keen understanding of human miseries in the society in which he lived.

The tone of the poem rejects the optimistic pursuit of pleasure found within Keats's earlier poems and explores the themes of nature, transience and mortality, the latter being particularly personal to Keats. Instead, the songbird is capable of living through its song, which is a fate that humans cannot expect. The poem ends with an acceptance that pleasure cannot last and that death is an inevitable part of life. The nightingale's song is the dominant image and dominant "voice" within the ode. Keats seems to write the nightingale, but in fact he uses the nightingale to express his colorful imagination.

Selected Reading

Ode to a Nightingale

My heart aches, and a drowsy① numbness pains
My sense, as though of hemlock② I had drunk,
Or emptied some dull opiate to the drains③
One minute past, and Lethe-wards④ had sunk:
'Tis not through envy of thy happy lot,
But being too happy in thine happiness, —
That thou, light-winged Dryad⑤ of the trees
In some melodious⑥ plot
Of beechen⑦ green, and shadows numberless,
Singest of summer in full-throated ease.

O, for a draught of vintage⑧! that hath been

---

①drowsy [TOEFL]：昏昏欲睡的；沉寂的
②hemlock：毒药
③to the drains：to the last dreg
④Lethe-wards：toward Lethe, meaning "forgetful of all things"
⑤Dryad：fairy in the woods, the nightingale
⑥melodious [TOEFL]：悦耳的
⑦beechen：山毛榉制的
⑧vintage：古老的，葡萄收获期

Cool'd a long age in the deep-delved earth,
Tasting of Flora① and the country green,
Dance, and Provencal song②, and sunburnt mirth③!
O for a beaker full of the warm South,
Full of the true, the blushful④ Hippocrene⑤,
With beaded bubbles winking⑥ at the brim,
And purple-stained mouth;
That I might drink, and leave the world unseen,
And with thee fade away into the forest dim:

Fade far away, dissolve, and quite forget
What thou among the leaves hast never known,
The weariness, the fever, and the fret⑦
Here, where men sit and hear each other groan;
Where palsy⑧ shakes a few, sad, last gray hairs,
Where youth grows pale, and spectre-thin, and dies;
Where but to think is to be full of sorrow
And leaden-eyed despairs,
Where Beauty cannot keep her lustrous⑨ eyes,

---

①Flora[TOEFL][IELTS]: god of flower in Roman myth Flora. Here it refers to the fragrance of flowers.

②Provencal song: the love lyrics of the native minstrels in Provence, France in the 12th century

③sunburnt mirth: the joy of people living in the south of Europe where people enjoy the sunshine very much

④blushful: 脸红的

⑤Hippocrene: the spring on Mount Helicon where Apollo and the Nine Muses reside. If someone drinks the spring he will have the inspiration for poetry, (赫利孔山上的)灵泉;诗之灵感 Here in this line, it refers to wine

⑥wink: 眨眼

⑦fret: 烦躁

⑧palsy: 麻痹

⑨lustrous[TOEFL]: 有光泽的

Or new Love pine at them① beyond tomorrow.

Away! away! for I will fly to thee,
Not charioted② by Bacchus③ and his pards④,
But on the viewless wings of Poesy,
Though the dull brain perplexes and retards⑤:
Already with thee! tender is the night,
And haply the Queen-Moon is on her throne,
Cluster'd around by all her starry Fays⑥;
But here there is no light,
Save what from heaven is with the breezes blown
Through verdurous⑦ glooms and winding mossy⑧ ways.

I cannot see what flowers are at my feet,
Nor what soft incense hangs upon the boughs,
But, in embalmed darkness, guess each sweet
Wherewith the seasonable month endows⑨
The grass, the thicket, and the fruit-tree wild;
White hawthorn⑩, and the pastoral⑪ eglantine⑫;
Fast fading violets cover'd up in leaves;

---

①them:"her lustrous eyes" in line 29
②charioted:驾驭
③Bacchus: god of wine riding a chariot led by pards (leopards), 酒神巴克斯
④pards:伙伴
⑤retard:延迟
⑥Fays: fairies
⑦verdurous:碧绿的
⑧mossy:生苔的
⑨endows[TOEFL]:赋予
⑩hawthorn:山楂;山楂树
⑪pastoral:牧歌;田园诗
⑫eglantine:野蔷薇的一种

And mid-May's eldest child①,
The coming musk-rose, full of dewy② wine,
The murmurous haunt of flies on summer eves.

Darkling③ I listen; and, for many a time
I have been half in love with easeful Death,
Call'd him soft names in many a mused rhyme,
To take into the air my quiet breath④;
Now more than ever seems it rich to die,
To cease upon the midnight with no pain,
While thou art pouring forth thy soul abroad⑤
In such an ecstasy!
Still⑥ wouldst thou sing, and I have ears in vain—
To thy high requiem⑦ become a sod.

Thou wast⑧ not born for death, immortal Bird⑨!
No hungry generations⑩ tread thee down;
The voice I hear this passing night was heard
In ancient days by emperor and clown⑪:
Perhaps the self-same song that found a path

---

①mid-May's eldest child: the flower that is earliest in blossom in May, musk-rose in line 49

②dewy: 带露水的

③darkling: in the dark 在暗处

④breath[TOEFL]: life 生命

⑤abroad: out 异国

⑥still: always 永远

⑦requiem: 安魂曲

⑧wast: the archaic form of "were" for the second person singular, 古老的形式的"是"第二人称单数

⑨immortal Bird: the nightingale 夜莺

⑩hungry generations: meaning "the devouring time"

⑪emperor and clown: emperor and peasant, meaning "everyday"

Through the sad heart of Ruth[①], when, sick for home,
She stood in tears amid the alien corn[②];
The same that oft-times hath
Charm'd magic casements, opening on the foam
Of perilous[③] seas, in faery lands[④] forlorn[⑤].

Forlorn! the very word is like a bell
To toll me back from thee to my sole self!
Adieu! the fancy cannot cheat so well
As she is fam'd[⑥] to do, deceiving elf.
Adieu! adieu! thy plaintive[⑦] anthem[⑧] fades
Past the near meadows, over the still stream,
Up the hill-side; and now, 'tis buried deep
In the next valley-glades:
Was it a vision, or a waking dream?
Fled is that music:—Do I wake or sleep?

---

① Ruth: ancestor of King David. After her husband's death in the famine, she fled with her mother-in-law to the foreign land and made a living on the remnant of wheat left in the field. Here Keats imagined that Ruth was standing in the wheat field of the foreign land missing her home
② corn: wheat 小麦
③ perilous: 危险的
④ faery lands: fairy lands 仙境
⑤ forlorn: remote and far away 孤独的
⑥ fam'd: famed, namely widely known
⑦ plaintive: 哀伤的
⑧ anthem: 赞美诗；圣歌

Questions for Discussion

1. What are the artistic features of *Ode to a Nightingale*?
2. What is the theme of *Ode to a Nightingale*?
3. Why is the bird—Nightingale immortal?

Appreciation

此地长眠者,声名水上书。

——济慈的墓志铭

Stanza 1

Brief introduction

In the beginning of this poem, the poet enters the world of the urn and has a spiritual communication with those trees and people which are engraved on the urn. It shows that Keats has absorbed himself into the timeless beautiful scenery and the Grecian urn. Keats shows a more vigorous world and shifts the poem from the quietness of the first part to the musical and sounding world. The poet says that the pipe's unheard melodies are sweeter than mortal melodies because they are unaffected by time. "Pipe", along with the youth, the trees attract the poet's endless fantasy about a lovely spot.

Kids depicts the feeding of ecstasy and emphasizes that art can help us find the eternal happiness by repetition. The poet feels happy for trees surrounding the lovers that they will never shed their leaves. He feels happy for the piper because his song will be "forever new", and happy that the boy's love will last forever, unlike mortal love, which only "a burning forehead, and a parching tongue" and eventually vanishes.

Nature images became an enduring passion that subtly belies the poem's conclusion, "Beauty is truth, truth beauty". In Keats' view, all of the natural pure beauties have been frozen and kept a freshness by art. Our life is transient, but art works' life can be perpetual. Then he comes back to the realities and again addresses the urn itself, saying that when his generation is long dead, the urn will remain, telling future generations its lesson: "Beauty is truth, truth beauty".

In the urn, which captures moments of intense experience in attitudes of a grace and freezes them into marble immobility, Keats found that the perfect correlative for his persistent concern with the longing for permanence in the world of change. Keats told us a simple but useful truth that whatever ordinary a thing it is judging from its appearance maybe has the purest beauty, because it expresses itself without any decoration compared with the other splendid things with masks on their faces, and it shows us the true one.

Selected Reading

Ode on a Grecian Urn

Stanza 1

Thou still unravish'd bride of quietness,
Thou foster-child① of silence and slow time,
Sylvan② historian, who canst thus express
A flowery tale more sweetly than our rhyme:
What leaf-fring'd legend haunts③ about thy shape
Of deities④ or mortals, or of both,
In Tempe⑤ or the dales of Arcady⑥?
What men or gods are these? What maidens loth⑦?
What mad pursuit? What struggle to escape?
What pipes and timbrels⑧? What wild ecstasy⑨?

Stanza 2

Heard melodies are sweet, but those unheard

---

①foster-child：养子
②Sylvan：living or located in the woods or forest 住在森林里的
③haunts[TOEFL]：萦绕，缠绕
④deities：神，女神
⑤tempe：a beautiful valley in Greece, regarded as sacred as the Apollo, the God of Poet. 溪谷
⑥Arcady：an ancient place in Greece, often used as a symbol of the pastoral ideal 世外桃源
⑦loth：不乐意的，不情愿的
⑧timbrels：小手鼓
⑨ecstasy：狂喜

Are sweeter; therefore, ye soft pipes, play on;
Not to the sensual ear, but, more endear'd,
Pipe to the spirit ditties① of no tone:
Fair youth, beneath the trees, thou canst not leave
Thy song, nor ever can those trees be bare;
Bold Lover, never, never canst thou kiss,
Though winning near the goal-yet, do not grieve;
She cannot fade, though thou hast not thy bliss②,
For ever wilt thou love, and she be fair!

Stanza 3

Ah, happy, happy boughs! that cannot shed
Your leaves, nor ever bid the Spring adieu③;
And, happy melodist, unwearied,
For ever piping songs for ever new;
More happy love! more happy, happy love!
For ever warm and still to be enjoy'd,
For ever panting④, and for ever young;
All breathing human passion far above,
That leaves a heart high-sorrowful and cloy'd⑤,
A burning forehead, and a parching⑥ tongue.

Stanza 4

Who are these coming to the sacrifice?
To what green altaraltar: O mysterious priest,
Lead'st thou that heifer⑦ lowing at the skies,
And all her silken flanks⑧ with garlands⑨ drest?

---

①ditties: 小曲，小调

②bliss: 快乐，极乐

③adieu: goodbye 再见

④panting: 喘气

⑤cloyed: to surfeit with an excess usually of sth. originally pleasing

⑥parching: 极干燥的

⑦heifer: 小母牛

⑧flanks: 侧面，侧翼

⑨garlands: 花环

What little town by river or sea shore,
Or mountain-built with peaceful citadel①,
Is emptied of this folk, this pious② morn?
And, little town, thy streets for evermore
Will silent be; and not a soul to tell
Why thou art desolate③, can e'er④ return.

Stanza 5

O Attic shape⑤! Fair attitude! with brede
Of marble men and maidens overwrought⑥,
With forest branches and the trodden weed;
Thou, silent form, dost tease us out of thought
As doth eternity: Cold Pastoral!
When old age shall this generation waste,
Thou shalt remain, in midst of other woe⑦
Than ours, a friend to man, to whom thou say'st,
"Beauty is truth, truth beauty,"-that is all
Ye know on earth, and all ye need to know.

Questions for Discussion

1. How do you understand "Beauty is truth, truth beauty"?
2. What is the beauty of the Grecian Urn?

---

①citadel:（旧时的）要塞，堡垒
②pious：虔诚的
③desolate：悲凉的
④e'er：曾，永远【诗】= ever
⑤Attic shape：阿提卡，古希腊一地区
⑥overwrought：过度紧张的，过度忧烦的
⑦woe：麻烦，困难

Unit 5　Percy Bysshe Shelley

Appreciation

冬天已经到来,春天还会远么?

——雪莱

希望是厄运的忠实的姐妹。

——雪莱

Author

Percy Bysshe Shelley was born on August 4, 1792, at Field Place, near Horsham, Sussex, England. On July 8, 1822, shortly before his thirtieth birthday, Shelley was drowned in a storm while attempting to sail from Leghorn to La Spezia, Italy, in his schooner, the *Don Juan*.

Shelley is perhaps best known for such classic poems as *Ozymandias*, *Ode to the West Wind*, *To a Skylark*, *Music*, *When Soft Voices Die*, *The Cloud* and *The Masque of Anarchy*. Long poems include *Queen Mab*(1813)麦布女王, *Alastor* 阿拉斯特, *Prometheus Unbound*(1819)解放的普罗米修斯.

He was one of the major English Romantic poets and regarded by critics as among the finest lyric poets in the English language. Shelley became an idol of the next three or four generations of poets, including important Victorian and Pre-Raphaelite poets.

Brief Introduction

The speaker invokes the *Wild West Wind* of autumn, which scatters the dead leaves and spreads seeds so that they may be nurtured by the spring, and asks that the wind, a "destroyer and preserver", hear him. The speaker calls the wind the "dirge of the dying year", and describes how it stirs up violent storms, and again implores it to hear him. The speaker says that the wind stirs the Mediterranean from "his summer dreams", and cleaves the Atlantic into choppy chasms, making the "sapless foliage" of the ocean tremble, and asks for a third time that it hear him.

The speaker says that if he were a dead leaf that the wind could bear, or a cloud it could carry, or a wave it could push, or even if he were, as a boy, "the comrade" of the wind's "wandering over heaven", then he would never have needed to pray to the wind and invoke its powers. He pleads with the wind to lift him "as a wave, a leaf, a cloud!"—for though he is like the wind at heart, untamable and proud—he is now chained and bowed with the weight of his hours upon the earth.

The speaker asks the wind to "make me thy lyre", to be his own Spirit, and to drive his thoughts across the universe, "like withered leaves, to quicken a new birth". He asks the wind, by the incantation of this verse, to scatter his words among mankind, to be the "trumpet of a prophecy". Speaking both in regard to the season and in regard to the effect upon mankind that he hopes his words to have, the speaker asks: "If winter comes, can spring be far behind?"

Selected Reading

Ode to the West Wind

I

O wild West Wind, thou breath of Autumn's being[①],
Thou, from whose unseen presence the leaves dead[②]
Are driven, like ghosts from an enchanter[③] fleeing[④],

Yellow, and black, and pale, and hectic red,
Pestilence[⑤]-stricken multitudes: O thou,
Who chariotest[⑥] to their dark wintry bed

[①] thou breath of Autumn's being: 你秋日生命的呼吸。being: the totality of all things that exist
[②] from whose unseen presence the leaves dead: the leaves (turn) dead from whose unseen presence
[③] enchanter: 使着迷
[④] like ghosts from an enchanter fleeting: like ghosts fleeting from an enchanter, 如同逃离巫师的鬼魂。enchanter: a sorcerer or magician, 巫师, 魔术师
[⑤] pestilence 瘟疫的
[⑥] chariotest 马车

The winged seeds, where they lie cold and low,
Each like a corpse within its grave, until
Thine azure① sister of the Spring shall blow
Her clarion② o'er the dreaming earth, and fill
(Driving sweet buds like flocks to feed in air)
With living hues and odours plain and hill③:

Wild Spirit, which art moving everywhere④;
Destroyer and Preserver; hear, O hear!

II

Thou on whose stream, 'mid the steep sky's commotion,
Loose clouds like Earth's decaying leaves are shed,
Shook from the tangled boughs of Heaven and Ocean⑤,

Angels⑥ of rain and lightning: there are spread
On the blue surface of thine airy surge,
Like the bright hair uplifted from the head

Of some fierce Maenad⑦, even from the dim verge
Of the horizon to the zenith's⑧ height,
The locks⑨ of the approaching storm. Thou dirge⑩

---

①azure 蔚蓝色的

②charion 号角

③With living hues and orders plain and hill: and fill plain and hill with living hues and orders

④Wild spirit, which art moving everywhere: 这里的 spirit 指西风

⑤Loose clouds like earth's decaying leaves are shed, / Shook from the tangled boughs of Heaven and Ocean: 诗人把海天景色比作秋日落叶, 使画面显得雄浑壮阔

⑥Angel: a divine messenger 报信者, 使者

⑦Maenad: 迈娜德, 希腊神话中酒神巴克斯的女祭司, 性情狂暴乖戾, 诗人把雷雨前的乱云比作妖女的蓬发

⑧zenith: 天顶(太阳或月亮在天空中的最高点)

⑨locks: 妖女的头发, 比喻暴雨来临之前纷乱的云彩

⑩dirge: a funeral hymn or lament, 哀歌, 挽歌

Of the dying year, to which this closing night
Will be the dome of a vast sepulchre①
Vaulted with all thy congregated might

Of vapours, from whose solid atmosphere
Black rain, and fire, and hail will burst: O hear!

III

Thou who didst② waken from his summer dreams
The blue Mediterranean, where he lay,
Lulled by the coil③ of his crystalline streams,

Beside a pumice isle in Baiae's bay④,
And saw in sleep old palaces and towers
Quivering within the wave's intenser day,

All overgrown with azure moss and flowers
So sweet, the sense faints picturing them! Thou
For whose path the Atlantic's level powers

Cleave⑤ themselves into chasms, while far below
The sea-blooms and the oozy woods which wear
The sapless⑥ foliage⑦ of the ocean, know
Thy voice, and suddenly grow grey with fear,
And tremble and despoil⑧ themselves: O hear!

IV

If I were a dead leaf thou mightest bear;

---

①sepulchre: 在岩石上凿出或用石头砌成
②didst: did
③coil: disturbance; a fuss 喧闹，骚扰，这里指海水的拍击声
④Baiae's bay: 意大利那不勒斯附近的一个旅游胜地，古罗马国王在此建了许多行宫
⑤cleave: 劈开
⑥sapless: 枯萎的，无活力的
⑦foliage: 叶子，枝叶
⑧despoil: 掠夺，破坏

If I were a swift cloud to fly with thee;
A wave to pant① beneath thy power, and share

The impulse of thy strength, only less free
Than thou, O Uncontrollable! If even
I were as in my boyhood, and could be

The comrade of thy wanderings over Heaven,
As then, when to outstrip thy skiey speed
Scarce seemed a vision; I would ne'er have striven

As thus with thee in prayer in my sore need.
Oh! lift me as a wave, a leaf, a cloud!
I fall upon the thorns of life! I bleed!

A heavy weight of hours has chained and bowed
One too like thee: tameless, and swift, and proud.

V

Make me thy lyre, even as the forest is②:
What if my leaves are falling like its own③!
The tumult of thy mighty harmonies④

Will take from both⑤ a deep, autumnal tone,
Sweet though in sadness. Be thou, Spirit fierce,
My spirit! Be thou me, impetuous one!

Drive my dead thoughts over the universe
Like withered leaves to quicken a new birth!
And, by the incantation of this verse,

---

① pant: to breathe rapidly in short gasps, 喘气，急促地呼吸
② even as the forest is: just as the forest is (thy lyre)
③ like its own: like the forest's own (leaves)
④ thy mighty harmonies: the sound of the west wind
⑤ both: the poet himself and the forest

Scatter, as from an unextinguished hearth
Ashes and sparks, my words among mankind!
Be through my lips to unawakened Earth

The trumpet of a prophecy①! O Wind,
If Winter comes, can Spring be far behind?

Questions for Discussion

1. What is the image of West Wind?
2. Please analyze the form of *Ode to the West Wind*.
3. Please analyze the theme of *Ode to the West Wind*.

Unit 6　Jane Austen

Appreciation

我认为婚姻最坚韧的纽带不是孩子，不是金钱，而是精神的共同成长。

——杨澜

Author

Jane Austen was born on December 16, 1775, at Steventon in Hampshire, where her father was a rector. She was the second daughter and seventh child in a family of eight. The household was lively and bookish. The family also enjoyed writing and performing plays for evening entertainment. Jane Austen began writing when she was still a little girl. In 1801 the family moved to Bath and after the death of her father in 1805, to Southampton, settling in 1809 with her mother and sisters in a house in Chawton, Hampshire, provided by her brother Edward (1768 – 1852). Jane Austen never married. She died quietly at Winchester in 1817 and was buried in the cathedral

---

①The trumpet of a prophecy: the clarion call for a new times. prophecy，预言

there. Between 1795 and 1798 she worked on three novels. The first to be published was *Sense and Sensibility*. The writing of *First Impressions* got under way and it eventually turned out to be her most famous work *Pride and Prejudice*, but *Northanger Abbey*, a skit on the contemporary Gothic novel.

Jane Austen's novels deal mainly with middle-class families, set usually in rural communities, though occasionally in a town, for example, Bath. Her plots hinge mostly on the development of a love affair leading to the heroine's marriage. Her penetrating observation of human behavior results in insights that transcend period.

Jane Austen is one of the realistic novelists. She drew vivid and realistic pictures of everyday life of the country society in her novels, whose main concern is about human beings in their personal relations, human beings with their families and neighbors. Stories of love and marriage provide the framework for all her novels and in them women are always taken as the major characters. Describing individuals coping with ordinary life and social pressures, she explores the centres of human experience, with a sharp, satiric wit to expose the follies, hypocrisies, and false truths of the world.

Although Jane Austen was a contemporary of the great Romantics, her novels retain a certain Regency classicism and detachment, keeping always a sense of proportion. She is successful in the employment of irony and frequent use of witty and delightful dialogues.

Jane Austen was an English novelist whose works of romantic fiction, set among the landed gentry, earned her a place as one of the most widely read writers in English literature. Her realism, biting irony and social commentary have gained her historical importance among scholars and critics.

Brief Introduction

Pride and Prejudice tells a story which centers on a series of misunderstandings between Elizabeth and Darcy. Elizabeth is a lively young middle-class woman who has a satirical temperament whereas Darcy, born in a wealthy upper-class family, is an unconsciously arrogant young man. He first offends Elizabeth with his haughty contempt for the "inferiority of her connections" and the "want of propriety" apparently displayed by her son-in-law hunting mother, officer-chasing younger sisters and kind but indolent and cynical father. On account of this, Elizabeth makes up her mind not to care about Darcy at all. However, Darcy reluctantly finds himself a suitor of Elizabeth. As he proposes to Elizabeth, he can't help showing his pride for his own status. What is more, he thinks that he is lowering himself and this he communicates to Elizabeth. Elizabeth, in return, develops a strong dislike for and prejudice against Darcy and rejects Darcy's proposal. Then the two part each other. Later, Darcy writes a letter explaining his past conducts to Elizabeth and frees himself from Elizabeth's charges against him. After a series of events, reconciliation of the two comes. As Darcy renews his proposal to Elizabeth, he realizes that it was his pride that made him arrogant and insensitive. Elizabeth, in turn, accepts his offer with the knowledge that her prejudice caused her to mistake his real character. When they join their hands together, they find happiness and a better understanding of each other.

The preoccupation with socially advantageous marriage in the 19th century England society manifests itself here, because in claiming that a single man in possession of a good fortune must be in want of a wife, the narrator reveals that the reverse is also true: a single woman, whose socially prescribed options are quite limited, is in (perhaps desperate) want of a husband.

Selected Reading

Pride and Prejudice

Chapter 1

It is a truth universally acknowledged, that a single man in possession of a good fortune must be in want of a wife.

However little known the feelings or views of such a man may be on his first entering a neighbourhood, this truth is so well fixed in the minds of the surrounding families, that he is considered as the rightful property of some one or other of their daughters.

"My dear Mr. Bennet," said his lady to him one day, "have you heard that Netherfield Park① is let② at last?"

Mr. Bennet replied that he had not.

"But it is," returned she; "for Mrs. Long③ has just been here, and she told

---

①Netherfield Park: the name of an estate in the neighborhood where the Bennets lived
②let: 出租
③Mrs. Long: a neighbor of the Bennets

me all about it."

Mr. Bennet made no answer.

"Do not you want to know who has taken it?" cried his wife impatiently.

"You want to tell me, and I have no objection to hearing it."

This was invitation enough.

"Why, my dear, you must know, Mrs. Long says that Netherfield is taken by a young man of large fortune from the north of England; that he came down on Monday in a chaise and four① to see the place, and was so much delighted with it that he agreed with Mr. Morris② immediately; that he is to take possession③ before Michaelmas④, and some of his servants are to be in the house by the end of next week."

"What is his name?"

"Bingley."

"Is he married or single?"

"Oh! single, my dear, to be sure! A single man of large fortune; four or five thousand a year. What a fine thing for our girls!"

"How so? How can it affect them?"

"My dear Mr. Bennet," replied his wife, "how can you be so tiresome! You must know that I am thinking of his marrying one of them."

"Is that his design in settling here?"

"Design! nonsense, how can you talk so! But it is very likely that he may fall in love with one of them, and therefore you must visit him as soon as he comes."

"I see no occasion for that. You and the girls may go, or you may send them by themselves, which perhaps will be still better; for, as you are as handsome as any of them, Mr. Bingley might like you the best of the party."

"My dear, you flatter⑤ me. I certainly have had my share of beauty, but I do not pretend to be any thing extraordinary now. When a woman has five

---

① a chaise and four: a carriage drawn by four horses, 一辆四轮马车

② Mr. Morris: the man who owns the Netherfield Park

③ take possession: 入住

④ Michaelmas: a church festival in honor of the archangel Michael. The day is set on Sepetmber 29, 米迦勒节(宗教节日)

⑤ flatter: 奉承, 阿谀

grown up daughters, she ought to give over thinking of her own beauty."

"In such cases, a woman has not often much beauty to think of."

"But, my dear, you must indeed go and see Mr. Bingley when he comes into the neighbourhood."

"It is more than I engage for, I assure you."

"But consider your daughters. Only think what an establishment it would be for one of them. Sir William and Lady Lucas[①] are determined to go, merely on that account, for in general, you know they visit no new comers. Indeed you must go, for it will be impossible for us to visit him, if you do not."

"You are over-scrupulous[②], surely. I dare say Mr. Bingley will be very glad to see you; and I will send a few lines by you to assure him of my hearty consent to his marrying which ever he chuses[③] of the girls; though I must throw in a good word for my little Lizzy[④]."

"I desire you will do no such thing. Lizzy is not a bit better than the others; and I am sure she is not half so handsome as Jane[⑤], nor half so good humoured as Lydia[⑥]. But you are always giving her the preference."

"They have none of them much to recommend them," replied he; "they are all silly and ignorant like other girls; but Lizzy has something more of quickness than her sisters."

"Mr. Bennet, how can you abuse your own children in such way? You take delight in vexing[⑦] me. You have no compassion[⑧] on my poor nerves."

"You mistake me, my dear. I have a high respect for your nerves. They are my old friends. I have heard you mention them with consideration these twenty years at least."

"Ah! You do not know what I suffer."

"But I hope you will get over it, and live to see many young men of four

---

① Sir William and Lady Lucas: a couple, neighbor of the Bennets
② scrupulous[IELTS]: 小心谨慎的
③ chuse: (古英语)选择
④ Lizzy: the second daughter of the Bennets
⑤ Jane: the eldest daughter of the Bennets
⑥ Lydia: the youngest daughter of the Bennets
⑦ vexing: 使恼火,使烦恼
⑧ have no compassion on: 不同情,不怜悯

thousand a year come into the neighbourhood."

"It will be no use to us if twenty such should come, since you will not visit them."

"Depend upon it, my dear, that when there are twenty I will visit them all."

Mr. Bennet was so odd a mixture of quick parts①, sarcastic② humour, reserve, and caprice③, that the experience of three and twenty years had been insufficient to make his wife understand his character. Her mind was less difficult to develope. She was a woman of mean understanding, little information, and uncertain temper. When she was discontented, she fancied④ herself nervous. The business of her life was to get her daughters married; its solace⑤ was visiting and news.

Questions for Discussion

1. Analyze the opening sentence: "It is a truth universally acknowledged that a single man in possession of a good fortune must be in want of a wife."
2. Make an analysis of the title *Pride and Prejudice*.
3. What are the special features of the novel?
4. What is the theme of the novel?
5. How many major couples have you found in this novel?
6. What's your attitude towards marriage?

Terms

1. Romanticism
2. Ode
3. Lyric
4. Terza rima

---

①quick parts: wit, 智慧
②sarcastic [TOEFL]: 讽刺的, 嘲讽的
③caprice: 反复无常, 善变
④fancied [IELTS][TOEFL]: 以为, 想要
⑤solace: 安慰, 慰藉

5. Image
6. Imagery
7. Byronic hero
8. Round character

Chapter 6

19th-Century English Literature

I. Historical Background

The Victorian Age

The mid-and-late 19th century is generally known as the Victorian age, controlled by the rule of Queen Victoria. This is a period of dramatic change leading England to the summit of development as a powerful nation. The rising bourgeoisie were getting political importance as well as wealth. England became the world's workshop and London the world's bank. London became the center of Western civilization.

Literacy increased as the masses started to be educated and started to think for themselves. This stage had got ready for the coming of the Golden Age of the English novel. Along with other forms of literature, they displayed a mirror of the Victorian society and a powerful weapon of its criticism. The English critical realists of the 19th century truthfully reflect the evil of the upper class in bourgeois society as well as of the lower class. Generally speaking, Victorian literature vividly portrays the reality of the age.

II. Literary Background

The Victorian Age is one of the greatest and most creative periods in the history of English literature, standing only next to the Elizabethan Age and the Age of Romanticism.

1. Diversity in Victorian Literature

Unlike the previous two periods of Neoclassicism and Romanticism, there was no dominant literary theory in Victorian literature. Several literary trends existed side by side.

(1) Chartist literature

(2) Realistic novels, the greatest literary achievement

(3) Poetry of the "Big Three"—Alfred Tennyson, Robert Browning & Matthew Arnold

(4) Aesthetic Movement which advocated the theory of "art for art's sake"

2. Major Literary Figures

A. Novel: The novel was the dominant form in Victorian literature. It was a principal form of entertainment.

(1) The Rise of the Women Novelists

(2) Types of Novels since the 18th century: Realistic novels (picaresque novels); Romantic novels (historical novels, Gothic novels)

Charles Dickens: *Oliver Twist*, *David Copperfield*

William Thackeray: *The Snobs of England*, *Vanity Fair*

Gorge Eliot: *The Mill on the Floss*

Charlotte Brontë: *Jane Eyre*

Emily Brontë: *Wuthering Heights*

Thomas Hardy: *Tess of the D'Urbervilles*, *Jude the Obscure*

B. Poetry:

In many ways, Victorian poetry is a continuation of the Romantic poetry of the previous age. Dramatic monologue is the great achievement of Victorian poetry, originally a soliloquy in drama. Here it refers to a narrative poem in which one character speaks to one or more imaginary listeners. Alfred Tennyson poet laureate & the spokesman of the age. He voices the doubt and the faith, the grief and the joy of English people in an age of fast social change.

(1) Alfred Tennyson: *In Memoriam*, *Idylls of the King*

(2) Robert Browning: *The King and the Book*

(3) Elizabeth Barrett Browning

C. Drama: Aestheticism & art for art's sake

Oscar Wilde: *The Picture of Dorian Gray*, *The Importance of Being Earnest*

Unit 1 Charles Dickens

Appreciation

It was the best of times, it was the worst of times, it was the age of wisdom, it was the age of foolishness, it was the epoch of belief, it was the epoch of incredulity, it was the season of Light, it was the season of Darkness, it was the spring of hope, it was the winter of despair...

这里最好的时代,也是最坏的时代;是智慧时代,也是愚蠢的时代;是信仰的时代,也是怀疑的时代;是光明的季节,也是黑暗的季节;是充满希望的春天,也是令人绝望的冬天。

Author

Charles Dickens, the greatest author of 15 novels, volumes of stories, travel books, sketches and essays, was the greatest representative of English realism. He was especially famous for the vivid comic characterizatio and his powerful social criticism. His works were created during the Victorian age.

Charles Dickens was born in February, 1812 at Landport, a district of Portsmouth. His father was a hardworking but imprudent clerk, who later showed his character as Mr. Micawber in *David Copperfield*. In 1850, Dickens published *David Copperfield*, a semi-autobiographical novel that was the author's own favorite. Then it was followed by three novels: *Hard Times* (1854), *Little Dorrit* (1857), and *A Tale of Two Cities* (1859). The next one, *Great Expectations* (1861) was meant to be his best and successful work. His influence on the development of the European novel was enormous, and his power has greatly lighted world literature.

Brief Introduction

It tells the story of the development of a young man's moral values in the process of his life—from childhood in the provinces to gentleman's status in London. Similar to Dickens' memories of his own childhood, in his early years the young Pip seems to have no power to stand against injustice or to ever realize his dreams for a better and rich life. However, as he grows into a technical worker and then an educated young man, he reaches an important realization: grand schemes and dreams are never what they first seem to be. Pip himself is not always honest, and careful readers can catch him in several obvious contradictions between his truth and imagination.

Selected Reading

Great Expectations

Chapter 39

I was three-and-twenty years of age. Not another word had I heard to enlighten me on the subject of my expectations, and my twenty-third birthday was a week gone. We had left Barnard's Inn more than a year, and lived in the Temple. Our chambers were in Garden-court, down by the river.

Mr. Pocket① and I had for some time parted company② as to our original relations, though we continued on the best terms. Notwithstanding③ my inability to settle to anything—which I hope arose out of the restless and incomplete tenure on which I held my means—I had a taste for reading, and read regularly so many hours a day. That matter of Herbert's④ was still progressing, and everything with me was as I have brought it down to the close of the last preceding chapter.

Business had taken Herbert on a journey to Marseilles 马赛. I was alone, and had a dull sense of being alone⑤. Dispirited and anxious, long hoping that tomorrow or next week would clear my way⑥, and long disappointed, I sadly

---

① Mr. Pocket：文中指匹普的监护人
② parted company：解除关系
③ notwithstanding：尽管，虽然
④ That matter of Herbert's：与赫伯特有关系，赫伯特是匹普童年的伙伴
⑤ a dull sense of being alone：文中指感到孤苦伶仃，索然无趣
⑥ clear my way：文中指事件等开始明朗起来

missed the cheerful face and ready response of my friend.

It was wretched weather①; stormy and wet, stormy and wet; and mud, mud, mud, deep in all the streets. Day after day, a vast heavy veil had been driving over London from the East, and it drove still, as if in the East there were an eternity② of cloud and wind. So furious had been the gusts, that high buildings in town had had the lead stripped off their roofs; and in the country, trees had been torn up, and sails of windmills carried away; and gloomy accounts③ had come in from the coast, of shipwreck and death. Violent blasts of rain had accompanied these rages of wind④, and the day just closed as I sat down to read had been the worst of all.

Alterations⑤ have been made in that part of the Temple since that time. And it has not now so lonely a character as it had then, nor is it so exposed to the river. We lived at the top of the last house, and the wind rushing up the river shook the house that night, like discharges of cannon, or breakings of a sea. When the rain came with it and dashed against the windows, I thought, raising my eyes to them as they rocked, that I might have fancied myself in a storm-beaten lighthouse. Occasionally, the smoke came rolling down the chimney as though it could not bear to go out into such a night; and when I set the doors open and looked down the staircase: the staircase lamps were blown out; and when I shaded my face with my hands and looked through the black windows (opening them, ever so little, was out of the question in the teeth of⑥ such wind and rain) I saw that the lamps in the court were blown out, and that the lamps on the bridges and the shore were shuddering, and that the coal fires in barges on the river were being carried away before the wind like red-hot splashes in the rain⑦.

---

① wretched weather: 糟糕透顶的天气
② eternity: 永恒的风云
③ gloomy accounts: 令人扫兴的事情
④ violent blasts of rain had accompanied these rages of wind: 风雨交加
⑤ alteration [TOEFL]: 变化
⑥ in the teeth of: 顶着狂风暴雨
⑦ like red-hot splashes in the rain: 像一阵阵红热的雨点

I read with my watch upon the table, purposing to close my book at eleven o'clock. As I shut it, Saint Paul's, and all the many church-clocks in the City①— some leading, some accompanying, some following—struck that hour. The sound was curiously flawed by the wind; and I was listening, and thinking how the wind assailed and tore it, when I heard a footstep on the stair.

What nervous folly made me start, and awfully connect it with the footstep of my dead sister, matters not. It was past in a moment, and I listened again, and heard the footstep stumble in coming on. Remembering then that the staircase-lights were blown out, I took up my reading-lamp and went out to the stair-head. Whoever was below had stopped on seeing my lamp, for all was quiet.

"There is some one down there, is there not?" I called out, looking down.

"Yes," said a voice from the darkness beneath.

"What floor do you want?"

"The top. Mr. Pip."

"That is my name.—There is nothing the matter?"

"Nothing the matter," returned the voice. And the man came on.

I stood with my lamp held out over the stair-rail, and he came slowly within its light. It was a shaded lamp, to shine upon a book, and its circle of light was very contracted②; so that he was in it for a mere instant, and then out of it. In the instant, I had seen a face that was strange to me, looking up with an incomprehensible air of being touched and pleased by the sight of me.

Moving the lamp as the man moved, I made out that he was substantially dressed, but roughly; like a voyager by sea. That he had long iron-grey hair. That his age was about sixty. That he was a muscular man, strong on his legs, and that he was browned and hardened by exposure to weather③. As he ascended the last stair or two, and the light of my lamp included us both, I saw, with a stupid kind of amazement, that he was holding out both his hands to me.

---

①the City：伦敦的市中心

②its circle of light was very contracted：灯光照射的范围有限

③exposure to weather：饱经风霜

"Pray① what is your business?" I asked him.

"My business?" he repeated, pausing. "Ah! Yes. I will explain my business, by your leave."

"Do you wish to come in?"

"Yes," he replied; "I wish to come in, Master."

I had asked him the question inhospitably enough, for I resented the sort of bright and gratified recognition that still shone in his face. I resented it, because it seemed to imply that he expected me to respond to it. But I took him into the room I had just left, and, having set the lamp on the table, asked him as civilly as I could② to explain himself.

He looked about him with the strangest air—an air of wondering pleasure, as if he had some part in the things he admired—and he pulled off a rough outer coat, and his hat. Then, I saw that his head was furrowed③ and bald, and that the long iron-grey hair grew only on its sides. But I saw nothing that in the least explained him. On the contrary, I saw him next moment once more holding out both his hands to me.

"What do you mean?" said I, half suspecting him to be mad.

He stopped in his looking at me, and slowly rubbed his right hand over his head. "It's disappointing to a man," he said, in a coarse broken voice, "after having looked forward so distant, and come so far; but you're not to blame for that—neither on us is to blame for that. I'll speak in half a minute. Give me half a minute, please."

He sat down on a chair that stood before the fire, and covered his forehead with his large brown veinous hands. I looked at him attentively then, and recoiled④ a little from him; but I did not know him.

"There's no one nigh⑤," said he, looking over his shoulder; "is there?"

---

①pray：请问

②as civilly as I could：我尽量客气地

③furrowe：深深的皱纹

④recoile：退缩

⑤nigh：near

"Why do you, a stranger coming into my rooms at this time of the night, ask that question?" said I.

"You're a game one①," he returned, shaking his head at me with a deliberate affection, at once most unintelligible and most exasperating; "I'm glad you've grown up a game one! But don't catch hold of me. You'd be sorry afterwards to have done it."

I relinquished the intention he had detected, for I knew him! Even yet I could not recall a single feature, but I knew him! If the wind and the rain had driven away the intervening year, had scattered all the intervening objects, had swept us to the churchyard where we first stood face to face on such different levels, I could not have known my convict more distinctly than I knew him now, as he sat in the chair before the fire. No need to take a file from his pocket and show it to me; no need to take the handkerchief from his neck and twist it round his head; no need to hug himself with both his arms, and take a shivering turn across the room, looking back at me for recognition. I knew him before he gave me one of those aids, though, a moment before, I had not been conscious of remotely suspecting his identity.

He came back to where I stood, and again held out both his hands. Not knowing what to do for, in my astonishment I had lost my self-possession—I reluctantly gave him my hands. He grasped them heartily, raised them to his lips, kissed them, and still held them.

"You acted noble, my boy," said he. "Noble, Pip! And I have never forgot it!"

At a change in his manner as if he were even going to embrace me, I laid a hand upon his breast and put him away.

"Stay!" said I. "Keep off! If you are grateful to me for what I did when I was a little child, I hope you have shown your gratitude by mending your way of life②. If you have come here to thank me, it was not necessary. Still, however, you have found me out, there must be something good in the feeling that has brought you

---

① a game one：这里指匹普长得英俊、潇洒
② mending your way of life：你改过自新了

here, and I will not repulse① you; but surely you must understand that I...?"

My attention was so attracted by the singularity② of his fixed look at me that the words died away on my tongue.

"You were saying, " he observed, when we had confronted one another in silence, "that surely I must understand. What, surely must I understand?"

"That I cannot wish to renew that chance intercourse with you of long ago, under these different circumstances. I am glad to believe you have repented and recovered yourself. I am glad to tell you so. I am glad that, thinking I deserve to be thanked, you have come to thank me. But our ways are different ways, none the less. You are wet, and you look weary. Will you drink something before you go?"

He had replaced his neckerchief loosely, and had stood, keenly observant of me, biting a long end of it. "I think, " he answered, still with the end at his mouth and still observant of me, "that I will drink (I thank you) afore I go."

There was a tray ready on a side-table. I brought it to the table near the fire, and asked him what he would have? He touched one of the bottles without looking at it or speaking, and I made him some hot rum and water③. I tried to keep my hand steady while I did so, but his look at me as he leaned back in his chair with the long draggled end of his neckerchief between his teeth—evidently forgotten—made my hand very difficult to master. When at last I put the glass to him, I saw with amazement that his eyes were full of tears.

Up to this time I had remained standing, not to disguise that I wished him gone. But I was softened by the softened aspect of the man, and felt a touch of reproach④. "I hope, " said I, hurriedly putting something into a glass for myself, and drawing a chair to the table, "that you will not think spoke harshly to you just now. I had no intention of doing it, and I am sorry for it if I did. I wish you well, and happy!"

---

①repulse[TOEFL]：驳斥,拒绝
②singularity：奇特,奇怪,异常
③rum and water：兑水的朗姆酒
④a touch of reproach：良心上的责备

Questions for Discussion

1. What role does social class play in *Great Expectations*?
2. What lessons does Pip learn from his experience as a wealthy gentleman?
3. How is the theme of social class central to the novel?

Appreciation

我觉得,描写这样一帮事实上存在的犯罪分子,刻画他们畸形的面目、顽劣的品质和可悲的生活,如实地表现他们老是怀着鬼胎潜行在最肮脏的生活小道上,无论他们转向哪一面,前景望到底只有黑漆漆、阴森森的巨大脚架;我觉得反映这些情形也就是尝试做一件需要的、于社会有益的事情。

这里包含着人类本性最好和最坏的方面:有许多色彩丑陋不堪,也有一些极其美丽。这是一种矛盾,一种异态,一种表面看来不可能的现象,然而这是真实。

——荣如德

Brief Introduction

Probably the best-known of all Dickens' works, *Oliver Twist* was originally published as a serial, and sought to bring the public's attention to various contemporary social evils, including the workhouse, child labor and the recruitment of children as criminals. The novel is full of drama, sarcasm and dark humor even as it reveals the hypocrisies of the time. It centers on orphan Oliver Twist, who spends his early years in grim institutions. Oliver is mistreated and even tortured in the workhouse and sold into apprenticeship with an undertaker. When he escapes to London, he is taken in by a gang of juvenile pickpockets in London.

This novel is notable for its portrayal of criminals and their sordid lives, as well as for exposing the cruel treatment of the many orphans in London in the mid-19th century. In Chapter 2, the narrator describes how the board regulates the amount of food those in the workhouse are allowed to eat; it is mostly "gruel," or water mixed with thin oatmeal, and many of the workers starve and die. Oliver, after three months of near starvation, approaches the master in the dining hall and asks if he might have more gruel. The master is flabbergasted, and calls for the beadle, who brings Oliver before the board again. It shows the horrible cruelty of the workhouse system of the time and reflects the extreme brutality and corruption of the oppressors and their agents under the mask of philanthropy.

Selected Reading

Oliver Twist

CHAPTER II

TREATS OF OLIVER TWIST'S GROWTH, EDUCATION, AND BOARD

Mr. Bumble walked on with long strides; little Oliver, firmly grasping his gold-laced cuff, trotted① beside him, inquiring at the end of every quarter of a mile whether they were "nearly there", to which interrogations② Mr. Bumble returned very brief and snappish replies; for the temporary blandness③ which gin and water awakens in some bosoms had by this time evaporated④, and he was once again a beadle.

Oliver had not been within the walls of the workhouse a quarter of an hour, and had scarcely completed the demolition⑤ of a second slice of bread, when Mr. Bumble, who had handed him over to the care of an old woman, returned, and, telling him it was a board night, informed him that the board had said he was to appear before it forthwith.

Not having a very clearly defined notion of what a live board was, Oliver was rather astounded⑥ by this intelligence, and was not quite certain whether he ought to laugh or cry. He had no time to think about the matter, however; for Mr. Bumble gave him a tap on the head with his cane to wake him up, and

---

①trot: 小步,快跑

②interrogations: 审讯;询问,这里指 Oliver 的问话

③blandness: 温柔,平和

④evaporate[TOEFL][IELTS]:蒸发,消失

⑤demolition: 拆除,破坏,这里指 Oliver 狼吞虎咽的样子

⑥astounded: 惊骇的

another on the back to make him lively, and, bidding him to follow, conducted him into a large white washed room, where eight or ten fat gentlemen were sitting round a table, at the top of which, seated in an arm-chair rather higher than the rest, was a particularly fat gentleman with a very round, red face.

"Bow to the board," said Bumble. Oliver brushed away two or three tears that were lingering in his eyes, and seeing no board but the table, fortunately bowed to that.

"What's your name, boy?" said the gentleman in the high chair.

Oliver was frightened at the sight of so many gentlemen, which made him tremble; and the beadle① gave him another tap behind, which made him cry; and these two causes made him answer in a very low and hesitating voice; where upon a gentleman in a white waistcoat said he was a fool, which was a capital way of raising his spirits, and putting him quite at his ease.

"Boy," said the gentleman in the high chair; "listen to me. You know you're an orphan②, I suppose?"

"What's that, sir?" inquired poor Oliver.

"The boy is a fool—I thought he was," said the gentleman in the white waistcoat, in very decided tone. If one member of a class be blessed with an intuitive③ perception④ of others of the same race, the gentleman in white waistcoat was unquestionably well qualified to pronounce an opinion on the matter.

"Hush!" said the gentleman who had spoken first. "You know you've got no father or mother, and that you were brought up by the parish⑤, don't you?"

"Yes, sir," replied Oliver, weeping bitterly.

"What are you crying for?" inquired the gentleman in the white waistcoat; and to be sure it was very extraordinary. What could the boy be crying for?

---

①beadle：教区干事,牧师助理
②orphan：孤儿
③intuitive：直觉的
④perception[TOEFL][IELTS]：感知,洞察力,见解
⑤parish：教区

"I hope you say your prayers every night," said another gentleman in a gruff voice, "and pray for the people who feed you, and take care of you, like a Christian."

"Yes, sir," stammered① the boy. The gentleman who spoke last was unconsciously right. It would have been very like a Christian, and a marvellously good Christian, too, if Oliver had prayed for the people who fed and took care of him. But he hadn't, because nobody had taught him.

"Well! You have come here to be educated, and taught a useful trade," said the red-faced gentleman in the high chair.

"So you'll begin to pick oakum② to-morrow morning at six o'clock," added the surly one in the white waistcoat.

For the combination of both these blessings in the one simple process of picking oakum, Oliver bowed low by the direction of the beadle, and was then hurried away to a large ward, where, on a rough hard bed, he sobbed himself to sleep. What a novel illustration of the tender laws of this favoured country③! They let the paupers④ go to sleep!

Poor Oliver! He little thought, as he lay sleeping in happy unconsciousness⑤ of all around him, that the board had that very day arrived at a decision which would exercise the most material influence over all his future fortunes⑥. But they had. And this was it:

The members of this board were very sage⑦, deep, philosophical⑧ men; and when they came to turn their attention to the workhouse, they found out at

---

①stammer：结结巴巴地说

②oakum：a material obtained by pulling old rope to pieces, a job done in the past by prisoners 麻絮（旧时由囚犯制造）

③this favoured country：这里是讽刺的说法，指英国

④pauper：穷人，贫民

⑤unconsciousness：毫无知觉，无意识

⑥fortunes[TOEFL]：这里译为命运

⑦sage[GRE]：睿智的

⑧philosophical：哲学的，达观的，处乱不惊的

once, what ordinary① folks would never have discovered, – the poor people liked it! It was a regular place of public entertainment② for the poorer classes, a tavern where there was nothing to pay, – a public breakfast, dinner, tea, and supper all the year round, – a brick and mortar elysium③ where it was all play and no work. "Oho!" said the board, looking very knowing; "we are the fellows to set this to rights; we'll stop it all in no time." So, they established④ the rule, that all poor people should have the alternative⑤ (for they would compel nobody, not they), of being starved by a gradual process in the house, or by a quick one out of it. With this view, they contracted⑥ with the waterworks to lay on an unlimited supply of water, and with a corn-factor to supply periodically⑦ small quantities⑧ of oatmeal⑨; and issued three meals of thin gruel⑩ a – day, with an onion twice a week, and half a roll of Sundays. They made a great many other wise and humane regulations⑪ having reference to the ladies, which it is not necessary to repeat; kindly undertook to divorce poor married people, in consequence of the great expense of a suit in Doctors' Commons⑫; and, instead of compelling⑬ a man to support his family as they had theretofore done, took his family away from him, and made him a bachelor⑭! There is no telling how

①ordinary:寻常的,普通的
②entertainment:娱乐
③a brick and mortar elysium:砖头和灰泥砌成的乐园
④establish[TOEFL][IELTS]:建立,制定
⑤alternative[TOEFL][IELTS]:可供选择的事物
⑥contract[TOEFL][IELTS]:合同;订立合同
⑦periodically:周期性地
⑧quantities:数量
⑨oatmeal:燕麦片
⑩gruel:白粥,泡饭
⑪regulations[TOEFL][IELTS]:规章制度
⑫doctors' Commons:律师学院,始建于十三世纪,其成员多处理离婚和遗嘱等事宜
⑬compel[TOEFL][IELTS]:强迫,迫使
⑭bachelor[TOEFL][IELTS]:单身汉;学士

many applicants① for relief② under these last two heads would not have started up in all classes of society, if it had not been coupled with the workhouse. But they were long-headed men, and they had provided for this difficulty. The relief was inseparable from the workhouse and the gruel; and that frightened people.

For the first three months after Oliver Twist was removed, the system was in full operation. It was rather expensive at first, in consequence of the increase in the undertaker③'s bill, and the necessity of taking in the clothes of all the paupers, which fluttered④ loosely on their wasted, shrunken forms, after a week or two's gruel. But the number of workhouse inmates got thin, as well as the paupers; and the board were in ecstasies⑤.

The room in which the boys were fed, was a large, stone hall, with a copper⑥ at one end, out of which the master, dressed in an apron for the purpose, and assisted by one or two women, ladled the gruel⑦ at meal-times; of which composition each boy had one porringer⑧, and no more,—except on festive occasions, and then he had two ounces and a quarter of bread besides. The bowls never wanted washing—the boys polished⑨ them with their spoons till they shone again; and when they had performed this operation (which never took very long, the spoons being nearly as large as the bowls), they would sit staring at the copper with such eager eyes as if they could have devoured⑩ the very bricks of which it was composed; employing themselves meanwhile in

---

①applicant[TOEFL]:申请人

②relief[IELTS]:救济

③undertaker:殡葬承办人

④flutter:飘动,摆动

⑤ecstasy:狂喜

⑥copper: a large cooking pot 一种大饭锅

⑦gruel:(尤指旧时穷人吃的)稀粥,燕麦粥

⑧porringer:小汤碗

⑨polish[TOEFL][IELTS]:磨光,擦亮

⑩devour[TOEFL]:吞食

sucking their fingers most assiduously①, with the view of catching up any stray splashes② of gruel that might have been cast thereon. Boys have generally excellent appetites: Oliver Twist and his companions suffered the tortures of slow starvation for three months; at last they got so voracious③ and wild with hunger, that one boy, who was tall for his age, and hadn't been used to that sort of thing, (for his father had kept a small cook's shop), hinted darkly to his companions, that unless he had another basin of gruel *per diem*④, he was afraid he might some night happen to eat the boy who slept next him, who happened to be a weakly youth of tender age. He had a wild, hungry eye; and they implicitly⑤ believed him. A council was held; lots were cast who should walk up to the master after supper that evening, and ask for more; and it fell to Oliver Twist.

The evening arrived: the boys took their places; the master in his cook's uniform stationed himself at the copper; his pauper assistants ranged themselves behind him; the gruel was served out, and a long grace was said over the short commons. The gruel disappeared, the boys whispered each other and winked at Oliver, while his next neighbors nudged him. Child as he was, he was desperate with hunger and reckless⑥ with misery. He rose from the table, and advancing, basin and spoon in hand, to the master, said, somewhat alarmed at his own temerity⑦—

"Please, sir, I want some more."

The master was a fat, healthy man, but he turned very pale. He gazed in stupefied⑧ astonishment on the small rebel for some seconds, and then clung for

---

① assiduously: 用功地,勤勉地
② stray splashes: 这里指溅出来的粥嘎巴儿(stray: 走失的, 走散的 splash: 溅上的液体, 溅洒后留下的污渍)
③ voracious: 狼吞虎咽的, 贪婪的
④ per diem: 每日补贴
⑤ implicitly: 深信不疑地
⑥ reckless: 鲁莽的, 不计后果的, 无所顾忌的
⑦ temerity: 鲁莽, 冒失
⑧ stupefy: 使惊讶或惊呆

support to the copper. The assistants were paralysed① with wonder, the boys with fear.

"What!" said the master at length, in a faint voice.

"Please, sir," replied Oliver, "I want some more."

The master aimed a blow at Oliver's head with the ladle②, pinioned③ him in his arms, and shrieked aloud for the beadle.

The board were sitting in solemn conclave④ when Mr. Bumble rushed into the room in great excitement, and addressing the gentleman in the high chair, said, —

"Mr. Limbkins, I beg your pardon, sir! —Oliver Twist has asked for more!" There was a general start. Horror was depicted on every countenance.

"For more!" said Mr. Limbkins. "Compose yourself, Bumble, and answer me distinctly. Do I understand that he asked for more, after he had eaten the supper allotted⑤ by the dietary?"

"He did, sir," replied Bumble.

"That boy will be hung," said the gentleman in the white waistcoat. "I know that boy will be hung."

Nobody controverted⑥ the prophetic gentleman's opinion. An animated discussion took place. Oliver was ordered into instant confinement⑦; and a bill was next morning pasted on the outside of the gate, offering a reward⑧ of five pounds to anybody who would take Oliver Twist off the hands of the parish: in other words, five pounds and Oliver Twist were offered to any man or woman who wanted an apprentice⑨ to any trade, business, or calling.

---

①paralyse:使瘫痪,使麻痹,使不能正常工作
②ladle:长柄勺
③pinion:捆住,缚住(双臂);固定住
④conclave:秘密会议
⑤allot:分配
⑥controvert:反驳,驳斥
⑦confinement:禁闭
⑧reward[TOEFL][IELTS]:奖励,回报,赏金
⑨apprentice:学徒

"I never was more convinced of① anything in my life," said the gentleman in the white waistcoat, as he knocked at the gate and read the bill next morning, — "I never was more convinced of anything in my life, than I am that that boy will come to be hung."

As I purpose to show in the sequel② whether the white-waistcoated gentleman was right or not, I should perhaps mar③ the interest of this narrative④, (supposing it to possess any at all), if I ventured⑤ to hint just yet, whether the life of Oliver Twist will be a long or a short piece of biography.

Questions for Discussion

1. Give a summary of the excerpt in *Oliver Twist*.
2. What kind of world is depicted in this novel?

Unit 2　Charlotte Brontë

Appreciation

Do you think I am an automaton? a machine without feelings?……Do you think, because I am poor, obscure, plain, and little, I am soulless and heartless? You think wrong! I have as much soul as you, and full as much heart! And if God had gifted me with some beauty and much wealth, I should have made it as hard for you to leave me, as it is now for me to leave you. I am not talking to you now through the medium of custom, conventionalities, nor even of mortal flesh; it is my spirit that addresses your spirit; just as if both had passed through the grave, and we stood at God's feet, equal, as we are!

---

①be convinced of:深信不疑
②sequel:续篇,后续
③mar:破坏,损害
④narrative:叙述
⑤venture[TOEFL][IELTS]:敢于去做

你以为我是一架机器?——一架没有感情的机器?难道就因为我一贫如洗、默默无闻、长相平庸、个子瘦小,就没有灵魂,没有心肠了?——你不是想错了吗?——我的心灵跟你一样丰富,我的心胸跟你一样充实!要是上帝赐予我一点姿色和充足的财富,我会使你同我现在一样难分难舍,我不是根据习俗、常规,甚至也不是血肉之躯同你说话,而是我的灵魂同你的灵魂在对话,就仿佛我们两人穿过坟墓,站在上帝脚下,彼此平等——本来就如此!"

Author

There were two great woman novelists during the Victorian age. They were the Brontë sisters, Charlotte (1816 – 1855) and Emily (1818 – 1848). They were born in Yorkshire. In 1820 the family moved to Haworth, a remote and gloomy village on the Yorkshire moors. During the following years, they had a great deal of freedom to explore the surrounding countryside. Their younger sister, Ann Brontë (1820 – 1849) was also a novelist with two works. None of the Brontë sisters enjoyed a long life span and all died young. Charlotte and Emily, together with their two elder sisters, were sent to a charity school with bad food and poor living conditions, where they were cruelly treated. Their two elder sisters did not survive under the hardship and died of health failure. Charlotte and Emily were removed from the school to start a basic knowledge learning at home. Formal schooling was not much in their youth, but wide reading and home education seemed to give freedom to their imagination.

In 1846, a small volume was published with the title of *Poems* under the pennames of Currer, Ellis and Acton Bell. In 1847, Charlotte's *Jane Eyre*, Emily's *Wuthering Heights* and Anne's *Agnes Grey* were all published. However, in 1848, Emily died and Charlotte died in 1855.

Charlotte Brontë is best known for her novel *Jane Eyre*, which tells the story of an orphaned girl who falls in love with a married man. Emily Brontë is now best remembered for her only novel *Wuthering Heights*, a classic of English literature. Initially criticized for its violent nature, this story of uncompromising passion gained recognition as an astute look at the nature of romantic love. Anne Brontë: *Agnes Grey* (1847) *and The Tenant of Wildfell Hall* (1848).

Although their literary output was relatively small, the Brontë sisters are noted for writing works that transcend Victorian conventions.

Brief Introduction

Jane Eyre lives a tragic life when she is a little child. After her parents' death, she becomes a poor orphan. And her wicked aunt Mrs. Reed adopts her on account of the last will of Jane's uncle. The woman obviously dislikes and looks down upon Jane, and also treats her badly. She is employed to be a governess who teaches a French girl Adele in Thornfield, and the host is called Mr. Rochester. Jane's kindness and faithfulness deeply attracts Mr. Rochester, who soon falls in love with her. Strangely, during the days when they're busy in preparing for the wedding, she finds that Mr. Rochester has been in a marriage with a mad woman called Bertha. After a series of events, Jane suddenly realizes who her true love is. It's Mr. Rochester. Jane returns to Thornfield only to find the manor ruined by a big fire. In the end, to Jane's joy, she finds her lover again and they hold each other's hands forever and live a happy life.

Selected Reading

Jane Eyre

Chapter 23

The vehemence① of emotion, stirred② by grief and love within me, was claiming mastery, and struggling for full sway, and asserting a right to predominate③, to overcome, to live, rise, and reign at last: yes, and to speak.

"I grieve to leave Thornfield④: I love Thornfield: I love it, because I have lived in it a full and delightful life, momentarily at least. I have not been trampled⑤ on. I have not been petrified⑥. I have not been buried with inferior

---

①vehemence: 愤怒
②stir[IELTS]: 使奋起；唤起
③predominate[TOEFL]: 占支配地位
④Thornfield: 桑菲尔德
⑤trample[TOEFL][IELTS]: 践踏；蹂躏
⑥petrifiy: 吓呆，使麻木

minds, and excluded from every glimpse of communion with what is bright and energetic and high. I have talked, face to face, with what I reverence①, with what I delight in, with an original, a vigorous, an expanded mind. I have known you, Mr. Rochester; and it strikes me with terror and anguish② to feel I absolutely must be torn from you forever. I see the necessity of departure; and it is like looking on the necessity of death."

"Where do you see the necessity?" he asked suddenly.

"Where? You, sir, have placed it before me."

"In what shape?"

"In the shape of Miss Ingram; a noble and beautiful woman, your bride."

"My bride! What bride? I have no bride!"

"But you will have."

"Yes; I will! I will!" He set his teeth.

"Then I must go: you have said it yourself."

"No: you must stay! I swear it—and the oath shall be kept."

"I tell you I must go!" I retorted, roused to something like passion. "Do you think I can stay to become nothing to you? Do you think I am an automaton③? A machine without feelings? And can bear to have my morsel of bread snatched from my lips, and my drop of living water dashed from my cup? Do you think, because I am poor, obscure, plain, and little, I am soulless and heartless? You think wrong! I have as much soul as you, and full as much heart! And if God had gifted me with some beauty and much wealth, I should have made it as hard for you to leave me, as it is now for me to leave you. I am not talking to you now through the medium of custom, conventionalities, nor even of mortal flesh; it is my spirit that addresses your spirit; just as if both had passed through the grave, and we stood at God's feet, equal, as we are!"

"As we are!" repeated Mr. Rochester "so," he added, enclosing me in his arms, gathering me to his breast, pressing his lips on my lips:

---

①reverence: 尊敬
②anguish[IELTS]: 痛苦; 苦恼
③automaton: 机器人

"So, Jane!"

"Yes, so, sir," I rejoined: "and yet not so; for you are a married man—or as good as a married man, and wed to one inferior to you—to one with whom you have no sympathy whom I do not believe you truly love; for I have seen and heard you sneer at her. I would scorn such a union: therefore I am better than you let me go!"

"Where, Jane? To Ireland?"

"Yes to Ireland. I have spoken my mind, and can go anywhere now."

"Jane, be still; don't struggle so, like a wild frantic① bird that is rending its own plumage② in its desperation."

"I am no bird; and no net ensnares③ me; I am a free human being with an independent will, which I now exert to leave you."

Another effort set me at liberty, and I stood erect before him.

"And your will shall decide your destiny," he said: "I offer you my hand, my heart, and a share of all my possessions."

"You play a farce, which I merely laugh at."

"I ask you to pass through life at my side—to be my second self, and best earthly companion."

"For that fate you have already made your choice, and must abide by④ it."

"Jane, be still a few moments, you are over-excited, I will be still too."

A waft of wind came sweeping down the laurel⑤—walk and trembled through the boughs⑥ of the chestnut. It wandered away-away—to an indefinite distance—it died. The nightingale's song was then the only voice of the hour, in listening to it, I again wept. Mr. Rochester sat quiet, looking at me gently and seriously. Some time passed before he spoke; he at last said—

"Come to my side, Jane, and let us explain and understand one another."

---

①frantic[IELTS]：发疯似的；发狂的

②plumage[TOEFL]：羽毛

③ensnare：诱捕，使入陷阱

④abide by：遵守……；依从……

⑤laurel：月桂树

⑥bough：大树枝

"I will never again come to your side: I am torn away now, and cannot return."

"But, Jane, I summon you as my wife: it is you only I intend to marry."

I was silent: I thought he mocked me.

"Come, Jane—come hither."

"Your bride stands between us."

He rose, and with a stride reached me.

"My bride is here," he said, again drawing me to him, "because my equal is here, and my likeness. Jane, will you marry me?"

Still I did not answer, and still I writhed myself from his grasp: for I was still incredulous①.

"Do you doubt me, Jane?"

"Entirely."

"You have no faith in me?"

"Not a whit."

"Am I a liar in your eyes?" he asked passionately. "Little sceptic②, you shall be convinced. What love have I for Miss Ingram? None, and that you know. What love has she for me? None, as I have taken pains to prove: I caused a rumour to reach her that my fortune was not a third of what was supposed, and after that I presented myself to see the result; it was coldness both from her and her mother. I would not—I could not—marry Miss Ingram. You you strange, you almost unearthly thing! I love as my own flesh. You poor and obscure, and small and plain as you are—I entreat to accept me as a husband."

"What, me!" I ejaculated③, beginning in his earnestness—and especially in his incivility④—to credit his sincerity: "me who have not a friend in the world but you—if you are my friend: not a shilling but what you have given me?"

"You, Jane, I must have you for my own—entirely my own. Will you be

---

①incredulous：怀疑的
②sceptic：怀疑论者
③ejaculate：突然说出
④incivility：非礼

mine? Say yes, quickly."

"Mr. Rochester, let me look at your face: turn to the moonlight."

"Why?"

"Because I want to read your countenance-turn!"

"There! you will find it scarcely more legible than a crumpled, scratched page. Read on: only make haste, for I suffer."

His face was very much agitated and very much flushed, and there were strong workings in the features, and strange gleams in the eyes.

"Oh, Jane, you torture me!" he exclaimed. "With that searching and yet faithful and generous look, you torture me!"

"How can I do that? If you are true, and your offer real, my only feelings to you must be gratitude and devotion—they cannot torture."

"Gratitude!" he ejaculated; and added wildly "Jane, accept me quickly. Say, Edward give me my name—Edward—I will marry you."

"Are you in earnest? Do you truly love me? Do you sincerely wish me to be your wife?"

"I do; and if an oath is necessary to satisfy you, I swear it."

"Then, sir, I will marry you."

"Edward—my little wife!"

"Dear Edward!"

"Come to me—come to me entirely now," said he; and added, in his deepest tone, speaking in my ear as his cheek was laid on mine, "Make my happiness—I will make yours."

"God pardon me!" he subjoined①; "and man meddle② not with me: I have her, and will hold her."

"There is no one to meddle, sir. I have no kindred③ to interfere."

"No—that is the best of it," he said. And if I had loved him less I should

---

①subjoin：增补，附加
②meddle[IELTS]：插手
③kindred：亲属

have thought his accent and look of exultation① savage②; but, sitting by him, roused from the nightmare of parting—called to the paradise of union—I thought only of the bliss given me to drink in so abundant a flow. Again and again he said, "Are you happy, Jane?"

And again and again I answered, "Yes," After which he murmured, "It will atone—it will atone. Have I not found her friendless, and cold, and comfortless? Will I not guard, and cherish, and solace③ her? Is there not love in my heart, and constancy in my resolves? It will expiate at God's tribunal④. I know my Maker sanctions what I do.

For the world's judgment—I wash my hands thereof. For man's opinion—I defy it."

But what had befallen⑤ the night? The moon was not yet set, and we were all in shadow: I could scarcely see my master's face, near as I was. And what ailed the chestnut tree? It writhed⑥ and groaned; while wind roared in the laurel walk, and came sweeping over us.

"We must go in," said Mr. Rochester, "the weather changes. I could have sat with thee till morning, Jane."

"And so," thought I, "could I with you." I should have said so, perhaps, but a livid⑦, vivid spark leapt out of a cloud at which I was looking, and there was a crack, a crash, and a close rattling peal; and I thought only of hiding my dazzled⑧ eyes against Mr. Rochester's shoulder.

The rain rushed down. He hurried me up the walk, through the grounds, and into the house; but we were quite wet before we could pass the threshold⑨.

---

①exultation：狂喜

②savage[IELTS]：未开化的；野蛮的

③solace：慰藉

④tribunal：裁决

⑤befall：发生，降临

⑥writhe：扭动，翻滚

⑦livid：乌青色的

⑧dazzled：使目眩，使眼花

⑨threshold[TOEFL][IELTS]：门槛

He was taking off my shawl① in the hall, and shaking the water out of my loosened hair, when Mrs. Fairfax emerged from her room. I did not observe her at first, nor did Mr. Rochester. The lamp was lit. The dock was on the stroke of twelve.

"Hasten to take off your wet things," said he; "and before you go, good-night-good-night, my darling!"

He kissed me repeatedly. When I looked up, on leaving his arms, there stood the widow, pale, grave, and amazed. I only smiled at her, and ran upstairs. "Explanation will do for another time," thought I. Still, when I reached my chamber, I felt a pang at the idea she should even temporarily misconstrue what she had seen. But joy soon effaced② every other feeling; and loud as the wind blew, near and deep as the thunder crashed, fierce and frequent as the lightning gleamed, cataract③—like as the rain fell during a storm of two hours' duration, I experienced no fear and little awe. Mr. Rochester came thrice to my door in the course of it, to ask if I was safe and tranquil, and that was comfort, that was strength for anything.

Before I left my bed in the morning, little Adele came running in to tell me that the great horse-chestnut④ at the bottom of the orchard had been struck by lightning in the night, and half of it split away.

Chapter 37

Very early the next morning, I heard him up and astir, wandering from one room to another. As soon as Mary came down I heard the question: "Is Miss Eyre here?" Then: "Which room did you put her into? Was it dry? Is she up? Go and ask if she wants anything; and when she will come down."

I came down as soon as I thought there was a prospect of breakfast. Entering the room very softly, I had a view of him before he discovered my

---

①shawl: 围巾，披肩
②efface: 擦掉；抹去
③cataract[IELTS]: 大瀑布
④horse-chestnut: 七叶树

presence. It was mournful, indeed, to witness the subjugation① of that vigorous spirit to a corporeal infirmity②. He sat in his chair-still, but not at rest: expectant evidently; the lines of now habitual sadness marking his strong features. His countenance reminded one of a lamp quenched, waiting to be re-lit—and alas! it was not himself that could now kindle the lustre③ of animated expression: he was dependent on another for that Office! I had meant to be gay and careless, but the powerlessness of the strong man touched my heart to the quick④: still I accosted⑤ him with what vivacity I could:

"It is a bright, sunny morning, sir," I said. "The rain is over and gone, and there is a tender shining after it: you shall have a walk soon."

I had wakened the glow: his features beamed.

"Oh, you are indeed there, my sky lark! Come to me. You are not gone: not vanished? I heard one of your kind⑥ an hour ago, singing high over the wood: but its song had no music for me, any more than the rising sun had rays. All the melody on earth is concentrated in my Jane's tongue to my ear (I am glad it is not naturally a silent one), all the sunshine I can feel is in her presence."

The water stood in my eyes to hear this avowal⑦ of his dependence: just as if a royal eagle, chained to a perch, should be forced to entreat a sparrow to become its purveyor⑧. But I would not be lachrymose⑨, I dashed off the salt drops, and busied myself with preparing breakfast.

Most of the morning was spent in the open air. I led him out of the wet and wild wood into some cheerful fields: I described to him how brilliantly green

---

①subjugation (to): 服从，屈服
②infirmity: 虚弱
③lustre: 光辉
④touched my heart to the quick: 深深地触痛了我的心。quick: 晦涩
⑤accost: 走近跟某人讲话
⑥one of your kind: 你的一个同类。文中罗切斯特将简比作云雀
⑦avowal: 坦率承认
⑧purveyor: 提供者
⑨lachrymose: 爱哭的

they were; how the flowers and hedges looked refreshed; how sparklingly blue was the sky. I sought a seat for him in a hidden and lovely spot, a dry stump of a tree; nor did I refuse to let him, when seated, place me on his knee. Why should I, when both he and I were happier near than apart? Pilot① lay beside us, all was quiet. He broke out suddenly while clasping me in his arms:

"Cruel, cruel deserter! Oh, Jane, what did I feel when I discovered you had fled from Thornfield, and when I could nowhere find you; and, after examining your apartment, ascertained that you had no money, nor anything which could serve as an equivalent! A pearl necklace I had given you lay untouched in its little casket; your trunks were left corded and locked as they had been prepared for the bridal tour. What could my darling do, I asked, left destitute② and penniless? And what did she do? Let me hear now."

Thus urged, I began the narrative of my experience for the fast year. I softened considerably what related to the three days of wandering and starvation, because to have told him all would have been to inflict unnecessary pain: the little I did say lacerated③ his faithful heart deeper than I wished.

I should not have left him thus, he said, without any means of making my way: I should have told him my intention. I should have confided in him: he would never have forced me to be his mistress. Violent as he had seemed in his despair, he, in truth, loved me far too well and too tenderly to constitute himself my tyrant: he would have given me half his fortune, without demanding so much as a kiss in return, rather than I should have flung myself friendless on the wide world. I had endured, he was certain, more than I had confessed to him.

"Well, whatever my sufferings had been, they were very short," I answered: and then I proceeded to tell him how I had been received at Moor House; how I had obtained the office of schoolmistress, etc. The accession of fortune, the discovery of my relations, followed in due order. Of course, St.

---

①Pilot：罗切斯特先生养的狗的名字
②destitute：匮乏的，一无所有
③lacerate：撕裂；折磨

John Rivers'name came in frequently in the progress of my tale. When I had done, that name was immediately taken up.

"This St. John, then, is your cousin?"

"Yes."

"You have spoken of him often: do you like him?"

"He was a very good man, sir; I could not help liking him."

"A good man. Does that mean a respectable, well-conducted man of fifty? Or what does it mean?"

"St. John was only twenty-nine, sir."

" 'Jeune encore①,' as the French say. Is he a person of low stature, phlegmatic②, and plain? A person whose goodness consists rather in his guiltlessness of vice, than in his prowess③ in virtue?"

"He is untiringly active. Great and exalted deeds are what he lives to perform."

"But his brain? That is probably rather soft? He means well: but you shrug your shoulders to hear him talk?"

"He talks little, sir, what he does say is ever to the point. His brain is first-rate, I should think: not impressible, but vigorous."

"Is he an able man, then?"

"Truly able."

"A thoroughly educated man?"

"St. John is an accomplished and profound scholar."

"His manners, I think, you said are not to your taste? Priggish and parsonic④?"

"I never mentioned his manners; but, unless I had a very bad taste, they must suit it; they are polished, calm, and gentlemanlike."

---

①jeune encore:还很年轻(法语)

②phlegmatic:迟钝的;冷漠的

③prowess:杰出的才能

④priggish and parsonic:古板自负,一幅牧师腔。priggish:一本正经的; parsonic:牧师似的

"His appearance, I forget what description you gave of his appearance; a sort of raw curate①, half strangled with his white neckcloth, and stilted② up on his thick-soled high-lows③, eh?"

"St. John dresses well. He is a handsome man: tall, fair, with blue eyes, and a Grecian profile."

(Aside.) "Damn him!" (To me.) "Did you like him, Jane?"

"Yes, Mr. Rochester, I liked him, but you asked me that before."

I perceived, of course, the drift of my interlocutor④. Jealousy had got hold of him: she stung him; but the sting was salutary: it gave him respite⑤ from the gnawing fang⑥ of melancholy. I would not, therefore, immediately charm the snake.

"Perhaps you would rather not sit any longer on my knee, Miss Eyre?" was the next somewhat unexpected observation.

"Why not, Mr. Rochester?"

"The picture you have just drawn is suggestive of a rather too overwhelming contrast. Your words have delineated very prettily a graceful Apollo: he is present to your imagination, tall, fair, blue-eyed, and with a Grecian profile. Your eyes dwell on a Vulcan⑦, a real blacksmith, brown, broad-shouldered: and blind and lame into the bargain."

"I never thought of it, before; but you certainly are rather like Vulcan, sir."

"Well, you can leave me, ma'am, but before you go" (and he retained me by a firmer grasp than ever), "you will be pleased just to answer me a question or two." He paused.

"What questions, Mr. Rochester?"

Then followed this cross-examination.

---

①curate: 助理牧师
②stilt[TOEFL]: 踩高跷
③high-low: 高帮缚带靴
④interlocutor: 对话者
⑤respite: 暂时解脱
⑥fang: (毒蛇的)毒牙
⑦Vulcan: 伏尔甘, 古罗马宗教信奉的神, 后成为铁匠的守护神

"St. John made you schoolmistress of Morton before he knew you were his cousin?"

"Yes."

"You would often see him? He would visit the school sometimes?"

"Daily."

"He would approve of your plans, Jane? I know they would be clever, for you are a talented creature."

"He approved of them—yes."

"He would discover many things in you he could not have expected to find? Some of your accomplishments are not ordinary."

"I don't know about that."

"You had a little cottage near the school, you say, did he ever come there to see you?"

"Now and then."

"Of an evening?"

"Once or twice."

A pause.

"How long did you reside with him and his sisters after the cousinship was discovered?"

"Five months."

"Did Rivers spend much time with the ladies of his family?"

"Yes; the back parlour was both his study and ours: he sat near the window, and we by the table."

"Did he study much?"

"A good deal."

"What?"

"Hindustani①."

"And what did you do meantime?"

"I learnt German, at first."

"Did he teach you?"

---

①Hindostani：印度斯坦语

"He did not understand German."

"Did he teach you nothing?"

"A little Hindostani."

"Rivers taught you Hindostani?"

"Yes, sir."

"And his sisters also?"

"No."

"Only you?"

"Only me."

"Did you ask to learn?"

"No."

"He wished to teach you?"

"Yes."

A second pause.

"Why did he wish it? Of what use could Hindustani be to you?"

"He intended me to go with him to India."

"Ah! Here I reach the root of the matter. He wanted you to marry him?"

"He asked me to marry him."

"That is a fiction—an impudent invention to vex me."

"I beg your pardon, it is the literal truth: he asked me more than once, and was as stiff about urging his point as ever you could be."

"Miss Eyre, I repeat it, you can leave me. How often am I to say the thing? Why do you remain pertinaciously① perched on my knee, when I have given you notice to quit?"

"Because I am comfortable there."

"No, Jane, you are not comfortable there, because your heart is not with me: it is with this cousin—this St. John. Oh, till this moment, I thought my little Jane was all mine! I had a belief she loved me even when she left me, that was an atom of sweet in much bitter. Long as we have been parted, hot tears as I have wept over our separation, I never thought that while I was mourning her,

---

①pertinaciously：固执地，执着地

she was loving another! But it is useless grieving. Jane, leave me, go and marry Rivers."

"Shake me off, then, sir, push me away, for I'll not leave you of my own accord①."

"Jane, I ever like your tone of voice, it still renews hope, it sounds so truthful. When I hear it, it carries me back a year. I forget that you have formed a new tie. But I am not a fool—go—"

"Where must I go, sir?"

"Your own way—with the husband you have chosen."

"Who is that?"

"You know—this St. John Rivers."

"He is not my husband, nor ever will be. He does not love me. I do not love him. He loves (as he can love, and that is not as you love) a beautiful young lady called Rosamond. He wanted to marry me only because he thought I should make a suitable missionary's wife, which she would not have done. He is good and great, but severe; and, for me, cold as an iceberg. He is not like you, sir: I am not happy at his side, nor near him, nor with him. He has no indulgence for me—no fondness. He sees nothing attractive in me; not even youth—only a few useful mental points. Then I must leave you, sir, to go to him?"

I shuddered involuntarily, and clung instinctively closer to my blind but beloved master. He smiled.

"What, Jane! Is this true? Is such state of matters between you and Rivers?"

"Absolutely, sir. Oh, you need not be jealous! I wanted to tease you a little to make you less sad: I thought anger would be better than grief. But if you wish me to love you, could you but see how much I do love you, you would be proud and content. All my heart is yours, sir: it belongs to you; and with you it would remain, were fate to exile the rest of me from your presence for ever."

Again, as he kissed me, painful thoughts darkened his aspect.

---

①of one's own accord: 出于自愿

"My seared① vision! My crippled strength!" he murmured regretfully.

I caressed, in order to soothe him. I knew of what he was thinking, and wanted to speak for him, but dared not. As he turned aside his face a minute, I saw a tear slide from under the sealed eyelid, and trickle down the manly cheek. My heart swelled.

Questions for Discussion

1. Please make an analysis of major characters Jane Eyre and Edward Rochester.
2. What do the names mean in *Jane Eyre*? Some names to consider include: Jane Eyre, Gateshead, Lowood, Thornfield, Reed, Rivers, Miss Temple, and Ferndean.

Unit 3 Thomas Hardy

Appreciation

All waited in the growing light, their faces and hands as if they were silvered, the remainder of their figures dark, the stones glistening green-grey, the Plain still a mass of shade.

天越来越亮了，所有的人都在那儿等着，他们的脸和手都仿佛镀上了一层银灰色，而他们身体的其他部分则是黑色的，石头柱子闪耀着灰绿色的光，平原仍然是一片昏暗。

Author

Thomas Hardy was born in a small thatched cottage near Dorchester, Dorset, on June 2, 1840. He was the last one of the greatest Victorian novelists, and was also a great poet at the turn of the 19th century.

The young Hardy had a passion for books. He had expected to have further

---

①sear: 灼伤

education, but family finance situation did not support that far. Instead, he was apprenticed to a local architect at the age of 16, which forced Hardy to stay in Dorset, and provided him with the inspiration for his greatest books.

Hardy's novels were all Victorian in date. Most of them were set in Wessex, a fictional primitive and crude rural region which was Hardy's hometown he both loved and hated. These works, known as "novels of character and environment", were the most representative works. He believed in fate and attributed the tragic end of his hero or heroine to bad fortune. Therefore, he was considered to be a naturalistic writer.

1. Wessex Novels 威塞克斯小说

Dorset is the main background in his works, which he called Wessex—the fictional simple and beautiful though primitive rural region, threatened by the invading capitalism. The impact of scientific discoveries and modern philosophic thoughts upon man is quite obvious. Man is not the master of his destiny; he is at the mercy of indifferent forces which manipulate his behaviors and his relations to others.

Far from the Madding Crowd 远离尘嚣

The Woodlanders 林地居民

Under the Greenwood Tree 绿荫下

The Return of the Native 还乡

The Mayor of Casterbridge 卡斯特桥市长

Tess of the D'Urbervilles 德伯家的苔丝

Jude the Obscure 无名的裘德

Hardy had a deep sense of moral sympathy for England's lower classes, particularly for rural women. In 1891, Hardy published *Tess of the D'Urbervilles*: *A Pure Woman Faithfully Presented*. The novel, now a great classic of English literature, received mixed reviews when it first appeared, in part because it challenged the sexual morals of Hardy's day. The outcry and accusations of immortality greeted its attack on Victorian hypocrisy disgusted him. *Jude the Obscure* (1898) aroused even greater anger and Hardy stopped his writing. Most of his poems and novels reveal Hardy's love and observation of the natural world, often with symbolic effect.

2. Characteristics of Hardy's Novels

The underlying theme of his novels is the struggle of man against the mysterious force which rules the world, brings misfortune into man's life and predetermines his fate. This fatalism is strongly reflected in his writings. In his works, the strong elements of naturalism are combined with a tendency towards symbolism. These defects spoil the main realistic effect of his art. Hardy has a strong sense of humor and often describes nature with charm and impressiveness. He went on writing poetry and remained energetic right up to his death on January 11, 1928. He was buried in the Poets' Corner, Westminster Abbey.

Brief Introduction

Tess comes from a farmer's family, called the Durbeyfields. She has lived a poor but peaceful life. However, her father learns that they are descended from the D'Urbervilles, an ancient family once renowned in England. She meets Alec D'Urbervilles, who shows off the estate and always seduces her. Her tragic life has just begun. Despite the rumors all around, she gives birth to a child, who is called Sorrow but dies soon because of illness. For several weeks, Tess is overwhelmed by grief and sorrow. Nevertheless, without financial support, Tess has to leave home and goes to work as a dairymaid at a distant farm, where she meets Angel Claire. The two fall in love and become engaged. Then comes the wedding night, too honest to keep any secret, Tess admits about Alec D'Urbervilles and the child. She begs for forgiveness, but Angel leaves her in disgust. In the meantime, Alec D'Urbervilles, the evil person appears again. Tess stabs Alec in the heart and kills him. Then Tess and Angel Claire escape. They manage to hide for a while in a wood before they come to Stonehenge, where she is arrested. She is hanged later.

Selected Reading

Tess of the D'Urbervilles

Chapter 58

The night was strangely solemn and still. In the small hours she whispered to him the whole story of how he had walked in his sleep with her in his arms across the Froom stream①, at the imminent risk of both their lives, and laid her down in the stone coffin at the ruined abbey. He had never known of that till now.

"Why didn't you tell me next day!" he said. "It might have prevented much misunderstanding and woe②."

"Don't think of what's past!" said she. "I am not going to think outside of now. Why should we? Who knows what tomorrow has in store?"

But it apparently had no sorrow. The morning was wet and foggy, and Clare, rightly informed that the caretaker only opened the windows on fine days, ventured to creep out of their chamber and explore the house, leaving Tess asleep. There was no food on the premises③, but there was water; and he took advantage of the fog to emerge from the mansion and fetch tea, bread, and butter, from a shop in little place two miles beyond, and also a small tin kettle and spirit-lamp④, that they might get fire without smoke. His re-entry awoke her; and they breakfasted on what he had brought.

They were indisposed to stir abroad, and the day passed; and the night following; and the next; till almost without their being aware, five days had slipped by; in absolute seclusion, not a sight or sound of a human being disturbing their peacefulness—such as it was. The changes of the weather were their only events, the birds of the New Forest their only company. By tacit consent⑤ they hardly once spoke of any incident of the past subsequent to their wedding-day. The gloomy intervening time seemed to sink into chaos, over which the present and prior times closed as if it never had been. Whenever he suggested that they should leave their shelter and go forwards towards Southampton or London she showed a strange unwillingness to move. "Why

---

①the Froom stream: 佛鲁姆河
②woe: 不幸
③premises: 这里指苔丝与安吉尔在逃亡中暂时居住的一座空房子
④spirit-lamp: 酒精灯
⑤tacit consent: 默准

should we put an end to all that's sweet and lovely!" she deprecated①. "What must come will come." And, looking through the shutter-chink②: "All is trouble outside there; inside here content."

He peeped out also. It was quite true; within was affection, union, error forgiven; outside was the inexorable.

"And—and," she said, pressing her cheek against his; "I fear that what you think of me now may not last. I do not wish to outlive your present feeling for me. I would rather not. I would rather be dead and buried when the time comes for you to despise me, so that it may never be known to me that you despised me."

"I cannot ever despise you!"

"I also hope that. But considering what my life has been I cannot see why any man should, sooner or later, be able to help despising me... How wickedly mad I was! Yet formerly I never could bear to hurt a fly or worm, and the sight of a bird in a cage used often to make me cry."

They remained yet another day. In the night the dull sky cleared; and the result was that the old caretaker at the cottage awoke early. The brilliant sunrise made her unusually brisk; she decided to open the contiguous③ mansion immediately, and to air it thoroughly on such a day. Thus it occurred that having arrived and opened the lower rooms before six o'clock, she ascended to the bedchambers, and was about to turn the handle of the one wherein they lay.

At that moment she fancied she could hear the breathing of persons within. Her slipper and her antiquity had rendered her progress a noiseless one so far, and she made for instant retreat; then, deeming that her hearing might have deceived her she turned anew to the door and softly tried the handle. The lock was out of order, but a piece of furniture had been moved forward on the inside, which prevented her opening the door more than an inch or two. A stream of morning light through the shutter-chink fell upon the faces of the pair

---

①deprecate: 反对

②shutter-chink: 百叶窗窗缝

③contiguous[TOEFL]: 邻近的

wrapped in profound slumber, Tess's lips being parted like a half-opened flower near his cheek.

The caretaker was so struck with their innocent appearance and with the elegance of Tess's gown hanging across a chair, her silk stockings beside it, the pretty parasol, and the other habits in which she had arrived because she had none else, that her first indignation at the effrontery① of tramps and vagabonds gave way to momentary sentimentality over this genteel elopement, as it seemed. She closed the door and withdrew as softly as she had come, to go and consult with her neighbors on the odd discovery.

Not more than a minute had elapsed after her withdrawal when Tess woke, and then Clare. Both had a sense that something had disturbed them, though they could not say what: and the uneasy feeling which it engendered grew stronger. As soon as he was dressed he narrowly scanned the lawn through the two or three inches of shutter-chink.

"I think we will leave at once," said he. "It is a fine day. And I cannot help fancying somebody is about the house. At any rate the woman will be sure to come today."

She passively assented, arose, clothed herself, and putting the room in order they took up the few articles that belonged to them and departed noiselessly. When they had got into the forest she turned to take a last look at the house. "Ah, happy house—good-bye!" she said. "My life can only be a question of a few weeks; why should we not have stayed there?"

"Don't say it Tess! We shall soon get out of this district altogether. We'll continue our course as we've begun it, and keep straight north. Nobody will think of looking for us there. We shall be looked for at the Wessex ports if we are sought at all. When we are in the north we will get to a port and away."

Having thus persuaded her the plan was pursued, and they kept a bee line northward. Their long repose at the manor-house② lent them walking power now; and towards mid-day they found that they were approaching the steepled

---

① effrontery: 放肆
② manor-house: 庄园

city of Melchester①, which lay directly in their way. He decided to rest her in a clump of trees during the afternoon, and push onward under cover of darkness. At dusk Clare purchased food as usual, and their night march began, the boundary between Upper and Mid-Wessex being crossed about eight o'clock.

To walk across country without much regard to roads was not new to Tess, and she showed her old agility in the performance. The intercepting city, ancient Melchester, they were obliged to pass through in order to take advantage of the town bridge for crossing a large river that obstructed them. It was about midnight when they went along the deserted streets, lighted fitfully by the few lamps, keeping off the pavement that it might not echo their footsteps. The graceful pile of cathedral architecture rose dimly on their left hand, but it was lost upon them now. Once out of the town they followed the turnpike-road② which after a few miles plunged across an open plain.

Though the sky was dense with cloud a diffused light from some fragment of a moon had hitherto helped them a little. But the moon had now sunk, the clouds seemed to settle almost on their heads, and the night grew as dark as a cave. However, they found their way along, keeping as much on the turf as possible that their tread might not resound which it was easy to do, there being no hedge or fence of any kind. All around was open loneliness and black solitude, over which a stiff breeze blew.

They had proceeded thus gropingly two or three miles further when on a sudden, Clare became conscious of some vast erection close in his front, rising sheer from the grass. They had almost struck themselves against it.

"What monstrous place is this?" said Angel.

"It hums," said she, "Hearken!"

He listened. The wind, playing upon the edifice, produced a booming tune, like the note of some gigantic one-stringed harp. No other sound came from it, and lifting his hand and advancing a step or two, Clare felt the vertical surface of the structure. It seemed to be of solid stone, without joint or

---

①the steepled city of Melchester：尖塔之城，梅尔切斯特
②turnpike-road：收费公路

moulding. Carrying his fingers onward he found that what he had come in contact with was a colossal rectangular pillar; by stretching out his left hand he could feel a similar one adjoining. At an indefinite height overhead something made the black sky blacker, which had the semblance of a vast architrave uniting the pillars horizontally. They carefully entered beneath and between; the surfaces echoed their soft rustle; but they seemed to be still out-of-doors. The place was roofless. Tess drew her breath fearfully, and Angel, perplexed, said "What can it be?"

Feeling sideways they encountered another tower-like pillar, square and uncompromising as the first; beyond it another, and another. The place was all doors and pillars, some connected above by continuous architraves.

"A very Temple of the Winds①." he said.

The next pillar was isolated, others, composed a trilithon②; others were prostrate, their flanks forming a causeway wide enough for a carriage; and it was soon obvious that they made up a forest of monoliths③, grouped upon the grassy expanse of the plain. The couple advanced further into this pavilion of the night, till they stood in its midst.

"It is Stonehenge④!" said Clare.

"The heathen⑤ temple, you mean?"

"Yes. Older than the centuries; older than the D'Urbervilles! ... Well, what shall we do, darling? We may find shelter further on."

But Tess, really tired by this time, flung herself upon an oblong slab that lay close at hand, and was sheltered from the wind by a pillar. Owing to the action of the sun during the preceding day, the stone was warm and dry, in comforting contrast to the rough and chill grass around, which damped her skirts and shoes. "I don't want to go any further, Angel," she said stretching out her hand for

---

①Temple of the Winds：风神庙
②trililthon：三根连着的巨石
③monolith：独块巨石
④Stonehenge：英国南部史前巨石建筑遗址
⑤heathen：异教徒

his. "Can't we bide① here?"

"I fear not. This spot is visible for miles by day, although it does not seem so now."

"One of my mother's people was a shepherd, now I think of it. And you used to say at Talbothays that I was a heathen. So now I am at home." He knelt down beside her outstretched form, and put his lips upon hers. "Sleepy are you dear? I think you are lying on an altar."

"I like very much to be here," she murmured. "It is so solemn and lonely—after my great happiness—with nothing but the sky above my face. It seems as if there were no folk in the world but we two. And I wish there were not—except Liza-Lu."

Clare thought she might as well rest here till it should get a little lighter, and he flung his overcoat upon her, and sat down by her side.

"Angel, if anything happens to me, will you watch over Liza-Lu for my sake?" she asked, when they had listened a long time to the wind among the pillars.

"I will."

"She is so good, and simple, and pure. Oh Angel—I wish you would marry her, if you lose me, as you will do shortly. Oh if you would!"

"If I lose you I lose all. And she is my sister-in-law."

"That's nothing, dearest. People marry sister-in-laws continually about Marlott. And Liza-Lu is so gentle and sweet, and she is growing so beautiful. Oh I could share you with her willingly when we are spirits! If you would train her and teach her, Angel, and bring her up for your own self! ...

She has all the best of me without the bad of me; and if she were to become yours it would almost seem as if death had not divided us. ... Well—I have said it. I won't mention it again."

She ceased, and he fell into thought. In the far north-east sky, he could see between the pillars a level streak of light. The uniform concavity② of black cloud was lifting bodily like the lid of a pot, letting in at the earth's edge the coming day,

---

①bide: 停留

②concavity: 凹陷处

against which the towering monoliths and trilithons began to be blackly defined.

"Did they sacrifice to God here?" asked she.

"No," said he.

"Who to?"

"I believe to the sun. That lofty stone set away by itself is in the direction of the sun, which will presently rise behind it."

"This reminds me, dear," said she. "You remember you never would interfere with any belief of mine before we were married? But I knew your mind all the same, and I thought as you thought—not from any reasons of my own, but because you thought so. Tell me now, Angel, do you think we shall meet again after we are dead? I want to know."

He kissed her, to avoid a reply at such a time.

"Oh, Angel—I fear that means no!" said she with a suppressed sob. "And I want so to see you again so much, so much! What—not even you and I—Angel, who love each other so well?"

Like a greater than himself, to the critical question at the critical time he did not answer; and they were again silent. In a minute or two her breathing became more regular, her clasp of his hand relaxed, and she fell asleep. The band of silver paleness along the east horizon made even the distant parts of the Great plain appear dark and near; and the whole enormous landscape bore that impress of reserve, taciturnity①, and hesitation which is usual just before day. The eastward pillars and their architraves stood up blackly against the light, and the great flame-shaped sun-stone beyond them, and the stone of sacrifice midway. Presently the night wind died out, and the quivering little pools in the cup-like hollows of the stones lay still. At the same time something seemed to move on the verge of the dip eastward—a mere dot. It was the head of a man, approaching them from the hollow beyond the Sunstone. Clare wished they had gone onward, but in the circumstances decided to remain quiet. The figure came straight towards the circle of pillars in which they were.

He heard something behind him, the brush of feet. Turning, he saw over the prostrate columns another figure; then, before he was aware, another was at

---

①taciturnity: 沉默寡言

hand on the fight, under a trilithon, and another on the left. The dawn shone full on the front of the man westward, and Clare could discern from this that he was tall, and walked as if trained. They all closed in, with evident purpose. Her story, then, was true! Springing to his feet he looked around for a weapon, loose stone, means of escape, anything. By this time the nearest man was upon him.

"It's no use, sir, " he said. "There are sixteen of us on the Plain, and the whole country is reared. "

"Let her finish her sleep!" he implored in a whisper of the men, as they gathered round.

When they saw where she lay, which they had not done till then, they showed no objection; and stood watching her, as still as the pillars around. He went to the stone, and bent over her, holding one poor little hand; her breathing now was quick and small, like that of a lesser creature than a woman. All waited in the growing light, their faces and hands as if they were silvered, the remainder of their figures dark, the stones glistening green-grey, the Plain still a mass of shade. Soon the light was strong, and a ray shone upon her unconscious form, peering under her eyelids waking her.

"What is it, Angel?" she said starting up. "Have they come for me?" "Yes, dearest, " he said. "They have come. "

"It is as it should be!" she murmured. "Angel—I am almost glad—yes, glad! This happiness could not have lasted—it was too much—I have had enough; and now I shall not live for you to despise me. "

She stood up, shook herself, and went forward, neither of the men having moved. "I am ready, " she said quietly.

Questions for Discussion

1. Discuss the character of Tess. To what extent is she a helpless victim? When is she strong and when is she weak?
2. Discuss the role of landscape in the novel. How do descriptions of place match the development of the story? Does the passing of the seasons play any symbolic role?
3. The subtitle of the novel is *A Pure Woman Faithfully Portrayed*. All things considered, is Tess a pure woman? Why or Why not?
4. According to Hardy, Man is impotent before Fate, however he tries, he seldom escapes his doomed destiny. Then what causes the destruction of Tess? Is it fate, or some other force?

Unit 4 William Makepeace Thackeray

Appreciation

《名利场》描写的是什么呢? 马克思论英国的狄更斯、萨克雷等批判现实主义小说家时说:"他们用逼真而动人的文笔,揭露出政治和社会上的真相;一切政治家、政论家、道德家所揭露的加在一起,还不如他们揭露得多。他们描写了中等阶级的每个阶层:从鄙视一切商业的十足绅士气派的大股东,到小本经营的店掌柜以及律师手下的小书记。"《名利场》这部小说正是一个恰当的例子。

——杨绛

Author

William Makepeace Thackeray, (born July 18, 1811, Calcutta, India and died Dec. 24, 1863, London, Eng.), English novelist whose reputation rests chiefly on *Vanity Fair* (1847 – 1848), a novel of the Napoleonic period in England, and The History of Henry Esmond, Esq. (1852), set in the early 18th century.

Thackery was another representative of critical realism in the 19th century England. In his own time Thackeray was regarded as the only possible rival to Dickens. His pictures of contemporary life were obviously real and were accepted as such by the middle classes. A great professional, he provided novels, stories, essays, and verses for his audience, and he toured as a nationally known lecturer. In his early life, Thackeray wrote all kinds of articles, mainly short pieces for journals and relatively slim books. Up to 1847, a series of his satirical sketches were collected in *The Book of Snobs* (1846 – 1847). But it was not until the publication of *Vanity Fair* (1847 – 1848) that the world recognized the appearance of a new novelist of the first rank. Among his later historical works, the better known are *The History of Pendennis*, *The History of Henry Esmond*, *Esquire*, *The Newcomes*, and *The Virginians*.

Brief Introduction

Set in the second decade of the 19th century, the period of the Regency, the novel deals mainly with the interwoven fortunes of two contrasting women, Amelia Sedley and Rebecca Sharp. The latter, an unprincipled adventuress, is the leading personage and is perhaps the most memorable character Thackeray created.

The wealthy, wellborn, passive Amelia Sedley and the ambitious, energetic, scheming, provocative, and essentially amoral Rebecca Sharp, daughter of a poor drawing master, are contrasted in their fortunes and reactions to life, but the contrast of their characters is not the simple one between moral good and evil—both are presented with dispassionate sympathy. Becky is the character around whom all the men play their parts in an upper middle-class and aristocratic background. Amelia marries George Osborne, but George, just before he is killed at the Battle of Waterloo, is ready to desert his young wife for Becky, who has fought her way up through society to marriage with Rawdon Crawley, a young officer of good family. Crawley, disillusioned, finally leaves Becky, and in the end virtue apparently triumphs, Amelia marries her lifelong admirer, Colonel Dobbin, and Becky settles down to genteel living and charitable works.

The rich movement and color of this panorama of early 19th-century society make *Vanity Fair* Thackeray's greatest achievement; the narrative skill, subtle characterization, and descriptive power make it one of the outstanding novels of its period.

Throughout his works, Thackeray analyzed and deplored snobbery and frequently gave his opinions on human behavior and the shortcomings of society. He examined such subjects as hypocrisy, secret emotions, the sorrows sometimes attendant on love, remembrance of things past, and the vanity of much of life. Such moralizing being, in his opinion, is an important function of the novelist.

Selected Reading

Vanity Fair

HOW TO LIVE WELL ON NOTHING A - YEAR

Chapter XXVI

Some three or four years after his stay in Paris, when Rawdon Crawley and his wife were established in a very small comfortable house in Curzon Street, May Fair, there was scarcely one of the numerous friends whom they entertained at dinner that did not ask the above question regarding them. The novelist, it has been said before, knows everything, and as I am in a situation to be able to tell the public how Crawley and his wife lived without any income, may I entreat the public newspapers which are in the habit of extracting portions of the various periodical works now published not to reprint the following exact narrative and calculations—of which I ought, as the discoverer (and at some expense, too), to have the benefit? My son, I would say, were I blessed with a child—you may by deep inquiry and constant intercourse with him learn how a man lives comfortably on nothing a year. But it is best not to be intimate with gentlemen of this profession and to take the calculations at second hand, as you do logarithms, for to work them yourself, depend upon it, will cost you something considerable.

On nothing per annum① then, and during a course of some two or three years, of which we can afford to give but a very brief history, Crawley and his

---

①annum:一年,一岁

wife lived very happily and comfortably at Paris. It was in this period that he quitted the Guards and sold out of the army. When we find him again, his mustachios and the title of Colonel on his card are the only relics of his military profession①.

  It has been mentioned that Rebecca, soon after her arrival in Paris, took a very smart and leading position in the society of that capital, and was welcomed at some of the most distinguished② houses of the restored French nobility. The English men of fashion in Paris courted③ her, too, to the disgust of the ladies their wives, who could not bear the parvenue④. For some months the salons of the Faubourg St. Germain, in which her place was secured, and the splendours of the new Court, where she was received with much distinction, delighted and perhaps a little intoxicated⑤ Mrs. Crawley, who may have been disposed during this period of elation to slight the people—honest young military men mostly—who formed her husband's chief society.

  But the Colonel yawned sadly among the Duchesses and great ladies of the Court. The old women who played ecarte⑥ made such a noise about a five-franc piece that it was not worth Colonel Crawley's while to sit down at a card-table. The wit of their conversation he could not appreciate, being ignorant of their language. And what good could his wife get, he urged, by making curtsies every night to a whole circle of Princesses? He left Rebecca presently to frequent these parties alone, resuming his own simple pursuits and amusements amongst the amiable friends of his own choice.

  The truth is, when we say of a gentleman that he lives elegantly on nothing a year, we use the word "nothing" to signify something unknown; meaning, simply, that we don't know how the gentleman in question defrays the expenses of his establishment. Now, our friend the Colonel had a great aptitude⑦ for all

---

①profession[IELTS][TOEFL]:职业,行业
②distinguished[TOEFL]:卓越的,著名的,高贵的
③court[TOEFL]:求爱
④parvenue:女暴发户
⑤intoxicated:陶醉的,如痴如醉的
⑥ecarte:一种纸牌游戏
⑦aptitude:天赋

games of chance; and exercising himself, as he continually did, with the cards, the dice-box①, or the cue②, it is natural to suppose that he attained a much greater skill in the use of these articles than men can possess who only occasionally handle them. To use a cue at billiards③ well is like using a pencil, or a German flute, or a small-sword—you cannot master any one of these implements at first, and it is only by repeated study and perseverance, joined to a natural taste, that a man can excel in the handling of either. Now Crawley, from being only a brilliant amateur, had grown to be a consummate④ master of billiards. Like a great General, his genius used to rise with the danger, and when the luck had been unfavourable to him for a whole game, and the bets were consequently against him, he would, with consummate skill and boldness, make some prodigious⑤ hits which would restore the battle, and come in a victor at the end, to the astonishment of everybody—of everybody, that is, who was a stranger to his play. Those who were accustomed to see it were cautious how they staked their money against a man of such sudden resources and brilliant and overpowering skill.

At games of cards he was equally skilful; for though he would constantly lose money at the commencement⑥ of an evening, playing so carelessly and making such blunders, that newcomers were often inclined to think meanly of his talent; yet when roused to action and awakened to caution by repeated small losses, it was remarked that Crawley's play became quite different, and that he was pretty sure of beating his enemy thoroughly before the night was over. Indeed, very few men could say that they ever had the better of him. His successes were so repeated that no wonder the envious and the vanquished spoke sometimes with bitterness regarding them. And as the French say of the Duke of Wellington, who never suffered a defeat, that only an astonishing series of lucky

---

①the dice-box:掷色子
②the cue:台球等的球杆,弹子棒
③billiards:台球,撞球
④consummate:技艺高超的
⑤prodigious:非凡的
⑥commencement:开始

accidents enabled him to be an invariable① winner; yet even they allow that he cheated at Waterloo, and was enabled to win the last great trick: so it was hinted at headquarters in England that some foul play must have taken place in order to account for the continuous successes of Colonel Crawley.

  Though Frascati's and the Salon were open at that time in Paris, the mania② for play was so widely spread that the public gambling-rooms did not suffice③ for the general ardour④, and gambling went on in private houses as much as if there had been no public means for gratifying the passion. At Crawley's charming little reunions of an evening this fatal amusement commonly was practised—much to good-natured little Mrs. Crawley's annoyance. She spoke about her husband's passion for dice with the deepest grief; she bewailed it to everybody who came to her house. She besought⑤ the young fellows never, never to touch a box; and when young Green, of the Rifles, lost a very considerable sum of money, Rebecca passed a whole night in tears, as the servant told the unfortunate young gentleman, and actually went on her knees to her husband to beseech him to remit the debt, and burn the acknowledgement. How could he? He had lost just as much himself to Blackstone of the Hussars, and Count Punter of the Hanoverian Cavalry. Green might have any decent time; but pay? —of course he must pay; to talk of burning IOU's was child's play.

  Other officers, chiefly young—for the young fellows gathered round Mrs. Crawley—came from her parties with long faces, having dropped more or less money at her fatal card-tables. Her house began to have an unfortunate reputation. The old hands warned the less experienced of their danger. Colonel O'Dowd, of the —th regiment⑥, one of those occupying in Paris, warned Lieutenant Spooney of that corps. A loud and violent fracas took place between the infantry Colonel and his lady, who were dining at the Cafe de Paris, and

---

①invariable:始终如一的
②mania[TOEFL]:狂热
③suffice[IELTS]:满足
④ardour:激情,热情
⑤besought:beseech 的过去分词和过去式,恳求,哀求,乞求
⑥regiment:(军队的)团

Colonel and Mrs. Crawley; who were also taking their meal there. The ladies engaged on both sides. Mrs. O'Dowd snapped her fingers in Mrs. Crawley's face and called her husband "no betther than a black-leg." Colonel Crawley challenged Colonel O'Dowd, C. B. The Commander-in-Chief hearing of the dispute sent for Colonel Crawley, who was getting ready the same pistols "which he shot Captain Marker," and had such a conversation with him that no duel took place. If Rebecca had not gone on her knees to General Tufto, Crawley would have been sent back to England; and he did not play, except with civilians, for some weeks after.

But, in spite of Rawdon's undoubted skill and constant successes, it became evident to Rebecca, considering these things, that their position was but a precarious① one, and that, even although they paid scarcely anybody, their little capital② would end one day by dwindling③ into zero. "Gambling④," she would say, "dear, is good to help your income, but not as an income itself. Someday people may be tired of play, and then where are we?" Rawdon acquiesced⑤ in the justice of her opinion; and in truth he had remarked that after a few nights of his little suppers, gentlemen were tired of play with him, and, in spite of Rebecca's charms⑥, did not present themselves very eagerly.

Easy and pleasant as their life at Paris was, it was after all only an idle dalliance⑦ and amiable trifling; and Rebecca saw that she must push Rawdon's fortune in their own country. She must get him a place or appointment⑧ at home or in the colonies, and she determined to make a move upon England as soon as the way could be cleared for her. As a first step she had made Crawley sell out of the Guards and go on half-pay. His function as aide-de-camp to General Tufto

---

①precarious:不稳定的,岌岌可危的
②capital[IELTS][GRE]:资本,资金
③dwindle[IELTS][GRE]:逐渐减少
④gambling:赌博
⑤acquiesce:默认
⑥charm[GRE]:魅力
⑦dalliance:嬉戏
⑧appointment[IELTS][TOEFL]:任命,委任,职务;约见

had ceased previously. Rebecca laughed in all companies at that officer, at his toupee①(which he mounted on coming to Paris), at his waistband, at his false teeth, at his pretensions to be a lady-killer above all, and his absurd vanity in fancying② every woman whom he came near was in love with him. It was to Mrs. Brent, the beetle-browed wife of Mr. Commissary Brent, to whom the general transferred his attentions now—his bouquets, his dinners at the restaurateurs', his opera-boxes, and his knick-knacks. Poor Mrs. Tufto was no more happy than before, and had still to pass long evenings alone with her daughters, knowing that her General was gone off scented and curled to stand behind Mrs. Brent's chair at the play. Becky had a dozen admirers in his place, to be sure, and could cut her rival to pieces with her wit. But, as we have said, she was growing tired of this idle social life: opera-boxes and restaurateur dinners palled upon her: nosegays③ could not be laid by as a provision④ for future years: and she could not live upon knick-knacks⑤, laced handkerchiefs, and kid gloves. She felt the frivolity of pleasure and longed for more substantial benefits.

At this juncture⑥ news arrived which was spread among the many creditors of the Colonel at Paris, and which caused them great satisfaction. Miss Crawley, the rich aunt from whom he expected his immense inheritance⑦, was dying; the Colonel must haste to her bedside. Mrs. Crawley and her child would remain behind until he came to reclaim⑧ them. He departed⑨ for Calais, and having reached that place in safety, it might have been supposed that he went to Dover; but instead he took the diligence to Dunkirk, and thence travelled to

---

①toupee:(男用)小型遮秃假发
②fancy[IELTS][TOEFL]:自以为是,自命不凡
③nosegays:花束,花球
④provision[IELTS][TOEFL]:给养,饮食供应
⑤knick-knack:小装饰品,小摆设
⑥juncture:生死关头
⑦inheritance:继承
⑧reclaim:取回
⑨depart[IELTS][TOEFL]:离开,启程出发

Brussels, for which place he had a former predilection①. The fact is, he owed more money at London than at Paris; and he preferred the quiet little Belgian city to either of the more noisy capitals.

Her aunt was dead. Mrs. Crawley ordered the most intense mourning② for herself and little Rawdon. The Colonel was busy arranging the affairs of the inheritance. They could take the premier③ now, instead of the little entresol④ of the hotel which they occupied. Mrs. Crawley and the landlord had a consultation about the new hangings, an amicable⑤ wrangle⑥ about the carpets, and a final adjustment of everything except the bill. She went off in one of his carriages; her French bonne with her; the child by her side; the admirable landlord and landlady smiling farewell to her from the gate. General Tufto was furious⑦ when he heard she was gone, and Mrs. Brent furious with him for being furious; Lieutenant Spooney was cut to the heart; and the landlord got ready his best apartments previous to the return of the fascinating little woman and her husband. He *serréd*⑧ the trunks which she left in his charge with the greatest care. They had been especially recommended to him by Madame Crawley. They were not, however, found to be particularly valuable when opened some time after.

Questions for Discussion

1. What is depicted in Chapter 36?
2. Analyze the character of Rebecca Sharp (Mrs. Crawley).

---

①predilection：喜爱，偏爱，钟爱

②mourning[TOEFL]：丧服

③premier：first floor (second floor in American parlance) 二楼

④entresol：夹层，这里指底层和二楼之间的几间小屋子

⑤amicable：友好的

⑥wrangle：争吵

⑦furious[IELTS][TOEFL]：狂怒的，盛怒的

⑧*Serréd*：(Anglicized French) put in safe storage 细心照看

Unit 5　George Bernard Shaw

Appreciation

在萧伯纳一生的创作中,他始终秉持这样的信念,即戏剧要承载重要的社会使命。其目的不是供人娱乐,而是鞭挞社会。

——张中载　《萧伯纳最佳戏剧》译者

我年轻时注意到,我每做10件事有9件不成功,于是我就10倍地去努力做下去。

——萧伯纳

Author

George Bernard Shaw was an Irish playwright, novelist, critic and socialist who spent most of his adult life living and working in England. He is best known for his plays, particularly *Pygmalion* (performed 1914; published 1916), which was adapted into a screenplay in 1938, followed by the musical adaptation *My Fair Lady* (first performed on stage in 1956, followed by the film version in 1964). Shaw achieved both commercial popularity and critical acclaim during his lifetime, and is now regarded as one of the most significant playwrights in English literature of all time. He was also an active socialist, both as a public speaker and writer, and he helped to found the Fabian Society in 1884. His works includes: 60 plays, 5 novels, 3 volumes of music criticism, 4 volumes of dance and theatrical criticism, and heaps of social commentary, political theory, and correspondence.

One of Shaw's greatest contributions as a modern dramatist is in establishing drama as serious literature, no less important than the novel. Most of his plays explore the social and political issues with which he was concerned—particularly capitalism and the British class system; poverty; religion; education; and the institution of marriage—though this was usually intertwined with humour, irony and dry understatement.

In 1925, he was awarded the Nobel Prize for literature. Shaw accepted the honor but refused the money.

Brief Introduction

Pygmalion is a play by George Bernard Shaw based on the Greek myth of the same name. It tells the story of Henry Higgins, a professor of phonetics (based on phonetician Henry Sweet), who makes a bet with his friend Colonel Pickering that he can successfully pass off a Cockney flower girl, Eliza Doolittle, as a refined society lady by teaching her how to speak with an upper class accent and training her in etiquette. In the process, Higgins and Doolittle grow close, but she ultimately rejects his domineering ways and declares she will marry Freddy Eynsford Hill, a young, poor, gentleman. Eliza is not a self-contemptuous flower girl any more, she is a brave resistant who dares to pursue her own happiness. This play is based on Pygmalion, a sculptor from Greek Mythology who was a known misogynist—a trait somewhat shared by Prof Higgins in this play.

Do you hear of "the Pygmalion Effect"? The Pygmalion Effect is that people tend to behave as you expect they will. If you expect a person to take responsibility, they probably will. If you expect them not to even try, they probably won't.

Selected Reading

Pygmalion

ACT I

London at 11.15 p.m. Torrents of heavy summer rain. Cab whistles① blowing frantically in all directions. Pedestrians running for shelter into the market and under the portico② of St. Paul's Church (not Wren's cathedral but Inigo Jones's church in Covent Garden vegetable market), among them a lady and her daughter in evening dress. All are peering out gloomily at the rain, except one man with his back turned to the rest, who seems wholly preoccupied with a notebook in which he is writing busily.

---

①cab whistles: 叫车的哨子
②portico: 有圆柱的门廊

The church clock strikes the first quarter.

THE DAUGHTER [in the space between the central pillars, close to the one on her left] I'm getting chilled to the bone. What can Freddy be doing all this time? He's been gone twenty minutes.

THE MOTHER [on her daughters' right] Not so long. But he ought to have got us a cab by this.

A BYSTANDER [on the lady's right] He wont get no cab not until half-past eleven, missus①, when they come back after drop-ping their theatre fares.

THE MOTHER But we must have a cab. We cant stand here until half-past eleven. It's too bad.

THE BYSTANDER Well, it aint my fault, missus.

THE DAUGHTER If Freddy had a bit of gumption②, he would have got one at the Théatre door.

THE MOTHER What could he have done, poor boy?

THE DAUGHTER Other people got cabs. Why couldnt he?

Freddy rushes in out of the rain from the Southampton Street side, and comes between them closing a dripping umbrella. He is a young man of twenty, in evening dress, very wet around the ankles.

THE DAUGHTER Well, havnt you got a cab?

FREDDY Theres not one to be had for love or money③.

THE MOTHER Oh, Freddy, there must be one. You cant have tried.

THE DAUGHTER It's too tiresome. Do you expect us to go and get one ourselves?

FREDDY I tell you theyre all engaged. The rain was so sudden: nobody was prepared; and everybody had to take a cab. Ive been to Charing Cross one way and nearly to Ludgate Circus the other; and they were all engaged.

THE MOTHER Did you try Trafalgar Square?

FREDDY There wasnt one at Trafalgar Square.

THE DAUGHTER Did you try?

---

①missus: 即 Missis, 太太, 这是没有受过教育的用语, 正规英语为 Madam.
②gumption: 精明, 老练, 是口头语。
③for love or money: 无论是讲交情还是讲价钱, 这是习语, 只用于否定

FREDDY I tried as far as Charing Cross Station. Did you expect me to walk to Hammersmith?

THE DAUGHTER You havnt tried at all.

THE MOTHER You really are very helpless,

Freddy. Go again; and dont comeback until you have found a cab.

FREDDY I shall simply get soaked for nothing①.

THE DAUGHTER And what about us? Are we to stay here all night in this draught, with next to nothing on? You selfish pig –

FREDDY Oh, very well: I'll go, I'll go. [He opens his umbrella and dashes off Strandwards, but comes into collision with② a flower girl who is hurrying in for shelter, knocking her basket out of her hands. A blinding flash of lightning, followed instantly by a rattling peal of thunder, orchestrates the incident.]

THE FLOWER GIRL Nah then,

Freddy: look wh' y' gowin, deah.

FREDDY Sorry. [He rushes off.]

THE FLOWER GIRL [picking up her scattered flowers and replacing them in the basket] Theres menners f' yer! T? oo banches o voylets trod into themad. [She sits down on the plinth of the column, sorting her flowers, on the lady's right. She is not at all a romantic figure. She is perhaps eighteen, perhaps twenty, hardly older. She wears a little sailor hat③ of black straw that has long been exposed to the dust and soot of London 61 and has seldom if ever been brushed. Her hair needs washing rather badly: its mousy color can hardly be natural. She wears a shoddy④ blackcoat that reaches nearly to her knees and is shaped to her waist.

She has a brown skirt with a coarse apron. Her boots are much the worse for wear. She is no doubt as clean as she can afford to be; but compared to the ladies she is very dirty. Her features Pygmalion (1913) is a play by George Bernard Shaw based on the Greek myth of the same name. It tells the story of

---

①for nothing: 没来由地，白白地

②come into collision with: 和……相撞，撞着

③sailor hat: (妇女戴的)低顶草帽

④shoddy: 质量差的，以次充好的

Henry Higgins, a professor of phonetics (based on phonetician Henry Sweet), who makes a bet with his friend Colonel Pickering that he can successfully pass off a Cockney flower girl, Eliza Doolittle, as a refined society lady by teaching her how to speak with an upper class accent and training her in etiquette. In the process, Higgins and Doolittle grow close, but she ultimately rejects his domineering ways and declares she will marry Freddy Eynsford-Hill-bai a young, poor, gentleman. This play is based on Pygmalion, a sculptor from Greek Mythology who was a known misogynist — a trait somewhat shared by Prof Higgins in this play. are no worse than theirs; but their condition leaves something to be desired; and she needs the services of a dentist.]

THE MOTHER How do you know that my son's name is Freddy, pray?

THE FLOWER GIRL Ow, eez yə-ooa san, is e? Wal, fewd dan y' d? ooty bawmz a mather should, eed now bettern to spawl a pore gel's flahrzn than ran awyathaht pyin. Will ye-oo py me f'them? [Here, with apologies, this desperate attempt to represent her dialect without a phonetic alphabet must be abandoned as unintelligible outside London.]

THE DAUGHTER Do nothing of the sort, mother. The idea!

THE MOTHER Please allow me, Clara. Have you any pennies?

THE DAUGHTER No. Ive nothing smaller than six pence.

THE FLOWER GIRL [hopefully] I can give you change for a tanner①, kind lady.

THE MOTHER [to Clara] Give it to me. [Clara parts② reluctantly.] Now [to the girl] this is for your flowers.

THE FLOWER GIRL Thank you kindly, lady.

THE DAUGHTER Make her give you the change. These things are only a penny a bunch.

THE MOTHER Do hold your tongue, Clara. [to the girl] You can keep the change.

THE FLOWER GIRL Oh, thank you, lady.

THE MOTHER Now tell me how you know that young gentleman's name.

---

①tanner：(俚语)英国旧时的六便士银币

②parts：(口语)付款，出钱

THE FLOWER GIRL I didnt.

THE MOTHER I heard you call him by it. Dont try to deceive me.

THE FLOWER GIRL [protesting] Who's trying to deceive you? I called him Freddy or Charlie same as you might yourself if you was talking to a stranger and wished to be pleasant.

THE DAUGHTER Six pence thrown away! Really, mamma, you might have spared Freddy that. [She retreats in disgust behind the pillar.]

An elderly gentleman of the amiable military type rushes into the shelter, and closes a dripping umbrella. He is in the same plight as Freddy, very wet about the ankles. He is in evening dress, with a light overcoat. He takes the place left vacant by the daughter.

THE GENTLEMAN Phew!

THE MOTHER [to the gentleman] Oh, sir, is there any sign of its stopping?

THE GENTLEMAN I'm afraid not. It started worse than ever about two minutes ago. [He goes to the plinth beside the flower girl; puts up his foot on it; and stoops to turn down his trouser ends.]

THE MOTHER Oh dear! [She retires sadly and joins her daughter.]

THE FLOWER GIRL [taking advantage of the military gentleman's proximity to establish friendly relations with him] If it's worse, it's a sign it's nearly over. So cheer up, Captain; and buy a flower off a poor girl.

THE GENTLEMAN I'm sorry. I havnt any change.

THE FLOWER GIRL I can give you change 111, Captain.

THE GENTLEMAN For a sovereign①? Ive nothing less.

THE FLOWER GIRL Garn! Oh do buy a flower off me, Captain. I can change half-a-crown②. Take this for tuppence③.

THE GENTLEMAN Now dont be troublesome: theres a good girl. [trying his pockets] I really havnt any change-Stop: heres three hapence, if thats any use to you. [He retreats to the other pillar.]

---

①sovereign: 当时的一金镑硬币

②change half-a-crown: 兑开两先令六便士的硬币。当时英国有五先令的硬币, 称 crown; 也有两先令六便士的硬币, 称 half-a-crown。

③tuppence: two pence 两便士

THE FLOWER GIRL [disappointed, but thinking three halfpence better than nothing] Thank you, sir.

THE BYSTANDER [to the girl] You be careful: give him a flower for it. Theres a block① here behind taking down every blessed word you resaying. [All turn to the man who is taking notes.]

THE FLOWER GIRL [springing up terrified] I aint done nothing wrong by speaking to the gentleman. Ive a right to sell flowers if I keep off the kerb. [hysterically] I'm a respectable girl: so help me, I never spoke to him except to ask him to buy a flower off me. [General hubbub, mostly sympathetic to the flower girl, but deprecating her excessive sensibility. Cries of Dont start hollerin. Who's hurting you? Nobody's going to touch you. Whats the good of fussing? Steady on②. Easy, easy, etc., come from the elderly staid spectators, who pat her comfortingly. Less patient ones bid her shut her head, or ask her roughly what is wrong with her. A remoter group, not knowing what the matter is, crowd in and increase the noise with question and answer: Whats the row? What-shedo? Where is he? A tec taking her down. What! him? Yes: him over there: Took money off the gentleman, etc.]

THE FLOWER GIRL [breaking through them to the gentleman, crying wildly] Oh, sir, dont let him charge me. You dunno what it means to me. Theyll take away my character and drive me on the streets for speaking to gentlemen. They –

THE NOTE TAKER [coming forward on her right, the rest crowding after him] There! There! There! There! Who's hurting you, you silly girl? What do you take me for?

THE BYSTANDER It's aw rawt: e's a gentleman: look at his b? – oots. [explaining to the note taker] She thought you was a copper's nark, sir.

THE NOTE TAKER [with quick interest] Whats a copper's nark?

THE BYSTANDER [inapt at definition] It's a – well, it's a copper's nark, as you might say. What else would you call it? A sort of informer.

THE FLOWER GIRL [still hysterical] I take my Bible oath I never said a

---

①block：(俚语)家伙(只用来指男人)
②steady on：且慢，停下来

word –

THE NOTE TAKER [overbearing but good-humored] Oh, shut up, shut up. Do I like a policeman?

THE FLOWER GIRL [far from reassured] Then what did you take down my words for? How do I know whether you took me down right? You just shew me what youve wrote about me. [The note taker opens his book and holds it steadily under her nose, though the pressure of the mob trying to read it over his shoulders would upset a weaker man.] Whats that? That aint proper writing. I cant read that.

THE NOTE TAKER I can. [reads, reproducing her pronunciation exactly] 'Cheer ap, Keptin; n'baw ya flahrorf a pore gel.'

THE FLOWER GIRL [much distressed] It's because I called him Captain. I meant no harm. [to the gentleman] Oh, sir, dont let him lay a charge agen me for a word like that. You –

THE GENTLEMAN Charge! I make no charge. [to the note taker] Really, sir, if you are a detective, you need not begin protecting me against molestation by young women until I ask you. Anybody could see that the girl meant no harm.

THE BYSTANDERS GENERALLY [demonstrating against police espionage①] Course they coulda blooming. What business is it of yours? You mind your own affairs. He wants promotion, he does. Taking down people's words! Girl never said a word to him. What harm if she did? Nice thing a girl cant shelter from the rain without being insulted, etc., etc., etc. [She is conducted by the more sympathetic demonstrators back to her plinth, where she resumes her seat and struggles with her emotion.]

THE BYSTANDER He aint a tec②. He's a blooming busybody③: thats what he is. I tell you, look at his b? – oots.

THE NOTE TAKER [turning on him genially] And how are all your people down at Selsey?

---

①police espionage: 警察密探行为
②tec: (俚语), 即 detective 侦探
③a blooming busybody: 太爱管闲事的人

THE BYSTANDER [suspiciously] Who told you my people come from Selsey?

THE NOTE TAKER Never you mind. They did. [to the girl] How do you come to be up so far east? You were born in Lisson Grove.

THE FLOWER GIRL [appalled] Oh, what harm is there in my leaving Lisson Grove? It wasnt fit for a pig to live in; and I had to pay four-and-six a week. [in tears] Oh, boo-hoo-oo-

THE NOTE TAKER Live where you like; but stop that noise.

THE GENTLEMAN [to the girl] Come, come! He cant touch you: you have a right to live where you please.

A SARCASTIC BYSTANDER [thrusting himself between the note taker and the gentleman] Park Lane, for instance. Id like to go into the Housing Question with you, I would.

THE FLOWER GIRL [subsiding into a brooding melancholy① over her basket, and talking very low-spiritedly to herself] I'm a good girl, Iam.

THE SARCASTIC BYSTANDER [not attending to her] Do you know where I come from?

THE NOTE TAKER [promptly] Hoxton. Titterings. Popular interest in the note taker's performance in-creases.

THE SARCASTIC ONE [amazed] Well, who said I didn't? Bly me! you know everything, you do.

THE FLOWER GIRL [still nursing her sense of injury] Aint no call to meddle with me, he aint.

THE BYSTANDER [to her] Of course he aint. Dont you stand it from him. [to the note taker] See here: what call have you to know about people what never offered to meddle with you?

THE FLOWER GIRL Let him say what he likes. I dont want to have no truck with② him.

THE BYSTANDER You take us for dirt under your feet, dont you? Catch you

---

①brooding melancholy:闷闷不乐
②have no truck with:（口语）不交往，不打交道

taking liberties with① a gentleman!

THE SARCASTIC BYSTANDER Yes: tell him where he come from if you want to go fortune-telling.

THE NOTE TAKER Cheltenham, Harrow, Cambridge, and India.

THE GENTLEMAN Quite right. Great laughter. Reaction in the note taker's favor4. Exclamations of He knows all about it. Told him proper. Hear him tell the toff② where he come from? etc.

THE GENTLEMAN May I ask, sir, do you do this for your living at a music hall?

THE NOTE TAKER Ive thought of that. Perhaps I shall some day. The rain has stopped; and the persons on the outside of the crowd begin to drop off.

THE FLOWER GIRL [resenting the reaction] He's no gentleman, he aint, to interfere with a poor girl.

THE DAUGHTER [out of patience, pushing her way rudely to the front and displacing the gentleman, who politely retires to the other side of the pillar] What on earth is Freddy doing? I shall get pneumownia③ if I stay in this draught any longer.

THE NOTE TAKER [to himself, hastily making a note of her pronunciation of 'monia' Earlscourt.

THE DAUGHTER [violently] Will you please keep your impertinent remarks to yourself.

THE NOTE TAKER Did I say that out loud? I didnt mean to. I beg your pardon. Your mother's Epsom, unmistakably.

THE MOTHER [advancing between the daughter and the note taker] How very curious! I was brought up in Large lady Park, near Epsom.

THE NOTE TAKER [uproariously④ amused] Ha! Ha! What a devil of a name! Excuse me. [to the daughter] You want a cab, do you?

THE DAUGHTER Dont dare speak to me.

---

①take liberties with: 放肆，随意对待
②toff：(口语)上流人士，时髦人物
③pneumonia：肺炎
④uproariously：哄然大笑

THE MOTHER Oh please, please, Clara. [Her daughter repudiates[①] her with an angry shrug and retires haughtily.] We should be so grateful to you, sir, if you found us a cab. [The note taker produces a whistle.] Oh, thank you. [She joins her daughter.] The note taker blows a piercing blast.

THE SARCASTIC BYSTANDER There! I knowed he was a plain-clothescopper[②].

THE BYSTANDER That aint a police whistle: thats a sporting whistle.

THE FLOWER GIRL [still preoccupied with her wounded feelings] He's no right to take away my character. My character is the same to me as any lady's.

THE NOTE TAKER I dont know whether youve noticed it; but the rain stopped about two minutes ago.

THE BYSTANDER So it has. Why didnt you say so before? And us losing our time listening to your silliness! [He walks off towards the Strand.]

THE SARCASTIC BYSTANDER I can tell where you come from. You come from Anwell. Go back there.

THE NOTE TAKER [helpfully] Hanwell.

THE SARCASTIC BYSTANDER [affecting great distinction of speech] Thenk you, teacher. Haw haw! So long. [He touches his hat with mock respect and strolls off.]

THE FLOWER GIRL Frightening people like that! How would he like it himself?

THE MOTHER It's quite fine now, Clara. We can walk to a motor bus. Come. [She gathers her skirts above her ankles and hurries off towards the Strand.]

THE DAUGHTER But the cab-[Her mother is out of hearing.] Oh, how tiresome! [She follows angrily.]

All the rest have gone except the note taker, the gentleman, and the flower girl, who sits arranging her basket, and still pitying herself in murmurs.

THE FLOWER GIRL Poor girl! Hard enough for her to live without revigorated and chivied.

---

① repudiate: 拒绝，不听劝阻
② plain-clothes copper: 便衣警察

THE GENTLEMAN [returning to his former place on the note taker's left] How do you do it, if I may ask?

THE NOTE TAKER Simply phonetics. The science of speech. Thats my profession: also my hobby. Happy is the man who can make a living by his hobby! You can spot an Irishman or a Yorkshireman by his brogue. I can place any man within six miles. I can place him within two miles in London. Sometimes within two streets.

THE FLOWER GIRL Ought to be ashamed of himself, unmanly coward!

THE GENTLEMAN But is there a living in that?

THE NOTE TAKER Oh yes. Quite a flat one. This is an age of up-starts. Men begin in Kentish Town with £ 80 a year, and end in Park Lane with a hundred thousand. They want to drop Kentish Townb; but they give themselves away every time they open their mouths. Now I can teach them.

THE FLOWER GIRL Let him mind his own business and leave a poor girl

THE NOTE TAKER [explosively] Woman: cease this detestable boohooing① instantly; or else seek the shelter of some other place of worship.

THE FLOWER GIRL [with feeble defiance] Ive a right to be here if I like, same as you.

THE NOTE TAKER A woman who utters such depressing and disgusting sounds has no right to be anywhere-no right to live. Remember that you are a human being with a soul and the divine gift of articulate speech: that your native language is the language of Shakespeare and Milton and The Bible; and dont sit there crooning like a bilious pigeon②.

THE FLOWER GIRL [quite overwhelmed, looking up at him in mingled wonder and deprecation③ without daring to raise her head] Ah-ah-ah-ow-ow-ow-oo!

THE NOTE TAKER [whipping out his book] Heavens! What a sound! [He writes; then holds out the book and reads, reproducing her vowels exactly.] Ah-ah-ah-ow-ow-ow-oo!

---

①boohooing：哭闹
②crooning like a bilious pigeon：像生气的鸽子那样叽里咕噜
③deprecation[TOEFL]：不以为然，反对

THE FLOWER GIRL [tickled by the performance, and laughing in spite of herself] Garn!

THE NOTE TAKER You see this creature with her Kerbstone English: the English that will keep her in the gutter to the end of her days? Well, sir, in three months I could pass that girl off as a duchess at an ambassador's garden party. I could even get her a place as lady's maid or shop assistant, which requires better English.

THE FLOWER GIRL What's that you say?

THE NOTE TAKER Yes, you squashed cabbage leaf, you disgrace to the noble architecture of these columns, you incarnate insult to the English language: I could pass you off as the Queen of Sheba. [to the gentleman] Can you believe that?

THE GENTLEMAN Of course I can. I am myself a student of Indian dialects; and

THE NOTE TAKER [eagerly] Are you? Do you know Colonel Pickering, the author of Spoken Sanscrit?

THE GENTLEMAN I am Colonel Pickering. Who are you?

THE NOTE TAKER Henry Higgins, author of Higgins's Universal Alphabet.

PICKERING [with enthusiasm] I came from India to meet you.

HIGGINS I was going to India to meet you.

PICKERING Where do you live?

HIGGINS A Wimpole Street. Come and see me tomorrow.

PICKERING I'm at the Carlton. Come with me now and lets have a jaw① over some supper.

HIGGINS Right you are.

THE FLOWER GIRL [to Pickering, as he passes her] Buy a flower, kind gentleman. I'm short for my lodging.

PICKERING I really havnt any change. I'm sorry. [He goes away.]

HIGGINS [shocked at the girl's mendacity②] Liar. You said you could change half-a-crown.

---

①jaw[IELTS]：(口语)喋喋不休地说话
②mendacity：虚假,说谎

THE FLOWER GRIL [rising in desperation] You ought to be stuffed with nails, you ought. [flinging the basket at his feet] Take the whole blooming basket for sixpence. The church clock strikes the second quarter.

HIGGINS [hearing in it the voice of God, rebuking him for his Pharisaic want of charity to the poor girl] A reminder. [He raises his hat solemnly; then throws a handful of money into the basket and follows Pickering.]

THE FLOWER GIRL [picking up a half-crown] Ahow-ooh! [picking up a couple of florins① Aaahow-ooh! [picking up several coins] Aaaaaah-ow-ooh! [picking up a half-sovereign② Aaaaaaaaaaahow-ooh!!!

FREDDY [springing out of a taxicab] Got one at last. Hallo! [to the girl] Where are the two ladies that were here?

THE FLOWER GIRL They walked to the bus when the rain stopped.

FREDDY And left me with a cab on my hands! Damnation!

THE FLOWER GIRL [with grandeur] Never mind, young man. I'm going home in a taxi. [She sails off③ to the cab. The driver puts his hand behind him and holds the door firmly shut against her. Quite understanding his mistrust, she shews him her handful of money.] A taxi fare aint no object to me, Charlie. [He grins and opens the door.] Here. What about the basket?

THE TAXIMAN Give it here. Tuppence extra.

LIZA 374 No: I dont want nobody to see it. [She crushes it into the cab and gets in, continuing the conversation through the window.] Goodbye, Freddy.

FREDDY [dazedly raising his hat] Goodbye.

TAXIMAN Where to?

LIZA Bucknam Pellis [Buckingham Palace].

TAXIMAN What d'ye mean-Bucknam Pellis?

LIZA Dont you know where it is? In the Green Park, where the King lives. Goodbye, Freddy. Dont let me keep standing there. Goodbye.

FREDDY Goodbye. [He goes.]

TAXIMAN Here? Whats this about Bucknam Pellis? What business have you

---

①florins：两先令的银币
②half-sovereign：半英镑的金币
③sail off：昂然走去

at Bucknam Pellis?

LIZA Of course I havnt none. But I wasnt going to let him know that. You drive me home.

TAXIMAN And wheres home?

LIZA Angel Court, Drury Lane, next Meiklejohn's oil shop.

TAXIMAN That sounds more like it, Judy. [He drives off.] Let us follow the taxi to the entrance to Angel Court, a narrow little archway between two shops, one of them Meiklejohn's oil shop. When it stops there, Eliza gets out, dragging her basket with her.

LIZA How much?

TAXIMAN [indicating the taximeter] Cant you read? A shilling.

LIZA A shilling for two minutes!!

TAXIMAN Two minutes or ten: it's all the same.

LIZA Well, I dont call it right.

TAXIMAN Ever been in a taxi before?

LIZA [with dignity] Hundreds and thousands of times, young man.

TAXIMAN [laughing at her] Good for you, Judy. Keep the shilling, darling, with best love from all at home. Good luck! [He drives off.]

LIZA [humiliated] Impidence[①]! She picks up the basket and trudges up[②] the alley with it to her lodging: a small room with very old wall paper hanging loose in the damp places. A broken pane in the window is mended with paper. A portrait of a popular actor and a fashion plate of ladies' dresses, all wildly beyond poor Eliza's means, both torn from newspapers, are pinned up on the wall. A birdcage hangs in the window; but its tenant died long ago: it remains as a memorial only.

These are the only visible luxuries: the rest is the irreducible minimum of poverty's needs: a wretched bed heaped with all sorts of coverings that have any warmth in them, a draped packing case with a basin and jug on it and a little looking glass over it, a chair and table, the refuse of some suburban kitchen,

---

①impidence：是 impudence 的误读，意为大胆妄为,无礼，这里指 Taximan 对穷人的轻视态度

②trudges up：吃力地走

and an Americana arum clock on the shelf above the unused fireplace; the whole lighted with a gas lamp with a penny in the slot meter. Rent: four shillings a week. Here Eliza, chronically weary①, but too excited to go to bed, sits, counting her new riches and dreaming and planning what to do with them, until the gas goes out, when she enjoys for the first time the sensation of being able to put in another penny without grudging it. This prodigal mood does not extinguish her gnawing sense of the need for economy sufficiently to prevent her from calculating that she can dream and plan in bed more cheaply and warmly than sitting up without a fire. So she takes off her shawl and skirt and adds them to the miscellaneous bedclothes. Then she kicks off her shoes and gets into bed without any further change.

Question for Discussion

What changes happened in the inner world of the flower girl before and after her training?

Terms

1. Victorian Age
2. Critical Realism
3. Realism
4. Naturalism

---

①chronically weary: 极度疲劳

Chapter 7

20th-Century English Literature

I. Historical Background

The 20th century had the first global-scale war across multiple continents in World War I and World War II. It underwent a major shift in the way that vast numbers of people lived, as a result of changes in politics, ideology, economics, society, culture, science, technology, and medicine. Feminism demanded that women have equal rights to men. It was a century that started with horses and freighters but ended with cruise ships and the space shuttle. The 20th century saw more technological and scientific progress than all the other centuries combined since the dawn of civilization.

1. World War I

World War I was a global war centered in Europe that began on July 28, 1914 and lasted until November 11, 1918. The four years of the Great War was considered as the unprecedented levels of carnage and destruction. By the time World War I ended, more than 9 million soldiers had been killed and 21 million more wounded. The Treaty of Versailles, signed in 1919, established the League of Nations and punished Germany for its aggression with reparations and the loss of territory. Tragically, the instability caused by World War I would help make possible the rise of Nazi leader Adolf Hitler and would, only two decades later, lead to a second devastating international conflict.

World War I had greatly influenced English literature. The catastrophic World War I tremendously weakened the British Empire and brought about great sufferings to its people as well. Its appalling shock severely destroyed people's faith in the Victorian values; the postwar economic dislocation and spiritual disillusion produced a profound impact upon the British people, who came to see the prevalent wretchedness in capitalism.

2. World War II

World War II was a global war that lasted from 1939 to 1945. It involved the vast majority of the world's nations, eventually forming two opposing military alliances: the Allies and the Axis. It was the most widespread war in history, with more than 100 million people serving in military units from over 30 different countries. In a state of "total war", the major participants placed their entire economic, industrial, and scientific capabilities at the service of the war effort, erasing the distinction between civilian and military resources. Marked by mass deaths of civilians, including the Holocaust and the only use of nuclear weapons in warfare, it resulted in an estimated 50 million to 85 million fatalities. World War II altered the political alignment and social structure of the world. The United Nations (UN) was established to foster international co-operation and prevent future conflicts. The Soviet Union and the United States emerged as rival superpowers, setting the stage for the Cold War.

The two world wars, the most important influences on modern English literature, left their indelible marks of disillusionment and despair in many literary works of the time.

II. Literary Background

1. The characteristics

Although literature in the 20th century was diversified, it reflected the political, social and scientific events of the age.

Modernism is applied to the wide range of experimental trends in the literature of the early 20th century, including symbolism, futurism, expressionism, imagism, Dadaism, and surrealism. Modernist literature is characterized chiefly by a rejection and abandonment of all literary traditions and 19th century realism.

Modernism takes the irrational philosophy and psycho-analysis as its theoretical base. The major themes of the modernist literature are the distorted, alienated and ill relationships between man and nature, man and society, man and man, man and himself. The modernist writers concentrate more on the subjective than on the objective, more on the private than on the public. They are mainly concerned with the inner being of an individual. In their writings, the past, the present, and the future are mingled together and exist at the same time in the consciousness of an individual. Its favored techniques of juxtaposition, multiple points of view, stream-of-consciousness challenge the reader to reestablish a coherence of meaning from fragmentary forms.

2. The techniques

In the novel, vitality and interest in technical experimentation marked this period. Joseph Conrad, James Joyce, Virginia Woolf and David Herbert Lawrence were all giants of the giants. The modernist innovators were James Joyce and Virginia Woolf with the "stream of consciousness" technique and with the psychological penetration. A new view of time was developed, coupled with a deeper understanding of the consciousness. One's present was believed to be the sum of his past. Time was no longer a series of chronological moments to be presented by the novelist in sequence, but as a continuous flow in the consciousness of the individual.

3. The novelists and the poets

The novel *Ulysses* (1922), by the expatriate Irishman James Joyce, has been called "a demonstration and summation of the entire movement", which is set during one day in Dublin, and Joyce creates parallels with Homer's epic poem *Odyssey*. Although his books were controversial because of their freedom of language and content, Joyce's revolutions in narrative form, the treatment of time, and nearly all other techniques of the novel made him a master to be studied, but only intermittently copied. Though more conventional in form, the novels of Lawrence were equally challenging to convention; he was the first to champion both the primitive and the supercivilized urges of men and women.

The 20th century was also an era of high achievements in the fields of poetry and drama. W. B. Yeats and T. S. Eliot, both Nobel Prize winners, were the two greatest British poets of this century. Together with the American poet Ezra Pound, they led a revolution in the technique of modern poetry which has prevailed to the present day. Since the 1890s, there was a revival of English drama. Several important playwrights were part of a movement known as the Irish Literary Renaissance. However, the dominant force in the early 20th century drama was George Bernard Shaw, another Irish-born playwright, who was awarded the Nobel Prize in 1925.

Unit 1　Joseph Conrad

Appreciation

现代的基本特征,它容许任何事物都包含有它的反面。

马歇尔·伯曼

他在创作上的主要特征,是出色的环境描写,和细腻地刻画多半是处在海上险恶环境中的人物的心理活动。

黄雨石(《黑暗的心》译者)

Author

Joseph Conrad was a Polish-born English novelist and writer, a dreamer, adventurer, and gentleman. He is noted for his complex narratives and formal experiments, especially in point of view and temporal shift. He is also studied for his account of imperialism, colonialism, and for his depiction of man in his inner battles with good and evil when caught in extreme conditions.

Among Conrad's best-known works are *Lord Jim* (1900) and *Heart of Darkness* (1902). In 1890, he took command of a steamship in the Belgian Congo and began to fulfill his boyhood dream of traveling to the Congo River. His experiences in the Congo came out in *Heart of Darkness*.

In Conrad's life, he was admired for his rich prose and renderings of dangerous life at sea and in exotic places. But his initial reputation as a masterful teller of adventures masked his fascination with the individual when faced with his inner battles. He has been increasingly regarded as one of the greatest English novelists.

Brief Introduction

Heart of Darkness was first published in 1902 with the story *Youth* and thereafter published separately. The story reflects the physical and psychological shock Conrad himself experienced in 1890 when he worked briefly in the Belgian Congo. The narrator, Marlow, describes a journey he took on an African river. Assigned by an ivory company to take command of a cargo boat stranded in the interior, Marlow makes his way through the treacherous forest, witnessing the brutalization of the natives by white traders and hearing tantalizing stories of a Mr. Kurtz, the company's most successful representative. He reaches Kurtz's compound in a remote outpost only to see a row of human heads mounted on poles.

Heart of Darkness in particular, provides a bridge between Victorian values and the ideals of modernism. Like its Victorian predecessors, this novel relies on traditional ideas of heroism, which are nevertheless under constant attack in a changing world and in places far from England. Like much of the best modernist literature produced in the early decades of the twentieth century, *Heart of Darkness* is as much about alienation, confusion, and profound doubt as it is about imperialism.

Selected Reading

Heart of Darkness

The "Nellie①", a cruising yawl②, swung to her anchor without a flutter of the sails③, and was at rest. The flood had made, the wind was nearly calm, and being bound down the river, the only thing for us was to come to and wait for the turn of the tide.

The sea-reach of the Thames stretched before us like the beginning of an interminable waterway. In the offing the sea and the sky were welded together without a joint④, and in the luminous⑤ space the tanned sails of the barges⑥ drifting up with the tide seemed to stand still in red clusters of canvas sharply

---

①Nellie:"奈丽"号
②yawl:轻便帆船,小划艇
③without a flutter of the sails:纹丝未动
④the sky were welded together without a joint:海天一色
⑤luminous [TOEFL]:发光的,鲜艳的
⑥barges[IELTS][TOEFL]:驳船

peaked①, with gleams of varnished② sprits. A haze rested on the low shores that ran out to sea in vanishing flatness. The air was dark above Gravesend, and farther back still seemed condensed into a mournful gloom, brooding motionless over the biggest, and the greatest, town on earth.

The Director of Companies was our captain and our host. We four affectionately watched his back as he stood in the bows looking to seaward. On the whole river there was nothing that looked half so nautical③. He resembled a pilot, which to a seaman is trustworthiness personified. It was difficult to realize his work was not out there in the luminous estuary, but behind him, within the brooding gloom.

Between us there was, as I have already said somewhere, the bond of the sea. Besides holding our hearts together through long periods of separation, it had the effect of making us tolerant of each other's yarns—and even convictions. The Lawyer—the best of old fellows—had, because of his many years and many virtues, the only cushion on deck, and was lying on the only rug. The Accountant had brought out already a box of dominoes④, and was toying architecturally with the bones. Marlow sat cross-legged right aft⑤, leaning against the mizzenmast⑥. He had sunken cheeks, a yellow complexion, a straight back, an ascetic aspect, and, with his arms dropped, the palms of hands outwards, resembled an idol. The Director, satisfied the anchor had good hold, made his way aft and sat down amongst us. We exchanged a few words lazily. Afterwards there was silence on board the yacht⑦. For some reason or other we did not begin that game of dominoes. We felt meditative, and fit for nothing but placid staring⑧. The day was ending in a serenity that had a still and

---

①stand still in red clusters of canvas sharply peaked：衬着尖尖的红帆布，释放着幽光
②varnish[TOEFL]：给……涂清漆
③nautical：航海的，海员的
④a box of dominoes：一盒多米诺骨牌
⑤aft：在船尾
⑥the mizzenmast：后桅杆
⑦yacht：帆船，快艇
⑧fit for nothing but placid staring：默然凝视着远方而无所事事

exquisite brilliance. The water shone pacifically; the sky, without a speck, was a benign immensity of unstained light①; the very mist on the Essex marshes was like a gauzy② and radiant fabric, hung from the wooded rises inland, and draping the low shores in diaphanous③ folds. Only the gloom to the west, brooding over the upper reaches, became more sombre every minute, as if angered by the approach of the sun.

And at last, in its curved and imperceptible fall, the sun sank low, and from glowing white changed to a dull red without rays and without heat, as if about to go out suddenly, stricken to death by the touch of that gloom brooding over a crowd of men.

Forthwith a change came over the waters, and the serenity became less brilliant but more profound. The old river in its broad reach rested unruffled at the decline of day, after ages of good service done to the race that peopled its banks, spread out in the tranquil dignity of a waterway leading to the uttermost ends of the earth. We looked at the venerable stream not in the vivid flush④ of a short day that comes and departs forever, but in the pacific yet august light of abiding memories. And indeed nothing is easier for a man who has, as the phrase goes, "followed the sea" with reverence and affection, than to evoke the great spirit of the past upon the lower reaches of the Thames. The tidal current runs to and fro in its unceasing service, crowded with memories of men and ships it had borne to the rest of home or to the battles of the sea. It had known and served all the men of whom the nation is proud, from Sir Francis Drake to Sir John Franklin⑤, knights all, titled and untitled—the great knights-errant of the sea. It had borne all the ships whose names are like jewels flashing in the

---

① without a speck, was a benign immensity of unstained light：天空纤尘不染，发着亮丽炫目的光彩
② gauzy：薄纱似的，轻薄透明的
③ diaphanous：轻柔细密的
④ the vivid flush：消逝的霞光
⑤ from Sir Francis Drake to Sir John Franklin：从弗朗西斯·德雷克爵士到约翰·富兰克林爵士

night of time, from the "Golden Hind"① returning with her round flanks full of treasure, to be visited by the Queen's Highness② and thus pass out of the gigantic tale, to the "Erebus" and "Terror"③, bound on other conquests—and that never returned. It had known the ships and the men. They had sailed from Deptford, from Greenwich, from Erith④—the adventurers and the settlers; kings' ships and the ships of men on 'Change; captains, admirals, the dark "interlopers⑤" of the Eastern trade, and the commissioned "generals" of East India fleets⑥. Hunters for gold or pursuers of fame, they all had gone out on that stream, bearing the sword, and often the torch, messengers of the might within the land, bearers of a spark from the sacred fire. What greatness had not floated on the ebb of that river into the mystery of an unknown earth? —The dreams of men, the seed of commonwealths, the germs of empires⑦.

Question for Discussion

Discuss the importance of the Congo River in this narrative. Why does Marlow travel primarily by boat and seldom on land?

Unit 2   William Butler Yeats

Appreciation

生命是一个过程,正如诗歌一样。当你青春年少时,生命就象枝叶婆娑的绿

---

①the "Golden Hind":"金鹿"号

②the Queen's Highness:女王

③the "Erebus" and "Terror":"爱勒巴斯"号和"恐怖"号

④sailed from Deptford, from Greenwich, from Erith:从德特福特,从格林威治,从艾瑞斯出海

⑤interlopers:闯入者

⑥East India fleets:东印度公司船队

⑦the seed of commonwealths, the germs of empires:共和国的种子和帝国的萌芽

树,在夏日的流风中欢快地歌唱,快乐却缺乏思想的沉淀;而当你年老了,你的生命枝叶现出繁华落尽的凋零,但是你遒劲的枝干,通过根蒂和大地紧密相连,那就是你的根本所在,这种对生命的认识,只有在生命最后才能真正领悟。

———William Butler Yeats "*When You Are Old*"

获得诺贝尔文学奖的理由是"用鼓舞人心的诗篇,以高度的艺术形式表达了整个民族的精神风貌。(inspired poetry, which in a highly artistic form that gives expression to the spirit of a whole nation)"。

———1923 年诺贝尔文学奖评审委员会颁奖词

Author

William Butler Yeats was born and educated in Dublin, but spent his childhood in County Sligo. He was an Irish poet and one of the significant figures of 20th century literature. As a pillar of both the Irish and British literary establishments, in his later years of life, he served as an Irish Senator for two terms. Yeats was a driving force behind the Irish Literary Revival and, along with Lady Gregory, Edward Martyn, and others, founded the Abbey Theatre, where he served as its chief during its early years. He studied poetry in his youth and from an early age was fascinated by both Irish legends and the occult. His earliest volume of verse was published in 1889, and those slow-paced and lyrical poems attribute to Edmund Spenser, Percy Bysshe Shelley, and the Pre-Raphaelite poets. In the 20th century, Yeats' poetry was more physical and realistic and renounced the transcendental beliefs of his youth, though he remained preoccupied with physical and spiritual masks, as well as with cyclical theories of life. In 1923, he was awarded the Nobel Prize in Literature as the first Irishman.

Brief Introduction

It's not so hard to see *When You Are Old* is a poem to lover, showing the infinite love. Even though his well-beloved is no longer young and covered with forehead wrinkles, in his heart she is still the most beautiful. In his eyes, her beauty is eternal, and even beyond the passing of time. When recalling the wonderful old days, he is sweet. This kind of love is great and true, and the feelings have been sublimated after the test of time. She is his goddess, with love and fear. He is willing to wait for her. The love is low-key, is murmur. How evocative!

Selected Reading

When You Are Old

When you are old and grey and full of sleep
And nodding by the fire, take down this book[①];
And slowly read, and dream of the soft look
Your eyes had once, and of their shadows deep

How many loved your moments of glad grace[②],
And loved your beauty with love false or true[③].
But one man loved the pilgrim soul[④] in you,
And loved the sorrows of your changing face

And bending down beside the glowing bars[⑤],
Murmur, a little sadly, how love fled
And paced upon the mountains overhead,
And hid his face amid a crowd of stars[⑥].

Question for Discussion

How could you identify the theme of this poem?

①this book: 指写给 Maud Gonne 的诗集
②moments of glad grace: 欢畅的瞬间
③your beauty with love false or true: 假意或真心爱慕你娇艳的容颜
④the pilgrim soul: 朝圣者般的灵魂，纯真的灵魂
⑤the glowing bars: 闪耀的炉火旁
⑥a crowd of stars: 群星

Selected Reading

The lake Isle of Innisfree

I will arise and go now, and go to Innisfree①,
And a small cabin build there, of clay and wottles② made;
Nine bean-rows will I have there, a hive③ for the honey bee,
And live alone in the bee-loud glade④.

And I shall have some peace there, for peace comes dropping slow,
Dropping from the veils⑤ of the morning to where the cricket⑥ sings;
There midnight's all a glimmer⑦, and noon a purple glow,
And evening full of the linnet's⑧ wings.

I will arise and go now, for always night and day
I hear lake water lapping⑨ with low sounds by the shore;
While I stand on the roadway, or on the pavements⑩grey,
I hear in the deep hearts core.

---

①Innisfree:茵梦湖岛，位于爱尔兰
②wottles:编条；枝条编成的篱笆
③hive[IELTS]:蜂巢，蜂群
④glade:林中空地
⑤veil[IELTS][TOEFL]:面纱,面罩
⑥cricket:蟋蟀
⑦glimmer:微光,少许
⑧linner:红雀
⑨lapping:轻拍,轻打
⑩pavement[IELTS]:路面，人行道

Question for Discussion

What does Innisfree Isle mean to Yeats?

Unit 3 James Joyce

Appreciation

虽然我们的力量已不如初,远非昔日移天动地的雄姿,但我们仍然是我们。英雄的心尽管被时间消磨,被命运削弱。我们的意志和坚强依然如故,坚持着去奋斗,探索追求,绝不屈服。

——詹姆斯·乔伊斯

侮辱和仇恨并不是生命,真正的生命是爱。

——詹姆斯·乔伊斯

Author

James Joyce was an Irish novelist and poet. He contributed to the modernist avant-garde, and is regarded as one of the most influential and important authors of the twentieth century.

Joyce is best known for *Ulysses* (1922), a landmark work in which the episodes of Homer's *Odyssey* are paralleled in an array of contrasting literary styles, perhaps most prominent among these the stream of consciousness technique he utilized. Other well-known works are the short-story collection *Dubliners* (1914), and the novels *A Portrait of the Artist as a Young Man* (1916) and *Finnegans Wake* (1939). His other writings include three books of poetry, a play, occasional journalism, and his published letters.

Joyce was born in 41 Brighton Square, Rathgar, Dublin—about half a mile from his mother's birthplace in Terenure—into a middle-class family on the way down. A brilliant student, he excelled at the Jesuit schools Clongowes and Belvedere, despite the chaotic family life imposed by his father's alcoholism and unpredictable finance. He went on to attend University College, Dublin.

Chapter 7 20th-Century English Literature

In 1904, in his early twenties, Joyce emigrated permanently to continental Europe with his partner (and later wife) Nora Barnacle. They lived in Trieste, Paris, and Zurich. Though most of his adult life was spent abroad, Joyce's fictional universe centres on Dublin, and is populated largely by characters who closely resemble family members, enemies and friends from his time there. *Ulysses* in particular is set with precision in the streets and alleyways of the city. Shortly after the publication of *Ulysses*, he elucidated this preoccupation somewhat, saying, "For myself, I always write about Dublin, because if I can get to the heart of Dublin I can get to the heart of all the cities of the world. In the particular is contained the universal."

Brief Introduction

Ulysses was first serialised in parts in the American journal *The Little Review* from March 1918 to December 1920, and then published in its entirety by Sylvia Beach in February 1922, in Paris. It is considered to be one of the most important works of modernist literature, and has been called "a demonstration and summation of the entire movement". According to Declan Kiberd, "Before Joyce, no writer of fiction had so foregrounded the process of thinking."

Ulysses chronicles the peripatetic appointments and encounters of Leopold Bloom in Dublin in the course of an ordinary day, June 16, 1904. Ulysses is the Latinised name of Odysseus, the hero of Homer's epic poem *Odyssey*, and the novel establishes a series of parallels between the poem and the novel, with structural correspondences between the characters and experiences of Leopold Bloom and Odysseus, Molly Bloom and Penelope, and Stephen Dedalus and Telemachus, in addition to events and themes of the early 20th century context of modernism, Dublin, and Ireland's relationship to Britain. The novel imitates registers of centuries of English literature and is highly allusive.

Ulysses is approximately 265,000 words in length, uses a lexicon of 30,030 words (including proper names, plurals and various verb tenses), and is divided into eighteen episodes. Since publication, the book has attracted controversy and scrutiny, ranging from early obscenity trials to protracted textual "Joyce Wars". *Ulysses*' stream-of-consciousness technique, careful structuring, and experimental prose — full of puns, parodies, and allusions — as well as its rich characterisation and broad humour, made the book a highly regarded novel in the modernist pantheon. Joyce fans worldwide now celebrate June 16 as Bloomsday. In 1998, the American publishing firm Modern Library ranked *Ulysses* first on its list of the 100 best English-language novels of the 20th century.

Selected Reading

Ulysses

Chapter 1

Solemnly① he came forward and mounted② the round gunrest③. He faced about and blessed gravely thrice the tower, the surrounding land and the awaking mountains. Then, catching sight of Stephen Dedalus, he bent towards him and made rapid crosses in the air, gurgling④ in his throat and shaking his head. Stephen Dedalus, displeased and sleepy, leaned his arms on the top of the staircase and looked coldly at the shaking gurgling face that blessed him, equine in its length, and at the light untonsured⑤ hair, grained and hued like pale oak.

Buck Mulligan peeped an instant under the mirror and then covered the bowl smartly.

—Back to barracks⑥! he said sternly.

He added in a preacher's tone:

—For this, O dearly beloved, is the genuine Christine: body and soul and blood and wounds. Slow music, please.

Shut your eyes, gents. One moment. A little trouble about those white corpuscles. Silence, all.

①solemnly:庄严地
②mounte[IELTS]:登上
③gunrest:炮座
④gurge:嗓子里发出的咯咯声音
⑤untonsure:未剃光
⑥barracks:营房

He peered sideways up and gave a long slow whistle of call, then paused awhile in rapt attention, his even white teeth glistening here and there with gold points. Chrysostomos①. Two strong shrill whistles answered through the calm.

—Thanks, old chap, he cried briskly. That will do nicely. Switch off the current, will you?

He skipped off the gunrest and looked gravely at his watcher, gathering about his legs the loose folds of his gown. The plump shadowed face and sullen oval jowl recalled a prelate②, patron of arts in the middle ages. A pleasant smile broke quietly over his lips.

—The mockery of it! He said gaily. Your absurd name, an ancient Greek!

He pointed his finger in friendly jest③ and went over to the parapet④, laughing to himself. Stephen Dedalus stepped up, followed him wearily halfway and sat down on the edge of the gunrest, watching him still as he propped his mirror on the parapet, dipped the brush in the bowl and lathered⑤ cheeks and neck.

Buck Mulligan's gay voice went on.

—My name is absurd too: Malachi Mulligan, two dactyls. But it has a Hellenic ring⑥, hasn't it? Tripping and sunny like the buck himself. We must go to Athens. Will you come if I can get the aunt to fork out twenty quid?

He laid the brush aside and, laughing with delight, cried:

—Will he come? The jejune jesuit!⑦

Ceasing, he began to shave with care.

—Tell me, Mulligan, Stephen said quietly.

—Yes, my love?

—How long is Haines going to stay in this tower?

---

①Chrysostomos:克里索斯托
②prelate:中世纪作为艺术保护者的高僧
③jest:笑话
④parapet:栏杆
⑤lathered:肥皂沫
⑥Hellenic ring:古希腊的味道
⑦The jejune jesuit:枯燥乏味的耶稣会士

Buck Mulligan showed a shaven cheek over his right shoulder.

—God, isn't he dreadful? He said frankly. A ponderous① Saxon. He thinks you're not a gentleman. God, these bloody English! Bursting with money and indigestion②. Because he comes from Oxford. You know, Dedalus, you have the real Oxford manner. He can't make you out. O, my name for you is the best: Kinch, the knife-blade.

He shaved warily③ over his chin.

—He was raving④ all night about a black panther⑤, Stephen said. Where is his guncase⑥?

—A woful lunatic⑦! Mulligan said. Were you in a funk?

—I was, Stephen said with energy and growing fear. Out here in the dark with a man I don't know raving and moaning to himself about shooting a black panther. You saved men from drowning. I'm not a hero, however. If he stays on here I am off.

Buck Mulligan frowned at the lather on his razorblade. He hopped down from his perch and began to search.

His trouser pockets hastily.

—Scutter! He cried thickly.

He came over to the gunrest and, thrusting a hand into Stephen's upper pocket, said:

—Lend us a loan of your noserag⑧ to wipe my razor.

Stephen suffered him to pull out and hold up on show by its corner a dirty crumpled handkerchief.

Buck Mulligan wiped the razorblade neatly. Then, gazing over the

---

①ponderous:笨头笨脑
②indigestion[TOEFL]:消化不良,此处指脑满肠肥的英国人
③warily:仔细地
④rave:狂言
⑤panther:豹
⑥guncase:枪套
⑦A woful lunatic:一个可怜可悲的疯子
⑧noserag:鼻涕布

handkerchief, he said.

—The bard's noserag! A new art colour for our Irish poets: snotgreen. You can almost taste it, can't you?

He mounted to the parapet again and gazed out over Dublin bay, his fair oakpale hair stirring slightly.

—God! he said quietly. Isn't the sea what Algy calls it: a great sweet mother? The snotgreen sea. The scrotumtightening sea. EPI OINOPA PONTON①. Ah, Dedalus②, the Greeks! I must teach you. You must read them in the original. THALATTA! THALATTA③! She is our great sweet mother. Come and look.

Stephen stood up and went over to the parapet. Leaning on it he looked down on the water and on the mailboat clearing the harbormouth of Kingstown.

—Our mighty mother! Buck Mulligan said.

He turned abruptly④ his grey searching eyes from the sea to Stephen's face.

—The aunt thinks you killed your mother, he said. That's why she won't let me have anything to do with you.

—Someone killed her, Stephen said gloomily.

—You could have knelt down, damn it, Kinch, when your dying mother asked you, Buck Mulligan said. I'm hyperborean as much as you. But to think of your mother begging you with her last breath to kneel down and pray for her. And you refused. There is something sinister in you ...

He broke off and lathered again lightly his farther cheek. A tolerant smile curled his lips.

—But a lovely mummer! He murmured to himself. Kinch, the loveliest mummer of them all!

He shaved evenly and with care, in silence, seriously.

Stephen, an elbow rested on the jagged granite⑤, leaned his palm against

---

①EPI OINOPA PONTON:到葡萄紫的大海上去
②Dedalus:迪达勒斯
③THALATTA:大海
④abruptly[TOEFL]:突然
⑤the jagged granite:坑洼不平的花岗石

his brow and gazed at the fraying① edge of his shiny black coat-sleeve. Pain, that was not yet the pain of love, fretted his heart. Silently, in a dream she had come to him after her death, her wasted body within its loose brown graveclothes giving off an odour② of wax and rosewood, her breath, that had bent upon him, mute, reproachful, a faint odour of wetted ashes. Across the threadbare cuff edge③ he saw the sea hailed as a great sweet mother by the wellfed voice beside him. The ring of bay and skyline held a dull green mass of liquid. A bowl of white china had stood beside her deathbed holding the green sluggish bile④ which she had torn up from her rotting liver by fits of loud groaning vomiting⑤.

Buck Mulligan wiped again his razorblade⑥.

—Ah, poor dogsbody! he said in a kind voice. I must give you a shirt and a few noserags. How are the secondhand breeks?

—They fit well enough, Stephen answered.

Buck Mulligan attacked the hollow beneath his underlip.

—The mockery of it, he said contentedly. Secondleg they should be. God knows what poxybowsy⑦ left them off. I have a lovely pair with a hair stripe, grey. You'll look spiffing⑧ in them. I'm not joking, Kinch. You look damn well when you're dressed.

—Thanks, Stephen said. I can't wear them if they are grey.

—He can't wear them, Buck Mulligan told his face in the mirror. Etiquette⑨ is etiquette. He kills his mother but he can't wear grey trousers.

---

①fray:磨损

②odour[IELTS]:气味

③threadbare cuff edge:褴褛的袖口

④green sluggish bile:暗绿色的液体

⑤vomite[IELTS]:呕吐

⑥razorblade:剃刀刃

⑦poxybowsy:酒疯子

⑧spiff:好看

⑨etiquette[TOEFL]:礼仪

He folded his razor neatly and with stroking palps① of fingers felt the smooth skin.

Stephen turned his gaze from the sea and to the plump face with its smokeblue mobile eyes.

—That fellow I was with in the Ship last night, said Buck Mulligan, says you have g. p. i. He's up in Dottyville with Connolly Norman. General paralysis of the insane!

He swept the mirror a half circle in the air to flash the tidings abroad in sunlight now radiant on the sea. His curling shaven lips laughed and the edges of his white glittering teeth. Laughter seized all his strong wellknit trunk.

—Look at yourself, he said, you dreadful bard!

Stephen bent forward and peered at the mirror held out to him, cleft by a crooked crack. Hair on end. As he and others see me. Who chose this face for me? This dogsbody to rid of vermin. It asks me too.

—I pinched it out of the skivvy's room, Buck Mulligan said. It does her all right. The aunt always keeps plainlooking servants for Malachi. Lead him not into temptation. And her name is Ursula.

Laughing again, he brought the mirror away from Stephen's peering eyes.

—The rage of Caliban② at not seeing his face in a mirror, he said. If Wilde were only alive to see you!

Drawing back and pointing, Stephen said with bitterness:

—It is a symbol of Irish art. The cracked looking-glass of a servant.

Buck Mulligan suddenly linked his arm in Stephen's and walked with him round the tower, his razor and mirror clacking③ in the pocket where he had thrust them.

—It's not fair to tease you like that, Kinch, is it? He said kindly. God knows you have more spirit than any of them.

---

①palps:触须
②Caliban:凯列班
③clack:磕碰

Parried① again. He fears the lancet of my art as I fear that of his. The cold steelpen.

—Cracked looking-glass of a servant! Tell that to the oxy chap downstairs and touch him for a guinea. He's stinking with money and thinks you're not a gentleman. His old fellow made his tin by selling jalap to Zulus or some bloody swindle or other. God, Kinch, if you and I could only work together we might do something for the island. Helleniseit. Cranly'sarm. His arm.

—And to think of your having to beg from these swine. I'm the only one that knows what you are. Why don't you trust me more? What have you up your nose against me? Is it Haines? If he makes any noise here I'll bring down Seymour and we'll give him a ragging worse than they gave Clive Kempthorpe②. Young shouts of moneyed voices in Clive Kempthorpe's rooms. Palefaces: they hold their ribs with laughter, one clasping another. O, I shall expire③! Break the news to her gently, Aubrey④! I shall die! With slit ribbons of his shirt whipping the air he hops and hobbles round the table, with trousers down at heels, chased by Ades of magdalen⑤ with the tailor's shears. A scared calf's face gilded with marmalade⑥. I don't want to be debagged! Don't you play the giddy⑦ ox with me!

Shouts from the open window startling evening in the quadrangle. A deaf gardener, aproned⑧, masked with Matthew Arnold's face, pushes his mower on the sombre lawn watching narrowly the dancing motes of grasshalms.

To ourselves... new paganism omphalos⑨.

—Let him stay, Stephen said. There's nothing wrong with him except at

---

①parry:岔开话题
②Clive Kempthorpe:克莱夫·肯普索普
③expire[IELTS][TOEFL]:断气
④Aubrey:奥布里
⑤Ades of Magdalen:麦达伦学院那个手里拿着裁缝大剪刀的埃德斯
⑥marmalade:果酱
⑦giddy:头晕,惊惶
⑧aprone:穿着围裙
⑨paganism omphalos:异教教义中心

night.

—Then what is it? Buck Mulligan asked impatiently. Cough it up. I'm quite frank with you. What have you against me now?

They halted, looking towards the blunt cape of Bray Head that lay on the water like the snout① of a sleeping whale. Stephen freed his arm quietly.

—Do you wish me to tell you? He asked.

—Yes, what is it? Buck Mulligan answered. I don't remember anything.

He looked in Stephen's face as he spoke. A light wind passed his brow, fanning softly his fair uncombed hair and stirring silver points of anxiety in his eyes.

Stephen, depressed by his own voice, said:

—Do you remember the first day I went to your house after my mother's death?

Buck Mulligan frowned quickly and said:

—What? Where? I can't remember anything. I remember only ideas and sensations. Why? What happened in the name of God?

—You were making tea, Stephen said, and went across the landing to get more hot water. Your mother and some visitor came out of the drawingroom. She asked you who was in your room.

—Yes? Buck Mulligan said. What did I say? I forget.

—You said, Stephen answered, Oh, IT'S ONLY DEDALUS WHOSE MOTHER IS BEASTLY DEAD.

A flush which made him seem younger and more engaging rose to Buck Mulligan's cheek.

—Did I say that? He asked. Well? What harm is that?

He shook his constraint from him nervously.

—And what is death, he asked, your mother's or yours or my own? You saw only your mother die. I see them pop off every day in the Mater and Richmond and cut up into tripes in the dissectingroom②. It's a beastly thing and nothing else. It simply doesn't matter. You wouldn't kneel down to pray for your

---

①snout:酣睡
②dissectingroom:解剖室

mother on her deathbed when she asked you. Why? Because you have the cursed jesuit strain in you, only it's injected the wrong way. To me it's all a mockery and beastly. Her cerebral lobes are not functioning. She calls the doctor sir Peter Teazle and picks buttercups off the quilt. Humour her till it's over. You crossed her last wish in death and yet you sulk with me because I don't whinge① like some hired mute from Lalouette's. Absurd! I suppose I did say it. I didn't mean to offend the memory of your mother.

He had spoken himself into boldness. Stephen, shielding the gaping wounds which the words had left in his heart, said very coldly:

—I am not thinking of the offence to my mother.

—Of what then? Buck Mulligan asked.

—Of the offence to me, Stephen answered.

Buck Mulligan swung round on his heel. —O, an impossible person! He exclaimed.

He walked off quickly round the parapet. Stephen stood at his post, gazing over the calm sea towards the headland. Sea and headland now grew dim. Pulses were beating in his eyes, veiling their sight, and he felt the fever of his cheeks.

A voice within the tower called loudly:

—Are you up there, Mulligan?

Question for Discussion

Chapter One introduces us to Stephen's struggle with the ins and outs of Irish identity. Please carry out an analysis.

---

①whinge: 哀号，痛哭

Unit 4　Virginia Woolf

Appreciation

一个人一旦有了自我认识,也就有了独立人格,而一旦有了独立人格,也就不再浑浑噩噩虚度年华了。换言之,他一生都会有一种适度的充实感和幸福感。

——弗吉尼亚·沃尔夫

Author

Virginia Woolf, a British writer, became one of the most innovative literary figures of the early 20th century, with novels like *Mrs. Dalloway* (1925), *Jacob's Room* (1922), *To the Lighthouse* (1927), and *The Waves* (1931). Her other works include two biographies and many important critical studies of literature and British society. Woolf's works are often linked to the development of feminist criticism, but she was also an important writer in the modernist movement. She revolutionized the novel with stream of consciousness, which allowed her to depict the inner lives of her characters in all too intimate detail. Woolf continued her experiments with fiction, particularly interested in the passage of time. In *The Waves*, she pains herself much to expand the stream-of-consciousness method, depicting characters in the context of time philosophically. The six characters represent different kinds of consciousness. Virginia Woolf is regarded as one of the greatest novelists of the 20th century for her techniques, such as interior monologues and the stream of consciousness.

Brief Introduction

Created from two short stories, *Mrs. Dalloway in Bond Street* and the unfinished *The Prime Minister*, the novel's story is about Clarissa's preparations for a party of which she is to be hostess. With the interior perspective of the novel, the story travels forwards and backcoards in time and in and out of the characters' minds to construct an image of

Clarissa's life and of the inter-war social structure.

Selected Reading

Mrs. Dalloway

Mrs. Dalloway said she would buy the flowers herself.

For Lucy① had her work cut out for her. The doors would be taken off their hinges②; Rumpelmayer's men were coming. And then, thought Clarissa Dalloway, what a morning—fresh as if issued to children on a beach.

What a lark③! What a plunge④! For so it had always seemed to her, when, with a little squeak⑤ of the hinges, which she could hear now, she had burst open the French windows⑥ and plunged at Bourton⑦ into the open air. How fresh, how calm, stiller than this of course, the air was in the early morning; like the flap of a wave; the kiss of a wave; chill and sharp and yet (for a girl of eighteen as she then was) solemn, feeling as she did, standing there at the open window, that something awful was about to happen; looking at the flowers, at the trees with the smoke winding off them and the rooks⑧ rising, falling; standing and looking until Peter Walsh said, "Musing⑨ among the vegetables?"—was that it? —"I prefer men to cauliflowers⑩" —was that it? He must have said it at breakfast one morning when she had gone out on to the terrace—Peter Walsh. He would be back from India one of these days, June or July, she forgot which, for his letters were awfully dull; it was his sayings one

---

①Lucy：露西，达罗卫夫人家里的帮佣
②hinges[IELTS][TOEFL]：合页，铰链
③lark：云雀，百灵鸟
④plunge[TOEFL]：骤降,突然下落
⑤squeak：嘎吱嘎吱响
⑥French windows：法式落地窗
⑦Bourton：英格兰度假胜地
⑧rooks：秃鼻乌鸦
⑨muse：沉思
⑩cauliflowers：花椰菜

remembered; his eyes his pocket-knife, his smile, his grumpiness① and, when millions of things had utterly vanished—how strange it was! —a few sayings like this about cabbages.

She stiffened a little on the kerb②, waiting for Durtnall's van to pass. A charming woman, Scrope Purvis thought her (knowing her as one does know people who live next door to one in Westminster③); a touch of the bird about her, of the jay④, blue-green, light, vivacious⑤, though she was over fifty, and grown very white since her illness. There she perched, never seeing him, waiting to cross, very upright.

For having lived in Westminster—how many years now? over twenty, —one feels even in the midst of the traffic, or waking at night, Clarissa was positive, a particular hush, or solemnity; an indescribable pause, a suspense (but that might be her heart, affected, they said, by influenza) before Big Ben⑥ strikes. There! Out it boomed. First a warning, musical; then the hour, irrevocable⑦. The leaden circles dissolved in the air. Such fools we are, she thought, crossing Victoria Street⑧.

Question for Discussion

Motifs are recurring structures, contrasts, or literary devices that can help to develop and inform the text's major themes. What are the meanings of "Big Ben" and "trees & flowers" in *Mrs. Dalloway*?

---

①grumpiness：坏脾气
②kerb：人行道
③Westminster：威斯敏斯特(伦敦市的一个行政区，英国议会所在地)
④jay：松鸭
⑤vivacious：活泼的
⑥Big Ben：大本钟
⑦irrevocable[IELTS][TOEFL]：不可挽回的
⑧Victoria Street：伦敦市中心的维多利亚大街

Unit 5   David Herbert Lawrence

Appreciation

要活着,要做活人,做活得完整的人,这就是问题的根本。小说的最大好处,就是能够极大地帮助你,帮助你不做生活中的死人。

——戴维·赫伯特·劳伦斯

人生有两大快乐,一是没有得到你心爱的东西,于是你可以去追求和创造;一是得到了你心爱的东西,于是你可以去品味和体验。

——周国平

Author

Born in England on September 11, 1885 in Eastwood, Nottinghamshire, David Herbert Lawrence is regarded as one of the most influential writers of the 20th century. Lawrence published many novels and poetry volumes during his lifetime, including *Sons and Lovers* and *Women in Love*, but he is best known for his infamous novel *Lady Chatterley's Lover*. During his last years, Lawrence spent much of his time in Italy making only brief visits to England, the last in 1926. He died on March 2, 1930 at Vence in the south of France.

Lawrence was a prolific writer of poetry, novels, short stories, plays, essays, and criticism. His works are heavily autobiographical and the experiences of his early years in Nottinghamshire continued to exert a profound influence throughout his life. He had an extraordinary ability to convey a sense of specific time and place, and his writings often reflected his complex personality. Lawrence uses the terms "mental consciousness" and "blood consciousness" to distinguish between "sense" and "perception". He also wrote a number of plays, travel books such as *Etruscan Places* (1932), and volumes of literary criticism, notably *Studies in Classic American Literature* (1916).

Chapter 7 20th-Century English Literature

Brief Introduction

Lawrence rewrote *Sons and Lovers* four times until he was happy with it. Although before publication the work was usually entitled *Paul Morel*, Lawrence finally settled on *Sons and Lovers*. Just as the new title makes the work less focused on a central character, many of the later additions broadened the scope of the work, thereby making the work less autobiographical. While some of the editions by Garnett were on the grounds of propriety or style, others would once more narrow the emphasis back upon Paul.

Part I

The refined daughter of a "good old burgher family," Gertrude Coppard meets a rough-hewn miner, Walter Morel, at a Christmas dance and falls into a whirlwind romance characterised by physical passion. But soon after her marriage to Walter, she realises the difficulties of living off his meagre salary in a rented house. The couple fight and drift apart and Walter retreats to the pub after work each day. Gradually, Mrs. Morel's affections shift to her sons, beginning with the oldest, William.

As a boy, William is so attached to his mother that he doesn't enjoy the fair without her. As he grows older, he defends her against his father's occasional violence. Eventually, he leaves their Nottinghamshire home for a job in London, where he begins to rise up into the middle class. He is engaged, but he detests the girl's superficiality. He dies and Mrs. Morel is heartbroken, but when Paul catches pneumonia, she rediscovers her love for her second son.

Part II

Both repulsed by and drawn to his mother, Paul is afraid to leave her but wants to go out on his own, and needs to experience love. Gradually, he falls into a relationship with Miriam, a farmer's daughter who attends his church. The two take long walks and have intellectual conversations about books but Paul resists, in part because his mother disapproves. At Miriam's family's farm, Paul meets Clara Dawes, a young woman with, apparently, feminist sympathies, who has separated from her husband, Baxter.

After pressuring Miriam into a physical relationship, which he finds unsatisfying, Paul breaks with her as he grows more intimate with Clara, who is more passionate physically. But even she cannot hold him and he returns to his mother. When his mother dies soon after, he is alone.

Selected Reading

Sons and Lovers

Chapter 15

Clara went with her husband to Sheffield, and Paul scarcely saw her again. Walter Morel seemed to have let all the trouble go over him, and there he was, crawling about on the mud of it, just the same. There was scarcely any bond between father and son, save that each felt he must not let the other go in any actual want. As there was no one to keep on the home, and as they could neither of them bear the emptiness of the house, Paul took lodgings in Nottingham, and Morel went to live with a friendly family in Bestwood.

Everything seemed to have gone smash for the young man. He could not paint. The picture he finished on the day of his mother's death—one that satisfied him—was the last thing he did. At work there was no Clara. When he came home he could not take up his brushes again. There was nothing left.

So he was always in the town at one place or another, drinking, knocking about with the men he knew. It really wearied him. He talked to barmaids[1], to almost any woman, but there was that dark, strained[2] look in his eyes, as if he were hunting something.

Everything seemed so different, so unreal. There seemed no reason why people should go along the street, and houses pile up in the daylight. There seemed no reason why these things should occupy the space, instead of leaving it empty. His friends talked to him: he heard the sounds, and he answered. But why there should be the noise of speech he could not understand.

---

①barmaids：酒吧女招待（ barmaid 的名词复数 ）
②strain[TOEFL]：紧张；态度不自然，勉强

He was most himself when he was alone, or working hard and mechanically① at the factory. In the latter case there was pure forgetfulness, when he lapsed② from consciousness. But it had to come to an end. It hurt him so, that things had lost their reality. The first snowdrops came. He saw the tiny drop-pearls among the grey. They would have given him the liveliest emotion at one time. Now they were there, but they did not seem to mean anything. In a few moments they would cease to occupy that place, and just the space would be, where they had been. Tall, brilliant tram-cars ran along the street at night. It seemed almost a wonder they should trouble to rustle③ backwards and forwards. "Why trouble to go tilting down to Trent Bridges?" he asked of the big trams. It seemed they just as well might NOT be as be.

The realest thing was the thick darkness at night. That seemed to him whole and comprehensible and restful. He could leave himself to it. Suddenly a piece of paper started near his feet and blew along down the pavement. He stood still, rigid, with clenched fists, a flame of agony④ going over him. And he saw again the sick-room, his mother, her eyes. Unconsciously he had been with her, in her company. The swift hop of the paper reminded him she was gone. But he had been with her. He wanted everything to stand still, so that he could be with her again.

The days passed, the weeks. But everything seemed to have fused, gone into a conglomerated⑤ mass. He could not tell one day from another, one week from another, hardly one place from another. Nothing was distinct or distinguishable. Often he lost himself for an hour at a time, could not remember what he had done.

One evening he came home late to his lodging. The fire was burning low; everybody was in bed. He threw on some more coal, glanced at the table, and

---

① mechanically [IELTS][TOEFL]：机械地；呆板地
② lapse：倒退；丧失
③ rustle：发出沙沙的声音
④ agony：极大的痛苦；苦恼
⑤ conglomerate [TOEFL]：聚结；成团

decided he wanted no supper. Then he sat down in the arm-chair. It was perfectly still. He did not know anything, yet he saw the dim smoke wavering① up the chimney. Presently two mice came out, cautiously, nibbling② the fallen crumbs③. He watched them as it were from a long way off. The church clock struck two. Far away he could hear the sharp clinking of the trucks on the railway. No, it was not they that were far away. They were there in their places. But where was he himself?

The time passed. The two mice, careering wildly, scampered④ cheekily⑤ over his slippers. He had not moved a muscle. He did not want to move. He was not thinking of anything. It was easier so. There was no wrench⑥ of knowing anything. Then, from time to time, some other consciousness, working mechanically, flashed into sharp phrases.

"What am I doing?"

And out of the semi-intoxicated⑦ trance⑧ came the answer:

"Destroying myself."

Then a dull, live feeling, gone in an instant, told him that it was wrong. After a while, suddenly came the question:

"Why wrong?"

Again there was no answer, but a stroke of hot stubbornness inside his chest resisted his own annihilation⑨.

There was a sound of a heavy cart clanking down the road. Suddenly the electric light went out; there was a bruising thud⑩ in the penny-in-the-slot

---

①wavering：摇摆
②nibble：啃，一点一点地咬
③crumbs：碎屑（尤指面包屑或糕饼屑）
④scamper[IELTS]：蹦蹦跳跳地跑
⑤cheekily：厚脸皮地
⑥wrench：痛苦，愁楚
⑦intoxicated：喝醉的，极其兴奋的
⑧trance：出神；恍惚
⑨annihilation[TOEFL]：歼灭；灭绝
⑩thud：砰的一声

meter. He did not stir, but sat gazing in front of him. Only the mice had scuttled①, and the fire glowed red in the dark room.

Then, quite mechanically and more distinctly, the conversation began again inside him.

"She's dead. What was it all for—her struggle?"

That was his despair wanting to go after her.

"You're alive."

"She's not."

"She is—in you."

Suddenly he felt tired with the burden of it.

"You've got to keep alive for her sake," said his will in him.

Something felt sulky②, as if it would not rouse③.

"You've got to carry forward her living, and what she had done, go on with it."

But he did not want to. He wanted to give up.

"But you can go on with your painting," said the will in him. "Or else you can beget④ children. They both carry on her effort."

"Painting is not living."

"Then live."

"Marry whom?" came the sulky question.

"As best you can."

"Miriam?"

But he did not trust that.

He rose suddenly, went straight to bed. When he got inside his bedroom and closed the door, he stood with clenched fist.

"Mater⑤, my dear—" he began, with the whole force of his soul. Then he

---

①scuttle: 快跑, 急走
②sulky: 生闷气的; 闷闷不乐的
③rouse: 鼓励, 鼓舞
④beget: 成为……的父亲
⑤Mater: ＜英＞母亲, 妈妈

stopped. He would not say it. He would not admit that he wanted to die, to have done. He would not own that life had beaten him, or that death had beaten him. Going straight to bed, he slept at once, abandoning himself to the sleep.

So the weeks went on. Always alone, his soul oscillated①, first on the side of death, then on the side of life, doggedly②. The real agony was that he had nowhere to go, nothing to do, nothing to say, and was nothing himself. Sometimes he ran down the streets as if he were mad: sometimes he was mad; things weren't there, things were there. It made him pant. Sometimes he stood before the bar of the public-house where he called for a drink. Everything suddenly stood back away from him. He saw the face of the barmaid, the gobbling③ drinkers, his own glass on the slopped, mahogany④ board, in the distance. There was something between him and them. He could not get into touch. He did not want them; he did not want his drink. Turning abruptly, he went out. On the threshold⑤ he stood and looked at the lighted street. But he was not of it or in it. Something separated him. Everything went on there below those lamps, shut away from him. He could not get at them. He felt he couldn't touch the lamp-posts, not if he reached. Where could he go? There was nowhere to go, neither back into the inn, or forward anywhere. He felt stifled⑥. There was nowhere for him. The stress grew inside him; he felt he should smash.

"I mustn't," he said; and, turning blindly, he went in and drank. Sometimes the drink did him good; sometimes it made him worse. He ran down the road. For ever restless, he went here, there, everywhere. He determined to work. But when he had made six strokes, he loathed⑦ the pencil violently, got up, and went away,

①oscillate：动摇，犹豫

②doggedly：固执地，顽强地

③gobbling：狼吞虎咽地吃

④mahogany：桃花心木，红木

⑤threshold[IELTS][TOEFL]：门槛

⑥stifled[TOEFL]：窒息的

⑦loathe：憎恨，厌恶

hurried off to a club where he could play cards or billiards①, to a place where he could flirt② with a barmaid who was no more to him than the brass pump-handle she drew.

He was very thin and lantern-jawed③. He dared not meet his own eyes in the mirror; he never looked at himself. He wanted to get away from himself, but there was nothing to get hold of.

Questions for Discussion

1. What's the main theme of *Sons and Lovers*?
2. Please analyze the relationship between Paul Morel and Miriam, and that between Paul and Clara.

Unit 6　Katherine Mansfield

Appreciation

儿童的心灵是敏感的,他是为接受一切好的东西而敞开的。

——苏霍姆林斯基

怎样是幸福的童年呢？是父母之间毫无间隙,在温柔地爱他们的孩子时,同时维持着坚固的纪律,且在儿童之间保持着一视同仁的平等。

——安德烈·莫洛亚

Author

Katherine Mansfield has acquired an international reputation as a writer of short stories, poetry, letters, journals and reviews. Her work has been translated into more

---

①billiards：台球,弹子球
②flirt：调情,打情骂俏
③lantern-jawed：下巴突出的,瘦长脸的

than 25 languages. She was born in Wellington, New Zealand, into a middle-class colonial family.

In 1915, Mansfield's brother visited her in London, and they spent the summer days reminiscing, planning to return to New Zealand. In October he was killed in the war. Mansfield was suffering sadness of losing her brother. So she determined to do something to her country and begin to write *The Prelude*. The following years she continued to build her reputation and then made a lot of works. Such as *Bliss and Other Stories* (1920), *Garden Party and Othe Stories* (1922), *At the Bay* (1922), *The Canary* (1922), etc. Also her illness turned much more serious day by day, And she cherish the time very much and work hard.

In 1922, she went to London for what were to be final meetings with her father and friends. On January 9, 1923, Mansfield died. Her last words were: "I love the rain. I want the feeling of it on my face".

The incorporation of stream of consciousness into stories, the addresses and the glimpses the focus on the interior life of her characters rather than the contrivances of plots and people at Arco innovations in a short story and have been adopted by many of her contemporary and later writers.

Brief Introduction

The Sheridan family is preparing to host a garden party Laura is supposed to be in charge, but has trouble with the workers who appear to know better, and her mother Mrs. Sheridan has ordered Lilies to be delivered for the party without Laura's approval. Her sister Joes tests the piano and then sings a song in case she is asked to do so again later. After the furniture is rearranged, they learned that their working class neighborhood Mr. Scott has died. While Laura believes the party should be called off, neither Jose nor their mother agrees. The party is a success and later Mrs. Sheridan decides it would be good to bring a basket full of leftovers to the Scotts' house. She summons Laura to do so. Laura is shown into the poor neighbors house by Mrs. Scott's sister, then sees the window and her late husband's corpse. She suddenly has insight into a topic persistently concerned — the matter of life and death.

The theme of her stories are mostly some single moments of daily life, through which she tries to review the profound meaning of trivial things.

Selected Reading

The Garden Party

Chapter 23

"Egg and—" Mrs. Sheridan held the envelope away from her. "It looks like mice. It can't be mice, can it?"

"Olive, pet," said Laura, looking over her shoulder.

"Yes, of course, olive. What a horrible combination it sounds. Egg and olive."

They were finished at last, and Laura took them off to the kitchen. She found Jose there pacifying① the cook, who did not look at all terrifying.

"I have never seen such exquisite sandwiches," said Jose's rapturous② voice.

"How many kinds did you say there were, cook? Fifteen?"

"Fifteen, Miss Jose."

"Well, cook, I congratulate you."

Cook swept up crusts with the long sandwich knife, and smiled broadly.

"Godber's has come," announced Sadie, issuing out of the pantry③. She had seen the man pass the window.

That meant the cream puffs had come. Godber's were famous for their cream puffs. Nobody ever thought of making them at home.

"Bring them in and put them on the table, my girl," ordered cook.

Sadie brought them in and went back to the door. Of course Laura and Jose were far too grown-up to really care about such things. All the same, they couldn't help agreeing that the puffs looked very attractive. Very. Cook began

---

① pacifying: 安抚，安慰
② rapturous: 兴高采烈的
③ pantry: 食品储藏室

arranging them, shaking off the extra icing sugar.

"Don't they carry one back to all one's parties?" said Laura.

"I suppose they do," said practical Jose, who never liked to be carried back. "They look beautifully light and feathery, I must say."

"Have one each, my dears," said cook in her comfortable voice. "Yer ma won't know."

Oh, impossible. Fancy cream puffs so soon after breakfast. The very idea made one shudder①. All the same, two minutes later Jose and Laura were licking their fingers with that absorbed inward look that only comes from whipped cream.

"Let's go into the garden, out by the backway," suggested Laura. "I want to see how the men are getting on with the marquee②. They're such awfully nice men."

But the back door was blocked by cook, Sadie, Godber's man and Hans.

Something had happened.

"Tuk-tuk-tuk," clucked cook like an agitated③ hen. Sadie had her hand clapped to her cheek as though she had toothache. Hans's face was screwed up in the effort to understand. Only Godber's man seemed to be enjoying himself; it was his story.

"What's the matter? What's happened?"

"There's been a horrible accident," said Cook.

"A man killed."

"A man killed! Where? How? When?"

But Godber's man wasn't going to have his story snatched④ from under his very nose.

"Know those little cottages just below here, miss?" Know them? Of course,

---

① shudder: 战栗，发抖
② arquee: 帐篷
③ agitated: 激动地，焦虑不安地
④ snatch: 抢走，夺去

she knew them. "Well, there's a young chap living there, name of Scott, a carter①. His horse shied at a traction-engine②, corner of Hawke Street this morning, and he was thrown out on the back of his head. Killed."

"Dead!" Laura stared at Godber's man.

"Dead when they picked him up," said Godber's man with relish③. "They were taking the body home as I come up here." And he said to the cook, "He's left a wife and five little ones."

"Jose, come here." Laura caught hold of her sister's sleeve and dragged her through the kitchen to the other side of the green baize door. There she paused and leaned against it. "Jose!" she said, horrified, "however are we going to stop everything?"

"Stop everything, Laura!" cried Jose in astonishment. "What do you mean?"

"Stop the garden-party, of course." Why did Jose pretend?

But Jose was still more amazed. "Stop the garden-party? My dear Laura, don't be so absurd. Of course we can't do anything of the kind. Nobody expects us to. Don't be so extravagant.④"

"But we can't possibly have a garden-party with a man dead just outside the front gate."

That really was extravagant, for the little cottages were in a lane to themselves at the very bottom of a steep rise that led up to the house. A broad road ran between. True, they were far too near. They were the greatest possible eyesore⑤, and they had no right to be in that neighborhood at all. They were little mean dwellings painted a chocolate brown. In the garden patches there was nothing but cabbage stalks, sick hens and tomato cans. The very smoke coming out of their chimneys was poverty-stricken. Little rags and shreds of

---

①carter：马车夫
②traction-engine：拖拉车
③with relish：津津有味的
④extravagant[IELTS]：不切实际的，奢侈浪费的
⑤eyesore：眼中钉，碍眼的建筑

smoke, so unlike the great silvery plumes that uncurled from the Sheridan's' chimneys. Washerwomen lived in the lane and sweeps and a cobbler①, and a man whose house-front was studded② all over with minute bird-cages. Children swarmed③. When the Sheridans were little they were forbidden to set foot there because of the revolting language and of what they might catch. But since they were grown up, Laura and Laurie on their prowls④ sometimes walked through. It was disgusting and sordid⑤. They came out with a shudder. But still one must go everywhere; one must see everything. So through they went.

"And just think of what the band would sound like to that poor woman," said Laura.

"Oh, Laura!" Jose began to be seriously annoyed. "If you're going to stop a band playing every time some one has an accident, you'll lead a very strenuous⑥ life. I'm every bit as sorry about it as you. I feel just as sympathetic." Her eyes hardened. She looked at her sister just as she used to when they were little and fighting together. "You won't bring a drunken workman back to life by being sentimental," she said softly.

"Drunk! Who said he was drunk?" Laura turned furiously on Jose. She said, just as they had used to say on those occasions, "I'm going straight up to tell mother."

"Do, dear," cooed Jose.

"Mother, can I come into your room?" Laura turned the big glass door-knob.

"Of course, child. Why, what's the matter? What's given you such a colour?" And Mrs. Sheridan turned round from her dressing-table. She was trying on a new hat.

"Mother, a man's been killed," began Laura.

---

①cobbler：修鞋匠，工匠
②studded：镶嵌的
③swarmed[TOEFL]：成群地移动
④prowls：徘徊
⑤sordid：肮脏的
⑥strenuous[TOEFL]：艰苦的，紧张的

"Not in the garden?" interrupted her mother.

"No, no!"

"Oh, what a fright you gave me!" Mrs. Sheridan sighed with relief, and took off the big hat and held it on her knees.

"But listen, mother," said Laura. Breathless, half-choking, she told the dreadful story. "Of course, we can't have our party, can we?" she pleaded.

Chapter 24

"The band and everybody arriving. They'd hear us, mother; they're nearly neighbours!"

To Laura's astonishment her mother behaved just like Jose; it was harder to bear because she seemed amused. She refused to take Laura seriously.

"But, my dear child, use your common sense. It's only by accident we've heard of it. If someone had died there normally—and I can't understand how they keep alive in those poky little holes—we should still be having our party, shouldn't we?

Laura had to say "yes" to that, but she felt it was all wrong. She sat down on her mother's sofa and pinched the cushion frill.

"Mother, isn't it terribly heartless of us?" she asked.

"Darling!" Mrs. Sheridan got up and came over to her, carrying the hat. Before Laura could stop her she had popped it on. "My child!" said her mother, "the hat is yours. It's made for you. It's much too young for me. I have never seen you look such a picture. Look at yourself!" And she held up her hand-mirror.

"But, mother," Laura began again. She couldn't look at herself; she turned aside.

This time Mrs. Sheridan lost patience just as Jose had done.

"You are being very absurd, Laura," she said coldly. "People like that don't expect sacrifices from us. And it's not very sympathetic to spoil everybody's enjoyment as you're doing now."

"I don't understand," said Laura, and she walked quickly out of the room into her own bedroom. There, quite by chance, the first thing she saw was this charming girl in the mirror, in her black hat trimmed with gold daisies, and a long black velvet ribbon. Never had she imagined she could look like that. Is mother right? she thought. And now she hoped her mother was right. Am I being extravagant? Perhaps it was extravagant.

Just for a moment she had another glimpse of that poor woman and those little children, and the body being carried into the house. But it all seemed blurred①, unreal, like a picture in the newspaper. I'll remember it again after the party's over, she decided. And somehow that seemed quite the best plan...

Lunch was over by half-past one. By half-past two they were all ready for the fray②. The green-coated band had arrived and was established in a corner of the tennis-court.

"My dear!" trilled Kitty Maitland, "aren't they too like frogs for words? You ought to have arranged them round the pond with the conductor in the middle on a leaf."

Laurie arrived and hailed them on his way to dress. At the sight of him Laura remembered the accident again. She wanted to tell him. If Laurie agreed with the others, then it was bound to be all right. And she followed him into the hall.

"Laurie!"

"Hallo!" He was half-way upstairs, but when he turned round and saw Laura he suddenly puffed out his cheeks and goggled his eyes at her. "My word, Laura! You do look stunning," said Laurie. "What an absolutely topping hat!"

Laura said faintly "Is it?" and smiled up at Laurie, and didn't tell him after all.

Soon after that people began coming instreams. The band struck up; the hired waiters ran from the house to the marquee. Wherever you looked there were couples strolling③, bending to the flowers, greeting, moving on over the lawn. They were like bright birds that had alighted in the Sheridans' garden for this one afternoon, on their way to—where? Ah, what happiness it is to be with

---

①blurred: 模糊不清的，难以区分的
②fray: 热闹，喧闹
③strolling: 散步，闲逛

people who all are happy, to press hands, press cheeks, smile into eyes.

"Darling Laura, how well you look!"

"What a becoming hat, child!"

"Laura, you look quite Spanish. I've never seen you look so striking."

"And Laura, glowing, answered softly," Have you had tea? Won't you have an ice? The passion-fruit ices really are rather special. "She ran to her father and begged him. Daddy darling, can't the band have something to drink?"

"And the perfect afternoon slowly ripened, slowly faded, slowly its petals closed.

"Never a more delightful garden-party …" "The greatest success …" "Quite the most …"

Laura helped her mother with the good-byes. They stood side by side in the porch till it was all over.

"All over, all over, thank heaven," said Mrs. Sheridan. "Round up the others, Laura. Let's go and have some fresh coffee. I'm exhausted. Yes, it's been very successful. Booth, these parties, these parties! Why will you children insist on giving parties!" And they all of them sat down in the deserted marquee.

"Have a sandwich, daddy dear. I wrote the flag①."

"Thanks." Mr. Sheridan took a bite and the sandwich was gone. He took another. "I suppose you didn't hear of a beastly accident that happened today?" he said.

"My dear," said Mrs. Sheridan, holding up her hand, "we did. It nearly ruined the party. Laura insisted we should put it off."

"Oh, mother!" Laura didn't want to be teased about it.

"It was a horrible affair all the same," said Mr. Sheridan. "The chap was married too. Lived just below in the lane, and leaves a wife and half a dozen kiddies, so they say."

---

①flag：标语

An awkward little silence fell. Mrs. Sheridan fidgeted① with her cup.

Really, it was very tactless of father...

Suddenly she looked up. There on the table were all those sandwiches, cakes, puffs, all uneaten, all going to be wasted. She had one of her brilliant ideas.

"I know," she said. "Let's make up a basket. Let's send that poor creature some of this perfectly good food. At any rate, it will be the greatest treat for the children. Don't you agree? And she's sure to have neighbours calling in and so on. What a point to have it all ready prepared. Laura!" She jumped up. "Get me the big basket out of the stairs cupboard."

"But, mother, do you really think it's a good idea?" said Laura.

Again, how curious, she seemed to be different from them all. To take scraps② from their party. Would the poor woman really like that?

"Of course! What's the matter with you today? An hour or two ago you were insisting on us being sympathetic, and now—"

Question for Discussion

What can you infer from the description of those little cottages the young carter lives contrasted to the Sheridans' big house?

Unit 7 William Somerset Maugham

Appreciation

I forget who it was that recommended men for their soul's good to do each day two things they disliked: it was a wise man, and it is a precept that I have

---

①fidgeted：坐立不安地，烦躁地

②scraps：残羹剩饭

followed scrupulously; for every day I have got up and I have gone to bed.

——William Somerset Maugham

Author

William Somerset Maugham was a British playwright, novelist and short story writer. He was among the most popular writers of his era and reputedly the highest paid author during the 1930s. After losing both his parents by the age of 10, Maugham was raised by a paternal uncle who was emotionally cold. Maugham He later studied medicine at Heidelberg University in Germany, he never practiced, having decided at an early age to devote himself to literature. The first run of his first novel, *Liza of Lambeth* (1897), sold out so rapidly that Maugham gave up medicine to write full-time.

He achieved his first success with the sardonically humorous play *Lady Frederick* (1907). His masterpiece, the partly autobiographical novel of *Human Bondage* appeared in 1915, describes the story of the painful growth to self-realization of a lonely, sensitive physician with a club foot.

His other famous novels include *The Moon and Sixpence* (1919), *Cake and Ale* (1930), and *The Razor's Edge* (1944), *Catalina: A Romance* (1948), etc.

Brief Introduction

The Moon and Sixpence is a short novel of 1919 by William Somerset Maugham based on the life of the painter Paul Gauguin. The story is told in episodic form by the first-person narrator as a series of glimpses into the mind and soul of the central character, Charles Strickland, a middle-aged English stockbroker who abandons his wife and children abruptly to pursue his desire to become an artist.

The novel is written largely from the point of view of the narrator, who is first introduced to the character of Strickland through his (Strickland's) wife and strikes him (the narrator) as unremarkable. Certain chapters are entirely composed of the stories or narrations of others which the narrator himself is recalling from memory (selectively editing or elaborating on certain aspects of dialogue, particularly Strickland's, as Strickland is said by the narrator to be limited in his use of verbiage and tended to use gestures in his expression).

Strickland is a well-off, middle-class stockbroker in London some time in the late 19th or early 20th century. Early in the novel, he leaves his wife and children and goes to Paris, living a destitute but defiantly content life there as an artist (specifically a painter), lodging in run-down hotels and falling prey to both illness and hunger. Strickland, in his drive to express through his art what appears to continually possess and compel him inside, cares nothing for physical comfort and is generally indifferent to his surroundings, but is generously supported while in Paris by a commercially successful but hackneyed Dutch painter, Dirk Stroeve, a friend of the narrator's, who immediately recognizes Strickland's genius. After helping Strickland recover from a life-threatening condition, Stroeve is repaid by having his wife, Blanche, abandon him for Strickland. Strickland later discards the wife (all he really sought from Blanche was a model topaint, not serious companionship, and it is hinted in the novel's dialogue that he indicated this to her and she took the risk anyway), who then commits suicide-yet another human casualty (the first ones being his own established life and those of his wife and children) in Strickland's single-minded pursuit of Art and Beauty.

Selected Reading

The Moon and Sixpence

Chapter One

I confess that when first I made acquaintance with Charles Strickland I never for a moment discerned① that there was in him anything out of the ordinary. Yet now few will be found to deny his greatness. I do not speak of that greatness which is achieved by the fortunate politician or the successful soldier; that is a quality which belongs to the place he occupies rather than to the man; and a change of circumstances reduces it to very discreet② proportions. The Prime

---

①discern[TOEFL]：觉察，了解
②discreet[TOEFL]：谨慎的，小心的

Minister out of office is seen, too often, to have been but a pompous① rhetorician, and the General without an army is but the tame hero of a market town. The greatness of Charles Strickland was authentic. It may be that you do not like his art, but at all events you can hardly refuse it the tribute of your interest. He disturbs and arrests. The time has passed when he was an object of ridicule, and it is no longer a mark of eccentricity② to defend or of perversity③ to extol④ him. His faults are accepted as the necessary complement to his merits. It is still possible to discuss his place in art, and the adulation⑤ of his admirers is perhaps no less capricious⑥ than the disparagement of his detractors; but one thing can never be doubtful, and that is that he had genius. To my mind the most interesting thing in art is the personality of the artist; and if that is singular, I am willing to excuse a thousand faults. I suppose Velasquez was a better painter than El Greco, but custom stales⑦ one's admiration for him: the Cretan, sensual and tragic, proffers the mystery of his soul like a standing sacrifice. The artist, painter, poet, or musician, by his decoration, sublime or beautiful, satisfies the aesthetic sense; but that is akin to the sexual instinct, and shares its barbarity⑧: he lays before you also the greater gift of himself. To pursue his secret has something of the fascination of a detective story. It is a riddle which shares with the universe the merit of having no answer. The most insignificant of Strickland's works suggests a personality which is strange, tormented, and complex; and it is this surely which prevents even those who do not like his pictures from being indifferent to them; it is this which has excited so curious an interest in his life and character.

It was not till four years after Strickland's death that Maurice Huret wrote

---

①pompous：自大的，浮夸的
②eccentricity[TOEFL]：古怪，怪癖
③perversity：变态，任性
④extol[IELTS][TOEFL]：颂扬，赞美
⑤adulation：奉承，吹捧
⑥capricious：反复无常的，任性的
⑦stale[IELTS]：使不新鲜
⑧barbarity：残暴，粗野

that article in the which rescued the unknown painter from oblivion① and blazed the trail which succeeding writers, with more or less docility②, have followed. For a long time no critic has enjoyed in France a more incontestable authority, and it was impossible not to be impressed by the claims he made; they seemed extravagant; but later judgments have confirmed his estimate, and the reputation of Charles Strickland is now firmly established on the lines which he laid down. The rise of this reputation is one of the most romantic incidents in the history of art. But I do not propose to deal with Charles Strickland's work except in so far as it touches upon his character. I cannot agree with the painters who claim superciliously③ docility that the layman can understand nothing of painting, and that he can best show his appreciation of their works by silence and a cheque-book. It is a grotesque④ misapprehension⑤ which sees in art no more than a craft comprehensible perfectly only to the craftsman: art is a manifestation of emotion, and emotion speaks a language that all may understand. But I will allow that the critic who has not a practical knowledge of technique is seldom able to say anything on the subject of real value, and my ignorance of painting is extreme. Fortunately, there is no need for me to risk the adventure, since my friend, Mr. Edward Leggatt, an able writer as well as an admirable painter, has exhaustively discussed Charles Strickland's work in a little book which is a charming example of a style, for the most part, less happily cultivated in England than in France.

Maurice Huret in his famous article gave an outline of Charles Strickland's life which was well calculated to whet⑥ the appetites of the inquiring. With his disinterested passion for art, he had a real desire to call the attention of the wise to a talent which was in the highest degree original; but he was too good a journalist to be unaware that the "human interest" would enable him more

---

①oblivion：遗忘，湮灭
②docility：顺从，孝顺
③superciliously：傲慢地，高傲地
④grotesque：可笑的，怪诞的
⑤misapprehension：误解，误会
⑥whet：刺激，促进

easily to effect his purpose. And when such as had come in contact with Strickland in the past, writers who had known him in London, painters who had met him in the cafes of Montmartre, discovered to their amazement that where they had seen but an unsuccessful artist, like another, authentic genius had rubbed shoulders with them there began to appear in the magazines of France and America a succession of articles, the reminiscences of one, the appreciation of another, which added to Strickland's notoriety, and fed without satisfying the curiosity of the public. The subject was grateful, and the industrious Weitbrecht-Rotholz in his imposing monograph has been able to give a remarkable list of authorities.

The faculty for myth is innate in the human race. It seizes with avidity upon any incidents, surprising or mysterious, in the career of those who have at all distinguished themselves from their fellows, and invents a legend to which it then attaches a fanatical belief. It is the protest of romance against the commonplace of life. The incidents of the legend become the hero's surest passport to immortality. The ironic philosopher reflects with a smile that Sir Walter Raleigh is more safely in shrined in the memory of mankind because he set his cloak for the Virgin Queen to walk on than because he carried the English name to undiscovered countries. Charles Strickland lived obscurely. He made enemies rather than friends. It is not strange, then, that those who wrote of him should haveeked out① their scanty② recollections with a lively fancy, and it is evident that there was enough in the little that was known of him to give opportunity to the romantic scribe; there was much in his life which was strange and terrible, in his character something outrageous③, and in his fate not a little that was pathetic. In due course④ a legend arose of such circumstantiality that the wise historian would hesitate to attack it.

But a wise historian is precisely what the Rev. Robert Strickland is not. He

---

①eke out: 竭力维持
②scanty: 稀有的，仅有的
③outrageous: 无法容忍的，反常的
④in due course: 在适当的时候

wrote his biography avowedly to "remove certain misconceptions which had gained currency" in regard to the later part of his father's life, and which had "caused considerable pain to persons still living." It is obvious that there was much in the commonly received account of Strickland's life to embarrass a respectable family. I have read this work with a good deal of amusement, and upon this I congratulate myself, since it is colorless and dull. Mr. Strickland has drawn the portrait of an excellent husband and father, a man of kindly temper, industrious habits, and moral disposition. The modern clergyman has acquired in his study of the science which I believe is called exegesis① an astonishing facility for explaining things away, but the subtlety with which the Rev. Robert Strickland has "interpreted" all the facts in his father's life which a dutiful son might find it inconvenient to remember must surely lead him in the fullness of time to the highest dignities of the Church. I see already his muscular calves encased in the gaiters episcopal②. It was a hazardous, though maybe gallant thing to do, since it is probable that the legend commonly received has had no small share in the growth of Strickland's reputation; for there are many who have been attracted to his art by the detestation in which they held his character or the compassion with which they regarded his death; and the son's well-meaning efforts threw a singular chill upon the father's admirers. It is due to no accident that when one of his most important works, The Woman of Samaria, was sold at Christie's shortly after the discussion which followed the publication of Mr. Strickland's biography, it fetched POUNDS 235 less than it had done nine months before when it was bought by the distinguished collector whose sudden death had brought it once more under the hammer. Perhaps Charles Strickland's power and originality would scarcely have sufficed to turn the scale if the remarkable mythopoeic faculty of mankind had not brushed aside with impatience a story which disappointed all its craving for the extraordinary. And presently Dr. Weitbrecht-Rotholz produced the work which finally set at rest the misgivings of all lovers of art.

---

①exegesis: 解释，注释
②gaiter episcopal: 牧师穿的绑腿

Chapter 7 20th-Century English Literature

Dr. Weitbrecht-Rotholz belongs to that school of historians which believes that human nature is not only about as bad as it can be, but a great deal worse; and certainly the reader is safer of entertainment in their hands than in those of the writers who take a malicious pleasure in representing the great figures of romance as patterns of the domestic virtues. For my part, I should be sorry to think that there was nothing between Anthony and Cleopatra but an economic situation; and it will require a great deal more evidence than is ever likely to be available, thank God, to persuade me that Tiberius was as blameless a monarch as King George V. Dr. Weitbrecht-Rotholz has dealt in such terms with the Rev. Robert Strickland's innocent biography that it is difficult to avoid feeling a certain sympathy for the unlucky parson. His decent reticence① is branded as hypocrisy②, his circumlocutions are roundly called lies, and his silence is vilified③ as treachery. And on the strength of peccadillos④, reprehensible in an author, but excusable in a son, the Anglo-Saxon race is accused of prudishness⑤, humbug⑥, pretentiousness⑦, deceit, cunning, and bad cooking. Personally I think it was rash of Mr. Strickland, in refuting the account which had gained belief of a certain "unpleasantness" between his father and mother, to state that Charles Strickland in a letter written from Paris had described her as "an excellent woman," since Dr. Weitbrecht-Rotholz was able to print the letter in facsimile⑧, and it appears that the passage referred to ran in fact as follows: God damn my wife. She is an excellent woman. I wish she was in hell. It is not thus that the Church in its great days dealt with evidence that was unwelcome.

Dr. Weitbrecht-Rotholz was an enthusiastic admirer of Charles Strickland,

---

①reticence：沉默寡言
②hypocrisy：虚伪，伪善
③vilify：诽谤，中伤
④peccadillos：轻罪，小过失
⑤prudishness：拘谨
⑥humbug：欺骗
⑦pretentiousness：自负，自命不凡
⑧in facsimile：毫厘不差

and there was no danger that he would whitewash him. He had an unerring① eye for the despicable motive in actions that had all the appearance of innocence. He was a psycho-pathologist②, as well as a student of art, and the subconscious had few secrets from him. No mystic ever saw deeper meaning in common things. The mystic sees the ineffable③, and the psycho-pathologist the unspeakable. There is a singular fascination in watching the eagerness with which the learned author ferrets out every circumstance which may throw discredit on his hero. His heart warms to him when he can bring forward some example of cruelty or meanness, and he exults like an inquisitor④ at the auto da fe of an heretic when with some forgotten story he can confound the filial piety⑤ of the Rev. Robert Strickland. His industry has been amazing. Nothing has been too small to escape him, and you may be sure that if Charles Strickland left a laundry bill unpaid it will be given you in extenso, and if he forebore to return a borrowed half-crown no detail of the transaction will be omitted.

Question for Discussion

What do you think of the decision of the main character, Charles Strickland, who abandons a profitable job and a normal family and go to pursues his dream and passion to become an artist?

Unit 8　David Lodge

Appreciation

And that seems just as well as Bernard struggles to overcome the obstacles that threaten the reunion. But Hawaii holds surprises undreamed of in overcast Rummidge.

---

①unerring：无过失的，不犯错误的
②psycho-pathologist：病理学家
③ineffable：不可言语的
④inquisitor：审问者
⑤filial piety：孝顺，孝道

As honeymooners, families nuclear and fissile, professional freeloaders and amateur cameramen avidly pursue their earthly visions of paradise, Bernard discovers the astonishing possibility of love.

——Penguin Books

很多人,由于人际关系层面上的失败或困难,过着悲伤而失意的生活,而命运已经把打开幸福之门的钥匙递到我们手中,对此,我们该心怀感激。亲爱的,让我们一起把它紧紧握住,永不松手。未来几年充满了不确定性、怀疑和艰巨的挑战,但有一点是明确的——我们稳固的爱情将使我们的道路清晰而笔直,即使困难重重。

——《生逢其时:戴维洛奇回忆录》

Author

David Lodge, in full David John Lodge, is an English novelist, literary critic, playwright, and editor known chiefly for his satiric novels about academic life. He was educated at University College, London, where he took his BA degree in 1955 and his MA in 1959. In between he did National Service in the British Army. He holds a doctorate from the University of Birmingham, where he taught in the English Department from 1960 to 1987, when he retired to become a full-time writer. He retains the title of Honorary Professor of Modern Literature at Birmingham. He is a Fellow of the Royal Society of Literature. In 1989 he was chairman of the judges for the Booker Prize.

Brief Introduction

The story concerns a successful sitcom writer, Laurence Passmore, plagued by middle-age neuroses and a failed marriage. His only problem seems to be an "internal derangement of the knee" but a mid-life crisis had struck and he is discovering angst. *Therapy* is a relatively late work of David Lodge, published in 1995, which reflects the change of Lodge's creative focus to "humanistic care", focusing on the pursuit of the meaning of life.

Selected Reading

Therapy

Chapter 4

I was driving eastwards along the N120 between Astorga and órbigo, a busy arterial road, when I saw her, walking towards me at the edge of the road — a plump①, solitary woman in baggy cotton trousers and a broadbrimmed straw hat. It was only a glimpse, and I was doing seventy miles an hour at the time. I trod on the brakes, provoking an enraged bellow from a huge petrol tanker on my tail. With heavy traffic in both directions on the two-lane road, it was impossible to stop until, after a kilometre or two, I came to a drive-in café with a dirt carpark. I did a three-point turn in a cloud of dust and raced back down the road, wondering if I had hallucinated the figure of Maureen. But no, there she was, plodding along ahead of me on the other side of the road — or there was somebody, largely concealed by a backpack, rolled bedmat and straw hat. I slowed down, provoking more indignant hooting from the cars behind me, and turned to look at the woman's face as I passed. It was Maureen alright. Hearing the noise of the car horns, she threw a casual glance in my direction, but I was concealed behind the Richmobile's dark-tinted glass, and unable to stop. A few hundred yards further on I pulled off the road where the verge was broad enough to park, got out of the car, and crossed the tarmac②. There was an incline at this point, and Maureen was walking downhill towards me. She walked slowly, with a limp, grasping③ a staff which she plonked down on the road in front of her at every second step. Nevertheless her gait was unmistakable, even at a distance. It was as if forty years had been pinched out of my existence, and I was back in Hatchford, outside the florist's shop on the corner of the Five

---

①plump[TOEFL]:丰腴的;微胖的
②Tarmac:(铺设路面的)碎石和沥青的混合材料
③grasp[IELTS][TOEFL]：抓住;理解;领会

Ways, watching her walk down Beecher's Road towards me in her school uniform.

If I had scripted the meeting I would have chosen a more romantic setting — the interior of some cool dark old church, perhaps, or a country road with wildflowers blowing in the breeze along its margins, where the bleating of sheep was the loudest noise. There would certainly have been background music (perhaps an instrumental arrangement of "Too Young"). As it was, we met on the edge of an ugly main road in one of the least attractive bits of Castile, deafened by the noise of tyres and engines, choked by exhaust fumes, and buffeted by gusts of gritty air displaced by passing juggernauts①. As she approached I began to walk towards her, and she took notice of me for the first time. She slowed, hesitated, and stopped, as if she feared my intentions. I laughed, smiled, and held out my arms in what was supposed to be a reassuring gesture. She looked at me with alarm, clearly thinking I was some kind of homicidal maniac② or rapist, and drew back, lifting her staff as if prepared to use it for self-defence.

I stopped, and spoke:

"Maureen! It's all right! It's me, Laurence."

She started. "What?" she said. "Laurence who?"

"Laurence Passmore. Don't you recognize me?"

I was disappointed that she obviously didn't — didn't seem even to remember my name. But as she reasonably explained later, she hadn't given me a thought for donkey's years, whereas I had been thinking of almost nothing else except her for weeks. While I had been scouring③ north-west Spain, hoping to run into her at every turn of the road, my sudden apparition on the N120 was to her as bizarre and surprising as if I had parachuted④ out of the sky, or popped up through a hole in the ground.

---

①juggernaut: 重型卡车
②maniac: 狂人;过激分子
③scour[IELTS][TOEFL]: 寻找;搜查;搜寻
④parachute[TOEFL]: 从天而降;空投;跳伞

I shouted above the howl and whine of traffic, "We used to go around together, years ago. In Hatchford."

Maureen's expression changed and the fear went from her eyes. She squinted at me, as if she were short-sighted, or dazzled by the sun, and took a step forward. "Is it really you? *Laurence Passmore*? What on earth are you doing here?"

"I've been looking for you."

"Why?" she said, and a look of anxiety returned to her face. "There's nothing wrong at home, is there?"

"No, nothing wrong," I reassured her. "Bede's worried about you, but he's OK."

"Bede? When did you see Bede?"

"Just the other day. I was trying to trace you."

"What for?" she said. We were now face to face.

"It's a long story," I said. "Get in the car, and I'll tell you." I gestured to my sleek① silver pet, crouched on the opposite verge. She gave it a momentary glance, and shook her head.

"I'm doing a pilgrimage," she said.

"I know."

"I don't go in cars."

"Make an exception today," I said. "You look as if you could do with a lift."

In truth she looked a wreck. As we parleyed, I was mentally coming to terms with the sad fact that Maureen was no longer the Maureen of my memories and fantasies. She had reached that point in a woman's life when her looks begin irretrievably to desert her. Sally hasn't quite reached it, and Amy is still several years on the right side of it. Both of them, anyway, are resisting the ageing process with everything short of plastic surgery, but Maureen seemed to have surrendered② without putting up much of a fight. There were crowsfeet at

---

①sleek[IELTS]:光亮的;阔气的

②surrender[TOEFL]:投降;屈服;屈从

the corners of her eyes, and bags under them. Her cheeks, once so plump and smooth, were slack jowls; her neck was creased like an old garment; and her figure had gone soft and shapeless, with no perceptible waistline between the cushiony mounds of her bosom and the broad beam of her hips. The general effect had not been improved by the weeks and months she had spent on the road: her nose was sunburnt and peeling, her hair lank and unkempt, her knuckles grubby and her nails broken. Her clothes were dusty and sweat-stained. I must admit that her appearance was a shock for which the posed and retouched photographs in Bede's living-room had not prepared me. I daresay the years have been even harder on me, but Maureen hadn't been nurturing any illusions to the contrary.

As she hesitated, leaning forward in her scuffed trainers to balance the weight of her backpack, I noticed that she had placed some lumps of sponge rubber under the shoulder straps to protect her collarbone from chafing. For some reason this seemed the most pathetic detail of all in her general appearance. I felt an overwhelming rush of tenderness towards her, a desire to look after her and rescue her from this daft, self-lacerating ordeal. "Just to the next village," I said, "Somewhere we can get a cold drink." The sun was basting my bald pate and I could feel sweat trickling① down my torso inside my shirt. I added coaxingly, "The car's air-conditioned."

Maureen laughed, wrinkling her sunburned nose in the way I remembered so well. "It had better be," she said. "I'm sure I stink to high heaven."

She sighed and stretched out luxuriously in the front seat of the Richmobile as we moved off down the highway with the silent speed of an electric train. "Well, this is very swish," she said, looking round the interior of the car. "What make is it?" I told her. "We have a Volvo, at home," she said. "Bede says they're very safe."

"Safety isn't everything," I said.

"No, it isn't," she said, with a little giggle.

"This is a dream come true, you, know," I said. "I've been fantasizing for

---

① trickle [TOEFL]: 淌;滴

months about driving you in this car."

"Have you?" She gave me a shy, puzzled smile. I didn't tell her that in my fantasies she was still in her teens.

A few kilometres further on we found a bar with some chairs and tables outside in the shade of an old oak, away from the of television and the hiss of the coffee machine. Over a beer and a *citron pressé* we had the first of many conversations that slowly filled in the information gap of thirty-five years. The first thing Maureen wanted to know, naturally enough, was why I had sought her out. I gave her a condensed account of what I have already written in these pages: that my life was in a mess, personally and professionally, that I had been suddenly reminded of our relationship and how shabbily I had treated her at the end of it, and had become consumed with a desire to see her again. "To get absolution," I said.

Maureen blushed① under her sunburn. "Goodness me, Laurence, you don't have to ask for that. It was nearly forty years ago. We were children, practically."

"But it must have hurt, at the time."

"Oh, yes, of course. I cried myself to sleep for ages "There you are, then."

"But young girls are always doing that. You were the first boy I cried over, but not the last." She laughed. "You look surprised." "You mean, Bede?" I said.

"Oh no, not *Bede*" She screwed up her face in a humorous grimace. "Can you imagine anybody crying over Bede? No, there were others, before him. A wildly handsome registrar I was hopelessly in love with, like every other student nurse at the hospital. I doubt if he even knew my name. And after I qualified there was a houseman I had an affair with." "You mean… in the full sense of the word?" I stared incredulously.

"I slept with him, if that's what you mean. I don't know why I'm telling you all these intimate details, but somehow the older you get, the less you care

---

①blush[TOEFL]:脸红;涨红了脸

what people know, don't you find? It's the same with your body. In hospital it's always the young patients who are most embarrassed about being washed and bedpanned and so on. The old ones couldn't give a damn."

"But what about your religion? When you had the affair."

"Oh, I knew I was committing a mortal sin. But I did it anyway, because I loved him. I thought he would marry me, you see. He said he would. But he changed his mind, or perhaps he was lying. So after I got over it I married Bede instead."

"Did you sleep with him first?" The question sounded crude as I formulated it, but curiosity overcame good manners.

Maureen rocked with laughter. "Good heavens, no! Bede would have been shocked at the very idea."

I pondered these surprising revelations in silence for a few moments. "So you haven't been bearing a grudge against me all this time?" I said at length.

"Of course not! Honestly, I haven't given you a thought for... I don't know how many years."

I think she was trying to reassure me, but I was hurt, I have to admit. "You haven't followed my career, then?" I said.

"No, should I have done? Are you terribly famous?"

"Not famous, exactly. But I've had some success as a TV writer. Do you ever watch *The People Next Door*?"

"Is that a comedy programme — the kind where you can hear a lot of people laughing but you can't see them?"

"It's a sitcom, yes."

"We tend to avoid those, I'm afraid. But now I know you write for it..."

"I write all of it. It was my idea. I'm known as Tubby Passmore," I said, desperate to strike some spark of recognition.

"Are you really?" Maureen laughed and wrinkled her nose. "Tubby!"

"But I'd rather you called me Laurence," I said, regretting the revelation①. "It reminds me of the old days."

---

①revelation[IELTS]:披露;揭露

But from then on she called me Tubby. She seemed delighted with the name and said she couldn't get it out of her head. "I try to say 'Laurence', but 'Tubby' comes out of my mouth instead," she said.

The day we met, Maureen was aiming to get to Astorga. She refused to let me drive her there from the café, but, admitting that her leg was painful, agreed to let me take her backpack on ahead. She was planning to spend the night at the local *refugio*, uninvitingly described in the pilgrim's guidebook as an "unequipped sports hall". Maureen pulled a face. "That means no showers." I said I would be bitterly disappointed if she wouldn't be my guest for dinner on this red-letter day, and she could shower in my hotel room. She accepted the offer with good grace, and we arranged to meet in the porch of the Cathedral. I drove to Astorga and checked into a hotel, booking an extra room for Maureen in the hope of persuading her to take it. (She did.) While I waited for Maureen I did the tourist bit in Astorga.

Maureen turned up at the Cathedral about three hours after we had parted, smiling and saying that, without the weight of her backpack, the walk had been like a Sunday-afternoon stroll. I asked to see her leg and didn't much like what I saw under the grimy[①] bandage. The calf was bruised and discoloured and the ankle joint swollen. "I think you should show that to a doctor," I said. Maureen said she had seen a doctor in León. He had diagnosed strained ligaments[②], recommended rest, and given her some ointment which had helped a little. She had rested the leg for four days, but it was still troubling her. "You need more like four months," I said. "I know a bit about this sort of injury. It won't go away unless you pack in the pilgrimage."

"I'm not going to give up now," she said. "Not after getting this far."

I knew her well enough not to waste breath trying to persuade her to drop out and go home. Instead I devised a plan to help her get to Santiago as comfortably as possible with honour. Each day I would drive with her pack to an agreed rendezvous, and book us into some modest inn or b. & b. Maureen had

---

①grimy[IELTS]:肮脏的;满是灰尘的
②ligament:韧带

no principled objection to such accommodation. She had treated herself to it occasionally, and the *refugios* were, she said, becoming increasingly crowded and unpleasant the nearer she got to Santiago. But her funds were low, and she hadn't wanted to ring up Bede and ask him to send her more money. She agreed to let me pay for our rooms on the understanding that she would repay her share when we got back to England, and kept scrupulous[①] note of our expenses.

We inched our way to Santiago in very short stages. Even without her backpack, Maureen wasn't capable of walking more than ten to twelve kilometres a day without discomfort, and it took her up to four hours to cover even that modest distance. Usually, after arranging our accommodation, I would walk back along the Camino eastwards to meet her, and keep her company on the home stretch. It pleased me that my knee stood up well to this exercise, even when the going was steep and rugged. In fact, I realized that I hadn't felt a single twinge in it since I got to St Jean Pied-de-Port. "It's St James," Maureen said, when I remarked on this. "It's a well-known phenomenon. He helps you. I'd never have got this far without him. I remember when I was climbing the pass through the Pyrenees, soaked[②] to the skin and utterly exhausted, feeling I couldn't go any further and would just roll into a ditch and die, I felt a force like a hand in the small of the back pushing me on, and before I knew where I was, I found myself at the top."

I wasn't sure how serious she was. When I asked her if she believed St James was really buried in Santiago, she shrugged[③] and said, "I don't know. We'll never know for sure, one way or the other." I said, "Doesn't it bother you that millions of people may have been coming here for centuries all because of a misprint?" I was showing off a bit of knowledge gleaned from one of my guidebooks: apparently the original association of St James with Spain all goes back to a scribe who wrote mistakenly that the Apostle's patch was

---

①scrupulous[IELTS]:一丝不苟的;细致的
②soak[IELTS]:浸透;湿透
③shrug[IELTS]:耸耸肩膀

"Hispaniam" instead of "Hierusalem" (i.e., Jerusalem.) "No," she said. "I think he's around the place somewhere. With so many people walking to Santiago to pay him homage, he could hardly stay away, could he?" But there was a twinkle in her eye as she spoke of these things, as if it were a private joke or tease, designed to scandalize① Protestant sceptics like me.

There was nothing frivolous about her commitment to the pilgrimage, however "*It's absurd, quite absurd,*" I remembered Bede saying, but the word had a Kierkegaardian resonance for me which he didn't intend. In the mediaeval town of Villafranca there's a church dedicated to St James with a porch known as the *Puerta del Perdón*, the Doorway of Pardon, and according to tradition if a pilgrim was ill and made it as far as this door, he could turn back and go home with all the graces and blessings of a fully completed pilgrimage. I pointed out this loophole② to Maureen when we got to Villafranca, and pressed her to take advantage of it. She laughed at first, but became quite annoyed when I persisted. After that I never attempted to dissuade her from trying to get to Santiago.

To tell the truth, I would have been almost as disappointed as Maureen herself if she had failed to make it. The pilgrimage, even in the bastardized, motorized form in which I was doing it, had begun to lay its spell upon me. I sensed, if only fragmentarily, what Maureen had experienced more deeply and intensely in the course of her long march from Le Puy. "You seem to drop out of time. You pay no attention to the news. The images you see on television in bars and cafés, of politicians and car bombs and bicycle races, don't hold your attention for more than a few seconds. All that matters are the basics: feeding yourself, not getting dehydrated③, healing your blisters, getting to the next stopping-place before it gets too hot, or too cold, or too wet. Surviving. At first you think you'll go mad with loneliness and fatigue, but after a while you resent the presence of other people, you would rather walk on your own, be alone

---

①scandalize:使震惊;使愤慨
②loophole:可钻的空子
③dehydrated[TOEFL]:使(身体)脱水;失水

with your own thoughts, and the pain in your feet."

"You wish I wasn't here, then?" I said.

"Oh no, I was almost at the end of my tether when you turned up, Tubby. I'd never have got this far without you."

I frowned, like Ryan Giggs when he's made a goal with a perfect cross. But Maureen wiped the frown off my face when she added, "It was like a miracle. St James again."

In our slow, looping dawdle① along the Camino we were frequently overtaken by younger, fitter, or fresher walkers. The nearer we got to Santiago, the more of them there were. The annual climax of the pilgrimage, the feast of St James on 25th July, was only a couple of weeks away, and everybody was anxious to get there in good time. Sometimes, from a high point on the road, you could look down on the Camino ribboning for miles ahead, with pilgrims in ones and twos and larger clusters strung out along it like beads as far as the horizon, just as it must have looked in the Middle Ages.

The days passed in a slow, regular rhythm. We rose early, so that Maureen could set off in the cool of the early morning. She usually arrived at our rendezvous② around noon. After a long, leisurely Spanish lunch we retired for a siesta and slept through the heat of the afternoon, coming to life again in the evening, when we would take the air with the natives, snacking③ in *tapas* bars and sampling the local *vino*. I can't describe how at ease I felt in Maureen's company, how quickly we seemed to resume our old familiarity. Although we talked a lot, we were often content to be together in a companionable silence, as if we were enjoying the sunset years of a long happy life together. Other people certainly assumed we were a married couple, or at least a couple; and the hotel staff always looked mildly surprised that we were occuping separate rooms.

---

①dawdle:拖延;磨蹭
②rendezvous:约会地点
③snack[IELTS]:吃点心(快餐或小吃)

Questions for Discussion

1. Discuss problems faced by Passmore as an embodiment of the middle-class middle-aged in the England.
2. Discuss the application of dramatic monologue in *Therapy*.

Appreciation

A wonderfully entertaining-and ultimately touching-introduction to a masterly writer's book.

——Penguin Books

洛奇在一系列优秀的文学作品中,以幽默的笔调探索人生的意义,寓训诫于巧妙的构思之中。该书为此类作品锦上添花。

——作家出版社

Brief Introduction

Paradise News is the ninth novel by David Lodge, a leading author of academic fiction. Bernard, a 40-year-old theology lecturer who suffers from intimacy phobia, accompanies his reluctant father to visit his ailing aunt in Hawaii. Unfortunately, the day after their arrival, Bernard's father is taken to hospital in a car accident. Bernard takes care of his father and aunt and happens to know a family scandal that has been hidden for years. After communication, the Walsh family reconcile. Hawaii is like a paradise on earth for Bernard where he regains confidence, hope and love.

Selected Reading

Paradise News

Part 3　Chapter 2

The next day, after they had shared an early lunch together, Tess took a cab to St Joseph's, and Bernard drove out to Makai Manor. The plan was that he would leave his car there and ride in the hired ambulance with Ursula, to and from the hospital, while Tess kept their father company. It wasn't a fully equipped ambulance like the one in which Bernard had accompanied his father to St Joseph's on the day of the accident, but a high-sided vehicle used for transporting patients in wheelchairs, with an electrically operated lift at the rear end. Ursula was excited and nervous. Her hair had been washed and waved that morning; her withered, yellow face was heavily powdered and her lips outlined with lipstick; the effect was well-intentioned but somewhat gruesome. She wore a silky blue and green *muu-muu*, and a fresh sling for her arm. A rosary of amber beads on a silver chain was wound around her wasted fingers.

"This was my mother's," she said. "She gave it to me when I left home to marry Rick. I think she thought of it as a kind of leash that would bring me back into the fold one day. She had a great devotion to Our Lady, like your own mother, Bernard. I thought Jack might like to have it."

Bernard asked if she didn't want to keep the rosary for herself.

"I want to give Jack something, something to remind him of today, when he goes back to England. I couldn't think of anything else. Anyway, I won't be needing it much longer."

"Nonsense," Bernard said with forced cheerfulness. "You're looking miles better today."

"Well, it feels good to be outside Makai Manor for a change, nice as it is. The sea looks so beautiful. I miss the sea."

They were running along the cliff-top road near Diamond Head at this point. Bernard asked her if she would like to stop somewhere and look at the view.

"Maybe on the way back," said Ursula. "I don't want to keep Jack waiting." Her fingers nervously twisted and untwisted the strands of the rosary. "Where are we meeting him? Has he got a private room?"

"No, he shares it with another man. But there's a nice sort of terrace① outside, where patients can walk up and down, or sit in the shade. I thought we'd go there. It will be more private."

When they arrived at St Joseph's, the driver lowered Ursula, strapped② into her wheelchair, to the ground, and pushed her up a ramp into the hospital's elevator. When they reached the right floor, Bernard asked the man to wait for them below, and took over the wheelchair. He went first to his father's room, but the bed was empty. Mr Winterspoon looked up from his miniature TV to say that Mr Walsh and his daughter were outside on the terrace. Bernard pushed the wheelchair down a corridor③ and through a pair of swing doors, out into the open air, round a corner—and there they were, at the end of the terrace. Mr Walsh was also seated in a wheelchair, and Tess was stooping to adjust his dressing-gown round his knees.

"Jack!" Ursula croaked, much too quietly for him to have heard, but he must have sensed her presence, for he looked round sharply, and said something to Tess. She smiled and waved and began to push the wheelchair towards Bernard and Ursula, so that they all met, almost collided④, in the middle of the terrace, in a clamour⑤ of laughter and tears and exclamations. Mr Walsh had obviously decided to control the emotion of the situation with a determined jocularity⑥.

"Whoa!" he exclaimed, as the two wheelchairs converged⑦, "Not so fast!

---

① terrace [IELTS] [TOEFL]:露天平台,梯田

② strap [IELTS] [TOEFL]:用带子系(或捆、扎、扣)好,带子

③ corridor [IELTS]:走廊

④ collide [TOEFL]:相撞,冲突

⑤ clamour:嘈杂声

⑥ jocularity:幽默

⑦ converge [TOEFL]:(人或车辆)汇集,(思想、政策、目标等)十分相似,相同

I don't want another traffic accident."

"Jack! Jack! It's wonderful to see you at last," Ursula cried, leaning across the interlocked wheels to clutch his arm and kiss his cheek.

"You too, Ursula. But aren't we a sight for sore eyes, propped up in these contraptions① like a couple of Guy Fawkes dolls?"

"You look marvellous, Jack. How's your hip?"

"It's mending well, I'm told. I don't know whether I'll ever be the same man again, mind you. And how are you, my dear?"

Ursula shrugged. "You can see for yourself," she said.

"Aye, you're very thin. I'm very sorry about your illness, Ursula. Don't cry, don't cry." He patted her bony hand nervously between his own.

Bernard and Tess parked the wheelchairs in a quiet, shady corner of the terrace, which was a kind of paved cloister, shaded by flowering vines growing over an open latticed roof. It had for Mr Walsh the attraction that he was allowed to smoke there, and he immediately broke out a packet of Pall Malls and offered them round. "No takers?" he said. "Well, I'll force myself, to keep the flies off the rest of you."

After some animated chatter about Ursula's ambulance ride, Mr Walsh's opinion of St Joseph's hospital, the view from the terrace, and similar trivia, a silence fell.

"Isn't it silly," Ursula sighed. "There's so much to talk about, you don't know where to start."

"We'll leave you two alone for a little while," said Bernard.

"There's no need," said his father. "You and Tess aren't in the way—are they, Ursula?"

Ursula murmured something non-committal. Tess supported Bernard's proposal, however, and they wandered off, leaving the two old people facing each other in their wheelchairs. Mr Walsh looked after them with a faintly cornered expression.

---

①contraption:奇异的机械

Bernard and Tess walked to the end of the terrace, and leaned on the balustrade①, looking out over the roofs of suburban houses shimmering in the heat, at the freeway with its unceasing currents of traffic, and in the distance the hazy flat industrial landscape around Honolulu harbour. A jumbo jet②, small as a child's toy, rose slowly into the sky and circled over the ocean before heading eastwards.

"Well," said Bernard. "We made it. We finally brought them together."

"It's nice of you to say "us", Bernard," said Tess. "You're the one who made it happen."

"Well, I'm very glad to have you here, anyway."

"As you know, my first reaction was that it was a mad idea, bringing Daddy all this way to see Ursula, and when I heard that he'd been knocked down, I thought it was a judgment on me for having changed my mind," said Tess, with the air of someone who had something she had decided to get off her chest. "But now I'm here, and knowing what I know now about their relationship in the past, I think you were right. It would have been terrible if Ursula had died alone, unreconciled, all these thousands of miles from home."

Bernard nodded. "I think it would have preyed on Daddy's mind, as he gets older. When he faces death himself."

"Don't," said Tess, clutching her arms, and hunching her shoulders. "I don't like to think of Daddy dying."

"They say," said Bernard, "that when your second parent dies, you finally accept your own mortality. I wonder if it's true. To accept death, to be ready for death whenever it happens, without letting that acceptance spoil your appetite for life—that seems to me the hardest trick of all."

They were silent for a few moments. Then Tess said: "When Mummy died, I said an unforgivable thing to you, Bernard, at the funeral."

"You're forgiven."

"I blamed you for Mummy's death. I shouldn't have. It was very wrong of

①jumbo jet:巨型喷气机
②balustrade:栏杆

me."

"That's all right," he said. "You were upset. We were all upset. I shouldn't have walked out. We should have talked. We should have talked a lot more, on many occasions."

Tess turned and gave him a quick kiss on the cheek. "Well, they seem to have found plenty to talk about at last," she said, nodding over his shoulder in the direction of Jack and Ursula, who were, indeed, deep in conversation.

They went for a rather aimless walk around the hospital's grounds, mostly car-park, and then sought out Father Luke. He showed them the chapel①, a cool, pleasant room, its white walls and polished hardwood furniture splashed with blotches of colour from the modern stained-glass windows. "I thought, as your aunt is in a wheelchair, we'd administer the sacrament② in here," he said. "Of course, it's usually done with the patient in bed, but in this case... After the anointing③, will you all be taking communion with Mrs Riddell?"

"Yes," said Tess.

"No," said Bernard.

"I could give you a blessing, if you like," said the priest. "I always invite people at mass who can't communicate for any reason, divorce for instance, to come to the altar for a blessing."

Bernard hesitated, then acquiesced. He was beginning to feel better disposed towards Father McPhee, who had put himself out to be helpful.

When they went back to the terrace, they found Mr Walsh smoking reflectively, gazing out over the balustrade at the sea, and Ursula asleep in her wheelchair.

"How long has she been asleep?" Bernard exclaimed, afraid that it had been for the duration④ of their absence.

"About five minutes ago," his father said. "She just nodded off in the

---

①chapel [IELTS] [TOEFL]:(教堂内的)分堂,小教堂
②sacrament:圣礼(如婚配、圣洗或圣餐等)
③anoint:涂(圣油、圣水)
④duration [IELTS] [TOEFL]:期间

middle of something I was saying."

"She does that occasionally," said Bernard. "She's very weak, poor thing."

"Did you have a nice talk, before that, Daddy?" Tess asked.

"Yes,' he said. 'There was a lot to talk about."

"There sure was," said Ursula. She seemed to have no awareness that she had been asleep.

On the way back to Makai Manor, Bernard asked their driver to pull into the clifftop parking place near Diamond Head and lower Ursula's wheelchair to the ground. Then he pushed her to the parapet①, so that she could look out over the blue and emerald sea, and at the dozen or so windsurfers scudding across its surface.

"What a wonderful day it's been," she said. "I feel so at peace. I could die now, quite happily."

"Don't be silly, Ursula," he said. "You've plenty of life in you yet."

"No, I mean it. I daresay it won't last for long, this feeling. I expect the fear and depression will come back tonight, as usual. But just now... I read in a magazine, the other day, that the old Hawaiians believed that when you died, your soul jumped off from a high cliff, into the sea of eternity. They had a special word for it, I can't remember it now, but it means, "jumping-off place". D'you think this was one?"

"I wouldn't be surprised," said Bernard.

"I have the strangest feeling that if I threw myself over the edge of this cliff now, I wouldn't feel any pain or terror. My body would fall off me like clothing, and flutter gently down to the beach, and my soul would fly up to heaven."

"Well, please don't try it," Bernard joked. "I think it would upset the people here." He gestured at the tourists who stood nearby, clicking and whirring with their cameras.

"I feel so strangely... light," said Ursula. "It must be the effect of

---

①parapet：防护矮墙

unburdening myself to Jack. Unburden is a good word. That's just what it feels like."

"So you talked about Sean, then?"

"Yes. Jack remembered that summer, of course. Perhaps not as vividly as I do, but as soon as I mentioned that old shed at the bottom of our garden in Cork, I could see from the expression on his face that he knew what I was going to say. He said that, at the time, he was frightened to report Sean to our Father and Mother, because Sean had got up to some dirty games with him, too, a couple of years before, and he was afraid it would all come out and all of us would be thrashed within an inch of our lives. Maybe he was right. He was a frightening man, when he was angry, I can tell you, our Father. Jack said he honestly thought I was too young to know what Sean was doing, too young to be harmed by it, and he assumed that in time I forgot all about it. He seemed genuinely shocked when I told him it had destroyed my marriage and pretty well ruined my life. He kept saying, "I'm sorry, Ursula, I'm sorry." I believe he is, too. I guess that's why he asked Father Luke if he could go to confession this afternoon, before he took communion. It was a beautiful service, wasn't it, the anointing? Some of the words were so beautiful, I wish I could remember them."

"I think I probably can,' said Bernard. 'I said them often enough. *Through this holy anointing, and through his own loving mercy, may the Lord forgive all the faults that you have committed through your eyes.*" And then the same for the nose, mouth, hands and feet."

"As matter of interest, how can you sin with your nose?"

Bernard guffawed. "Oh, that was a favourite teaser in Moral Theology, when I was a student."

"And what was the answer?"

"The textbooks suggested that you could overindulge in smelling perfumes and nosegays. It didn't seem very convincing. And there was a dark hint about lust being excited by bodily scents, but they didn't go very deeply into that in the seminary, for obvious reasons." He had a sharp memory-picture of himself kneeling at Yolande's feet with his face buried in her crotch, inhaling what smelled like the salty air of a tidal beach.

"That wasn't the bit I was thinking of, anyway," she said. "There was a lesson..."

"The Epistle of St James." "*Is any of you sick?*"

"That's it. Do you know how it goes?"

"*Is there any of you sick: let her call for the elders of the Church, and let them pray over her, anointing her with oil in the name of the Lord; and the prayer of faith will save the sick woman, and the Lord will raise her up; and if she has sinned, she will be forgiven. Therefore confess your sins to one another, and pray for one another, that you may be healed.*"

"That's it. What a pity you aren't a priest any more, Bernard, you say the words so beautifully. Did Father Luke say "woman" when he read that this afternoon?"

"No," said Bernard. "I changed it, for you."

Ursula was exhausted by the time they got back to Makai Manor. "Exhausted, but content," she said, when she was back in her bed. She stretched out her hand to clasp his. "Dear Bernard! Thankyou thankyou thankyou!"

"I'd better leave you to rest," he said.

"Yes," she said, but she did not release his hand.

"I'll come tomorrow."

"I know you will. I've come to count on it. I dread the day when you'll walk out that door for the last time. When I'll know you won't be coming back the next day, because you'll be in an airplane, on your way back to England."

"I don't know yet when I'll be leaving," he said, "so there's no point upsetting yourself about it. It all depends on Daddy's progress."

"He told me he expects to be discharged from the hospital next week."

"Tess could take him home, perhaps. I could stay on a few extra days."

"You're very sweet, Bernard. But sooner or later you'll have to go. You have a job to go back to."

"Yes," he admitted. "There's an induction① course at the College, for African and Asian students, coming up soon. I said I'd run it. It's supposed to introduce them to life in Britain," he elaborated, hoping to distract Ursula from her melancholy train of thought. "We have to demonstrate how to light a gas ring and how to eat a kipper, and take them to Marks and Spencer's to buy winter underwear."

Ursula smiled wanly. "I just hope I don't live too long after you've gone."

"You mustn't say that, Ursula. It's upsetting for me as well as for you."

"Sorry. I'm just trying to condition myself to doing without you. I've been spoiled these last couple of weeks, having you here, and then seeing Jack and Teresa. When you've all flown away, I'm going to feel terribly lonely."

"Who knows, I may come back to Hawaii."

Ursula shook her head. "It's too far, Bernard. You can't just hop into an airplane and fly halfway round the world because I'm feeling lonely."

"There's always the telephone," he said.

"Yes, there's always the telephone," Ursula said drily.

"And there's always Sophie Knoepflmacher," he joked. "I'm sure she'd be glad to visit you, when Daddy has gone."

Ursula made a grimace.

"There's somebody else who lives in Honolulu," he said. "Someone I know who would love to visit you—and I know you'd like her." A vivid proleptic image flashed into his head, of Yolande in her red dress, bounding into the room, swinging her brown tennis-player's arms, radiating health and energy, smiling at Ursula and pulling up a chair to talk. They would talk of himself, he thought fondly. "I'll bring her out to meet you tomorrow. Her name's Yolande Miller. She was the driver of the car that knocked Daddy down—that he walked into, I should say. That's how we met. We've become quite friendly since. Well, very friendly, actually." He blushed②. "You remember when you asked me to go to

---

①induction [IELTS]：入门
②blush [TOEFL]：(因尴尬或害羞)脸红

the Moana for cocktails①, to celebrate the discovery of your IBM shares? Well I didn't tell you at the time, but I invited Yolande." Without going into explicit② detail, he made clear that they had been seeing a lot of each other since.

"Well, Bernard, you're a dark horse!" said Ursula, highly amused. "So you have another motive for coming back to Hawaii, apart from seeing your poor old aunt."

"Absolutely," said Bernard. "The only problem is the fare."

"I'll pay your fare, any time you want to come," said Ursula. "After all, I'm leaving you all my money, anyway."

"Oh, I wouldn't do that," said Bernard.

"Why not? Who deserves it more than you do? Who needs it more than you?"

"Patrick," said Bernard. "Tess's Patrick is completely helpless."

Questions for Discussion

1. Analyse the symbol of the sea in the selected passage.
2. Discuss the function of "communication" in the selected passage.

Unit 9 J. K. Rowling

Appreciation

The knowledge that you have emerged wiser and stronger from setbacks means that you are, ever after, secure in your ability to survive. You will never truly know yourself, or the strength of your relationships, until both have been tested by adversity. Such knowledge is a true gift, for all that it is painfully won, and it has been worth more to me than any qualification I ever earned.

—— J. K. Rowling

---

①cocktail：鸡尾酒
②explicit [TOEFL]：直截了当的

Author

J. K. Rowling, in full Joanne Kathleen Rowling, is a British author. She is best known for her popular seven-book Harry Potter series, available in more than 200 countries and 60 languages. Film versions of the books were released in 2001-11 and became some of the top-grossing movies in the world. In 2007, Rowling was honoured as Companion of Honour, the highest rank of the British medal and title. Rowling makes great contributions to the development of children's literature in the world and becomes the first winner of the Hans Christian Andersen Literature Award in 2010.

Brief Introduction

Harry Potter and the Philosopher's Stone published in 1997 is an immediate success, appealing to both children, who are its intended audience, and adults. Featuring vivid descriptions and an imaginative story line, it followed the adventures of the unlikely hero Harry Potter, a lonely orphan who discovers that he is actually a wizard and enrols in the Hogwarts School of Witchcraft and Wizardry. It was the first book written by Rowling, and she was praised for creating well-rounded characters and a fully realized wizard universe that coexisted with the present world. The book received numerous awards, including the British Book Award for Children's Fiction.

Selected Reading

Harry Potter and the Philosopher's Stone

Chapter 16

They were standing on the edge of a huge chessboard, behind the black chessmen, which were all taller than they were and carved from what looked like black stone. Facing them, way across the chamber, were the white pieces. Harry, Ron and Hermione shivered slightly — the towering white chessmen had no faces.

"Now what do we do?" Harry whispered.

"It's obvious, isn't it?" said Ron. "We've got to play our way across the room."

Behind the white pieces they could see another door.

"How?" said Hermione nervously.

"I think," said Ron, "we're going to have to be chessmen."

He walked up to a black knight and put his hand out to touch the knights horse. At once, the stone sprang to life①. The horse pawed the ground and the knight turned his helmeted head to look down at Ron.

"Do we — er — have to join you to get across?"

The black knight nodded. Ron turned to the other two.

"This needs thinking about..." he said. "I suppose we've got to take the place of three of the black pieces...."

Harry and Hermione stayed quiet, watching Ron think. Finally he said, "Now, don't be offended or anything, but neither of you are that good at chess—"

"We're not offended," said Harry quickly. "Just tell us what to do."

"Well, Harry, you take the place of that bishop, and Hermione, you go there instead of that castle."

"What about you?"

"I'm going to be a knight," said Ron.

The chessmen seemed to have been listening, because at these words a knight, a bishop, and a castle turned their backs on the white pieces and walked off the board, leaving three empty squares that Harry, Ron, and Hermione took.

"White always plays first in chess," said Ron, peering across the board. "Yes... look..."

A white pawn② had moved forward two squares.

Ron started to direct the black pieces. They moved silently wherever he sent them. Harry's knees were trembling. What if they lost?

---

①spring to life：启动

②pawn：（国际象棋的）兵，典当

"Harry— move diagonally① four squares to the right."

Their first real shock came when their other knight was taken. The white queen smashed him to the floor and dragged him off the board, where he lay quite still, facedown.

"Had to let that happen," said Ron, looking shaken. "Leaves you free to take that bishop, Hermione, go on."

Every time one of their men was lost, the white pieces showed no mercy. Soon there was a huddle of limp black players slumped along the wall. Twice, Ron only just noticed in time that Harry and Hermione were in danger. He himself darted② around the board, taking almost as many white pieces as they had lost black ones.

"We're nearly there," he muttered suddenly. "Let me think— let me think..."

The white queen turned her blank face toward him.

"Yes..." said Ron softly, "it's the only way... I've got to be taken."

"NO!" Harry and Hermione shouted.

"That's chess!" snapped Ron. "You've got to make some sacrifices! I make my move and she'll take me— that leaves you free to checkmate the king, Harry!"

"But—"

"Do you want to stop Snape or not?"

"Ron—"

"Look, if you don't hurry up, he'll already have the Stone!"

There was no alternative.

"Ready?" Ron called, his face pale but determined. "Here I go— now, don't hang around③ once you've won."

He stepped forward, and the white queen pounced. She struck Ron hard across the head with her stone arm, and he crashed to the floor— Hermione

---

①diagonally [TOEFL]：斜对地
②dart [TOEFL]：突进，(朝某人猛然)看一眼
③hang around：(在某处)等待

screamed but stayed on her square— the white queen dragged Ron to one side. He looked as if he'd been knocked out.

Shaking, Harry moved three spaces to the left.

The white king took off his crown and threw it at Harry's feet. They had won. The chessmen parted and bowed, leaving the door ahead clear. With one last desperate look back at Ron, Harry and Hermione charged① through the door and up the next passageway.

"What if he's—?"

"He'll be all right," said Harry, trying to convince himself.

"What do you reckon's② next?"

"We've had Sprout's, that was the Devil's Snare; Flitwick must've put charms on the keys; McGonagall transfigured the chessmen to make them alive; that leaves Quirrell's spell, and Snape's . . ."

They had reached another door.

"All right?" Harry whispered.

"Go on."

Harry pushed it open.

A disgusting smell filled their nostrils, making both of them pull their robes up over their noses. Eyes watering, they saw, flat on the floor in front of them, a troll③ even larger than the one they had tackled, out cold with a bloody lump on its head.

"I'm glad we didn't have to fight that one," Harry whispered as they stepped carefully over one of its massive legs. "Come on, I can't breathe."

He pulled open the next door, both of them hardly daring to look at what came next— but there was nothing very frightening in here, just a table with seven differently shaped bottles standing on it in a line.

"Snape's," said Harry. "What do we have to do?"

They stepped over the threshold, and immediately a fire sprang up behind

---

①charge［IELTS］:向……方向冲去,控告,收(费)

②reckon［TOEFL］［IELTS］:认为,估算

③troll:(斯堪的纳维亚传说中的)山精,搜查

them in the doorway. It wasn't ordinary fire either; it was purple. At the same instant, black flames shot up in the doorway leading onward. They were trapped.

"Look!" Hermione seized a roll of paper lying next to the bottles. Harry looked over her shoulder to read it:

Danger lies before you, while safety lies behind,
Two of us will help you, whichever you would find,
One among us seven will let you move ahead,
Another will transport the drinker back instead,
*Two among our number hold only nettle wine*①,
Three of us are killers, waiting hidden in line.
Choose, unless you wish to stay here forevermore,
To help you in your choice, we give you these clues four:
First, however slyly the poison tries to hide
You will always find some on nettle wine's left side;
Second, different are those who stand at either end,
But if you would move onward, neither is your friend;
Third, as you see clearly, all are different size,
*Neither dwarf*② *nor giant holds death in their insides;*
Fourth, the second left and the second on the right
Are twins once you taste them, though different at first sight.

Hermione let out a great sigh and Harry, amazed, saw that she was smiling, the very last thing he felt like doing.

"*Brilliant,*" said Hermione. "This isn't magic— it's logic— a puzzle. A lot of the greatest wizards haven't got an ounce of logic, they'd be stuck in here forever."

"But so will we, won't we?"

---

①nettle wine: 荨麻酒
②dwarf [TOEFL]: 侏儒

"Of course not," said Hermione. "Everything we need is here on this paper. Seven bottles: three are poison; two are wine; one will get us safely through the black fire, and one will get us back through the purple."

"But how do we know which to drink?"

"Give me a minute."

Hermione read the paper several times. Then she walked up and down the line of bottles, muttering to herself and pointing at them. At last, she clapped her hands.

"Got it," she said. "The smallest bottle will get us through the black fire—toward the Stone."

Harry looked at the tiny bottle.

"There's only enough there for one of us," he said. "That's hardly one swallow."

They looked at each other.

"Which one will get you back through the purple flames?"

Hermione pointed at a rounded bottle at the right end of the line.

"You drink that," said Harry. "No, listen, get back and get Ron. Grab brooms from the flying-key room, they'll get you out of the trapdoor and past Fluffy— go straight to the owlery and send Hedwig to Dumbledore, we need him. I might be able to hold Snape off for a while, but I'm no match for him, really."

"But Harry— what if You-Know-Who's with him?"

"Well— I was lucky once, wasn't I?" said Harry, pointing at his scar. "I might get lucky again."

Hermione's lip trembled, and she suddenly dashed at Harry and threw her arms around him.

"*Hermione*!"

"Harry— you're a great wizard, you know."

"I'm not as good as you," said Harry, very embarrassed, as she let go of him.

"Me!" said Hermione. "Books! And cleverness! There are more important things— friendship and bravery and— oh Harry— be *careful*!"

"You drink first," said Harry. "You are sure which is which, aren't you?"

"Positive," said Hermione. She took a long drink from the round bottle at the end, and shuddered.

"It's not poison?" said Harry anxiously.

"No— but it's like ice."

"Quick, go, before it wears off."

"Good luck— take care—"

"GO!"

Hermione turned and walked straight through the purple fire.

Harry took a deep breath and picked up the smallest bottle. He turned to face the black flames.

"Here I come," he said, and he drained the little bottle in one gulp①.

It was indeed as though ice was flooding his body. He put the bottle down and walked forward; he braced himself, saw the black flames licking his body, but couldn't feel them— for a moment he could see nothing but dark fire— then he was on the other side, in the last chamber.

There was already someone there— but it wasn't Snape. It wasn't even Voldemort.

Chapter 17

It was Quirrell.

"*You*!" gasped Harry.

Quirrell smiled. His face wasn't twitching at all.

"Me," he said calmly. "I wondered whether I'd be meeting you here, Potter."

"But I thought— Snape—"

"*Severus*?" Quirrell laughed, and it wasn't his usual quivering treble, either, but cold and sharp. "Yes, Severus does seem the type, doesn't he? So useful to have him swooping around like an over grown bat. Next to him, who would suspect p–p–poor, st–stuttering P–Professor Quirrell?"

---

①gulp [TOEFL]:一大口,狼吞虎咽,深呼吸

Harry couldn't take it① in. This couldn't be true, it couldn't

"But Snape tried to kill me!"

"No, no, no. I tried to kill you. Your friend Miss Granger accidentally knocked me over as she rushed to set fire to Snape at that Quidditch match②. She broke my eye contact with you. Another few seconds and I'd have got you off that broom. I'd have managed it before then if Snape hadn't been muttering a countercurse, trying to save you."

"Snape was trying to save me?"

"Of course," said Quirrell coolly. "Why do you think he wanted to referee③ your next match? He was trying to make sure I didn't do it again. Funny, really... he needn't have bothered. I couldn't do anything with Dumbledore watching. All the other teachers thought Snape was trying to stop Gryffindor from winning, he did make himself unpopular... and what a waste of time, when after all that, I'm going to kill you tonight."

Quirrell snapped his fingers. Ropes sprang out of thin air and wrapped themselves tightly around Harry.

"You're too nosy to live, Potter. Scurrying around the school on Halloween like that, for all I knew you'd seen me coming to look at what was guarding the Stone."

"You let the troll in?"

"Certainly. I have a special gift with trolls— you must have seen what I did to the one in the chamber back there? Unfortunately, while everyone else was running around looking for it, Snape, who already suspected me, went straight to the third floor to head me off— and not only did my troll fail to beat you to death, that three-headed dog didn't even manage to bite Snape's leg off properly."

"Now, wait quietly, Potter. I need to examine this interesting mirror."

It was only then that Harry realized what was standing behind Quirrell. It

---

①take it:相信

②Quidditch match:魁地奇比赛

③referee [IELTS]:担任裁判,介绍人,调解人

Chapter 7 20th-Century English Literature

was the Mirror of Erised.

"This mirror is the key to finding the Stone," Quirrell murmured, tapping his way around the frame. "Trust Dumbledore to come up with something like this... but he's in London... I'll be far away by the time he gets back..."

All Harry could think of doing was to keep Quirrell talking and stop him from concentrating on the mirror.

"I saw you and Snape in the forest—" he blurted out①.

"Yes," said Quirrell idly, walking around the mirror to look at the back. "He was on to me by that time, trying to find out how far I'd got. He suspected me all along. Tried to frighten me— as though he could, when I had Lord Voldemort on my side..."

Quirrell came back out from behind the mirror and stared hungrily into it.

"I see the Stone... I'm presenting it to my master... but where is it?"

Harry struggled against the ropes binding him, but they didn't give. He had to keep Quirrell from giving his whole attention to the mirror.

"But Snape always seemed to hate me so much."

"Oh, he does," said Quirrell casually, "heavens, yes. He was at Hogwarts with your father, didn't you know? They loathed② each other. But he never wanted you dead."

"But I heard you a few days ago, sobbing— I thought Snape was threatening you."

For the first time, a spasm③ of fear flitted across Quirrell's face.

"Sometimes," he said, "I find it hard to follow my master's instructions — he is a great wizard and I am weak—"

"You mean he was there in the classroom with you?" Harry gasped.

"He is with me wherever I go," said Quirrell quietly. "I met him when I traveled around the world. A foolish young man I was then, full of ridiculous ideas about good and evil. Lord Voldemort showed me how wrong I was. There

---

① blurt out:脱口而出

② loathe [IELTS]:厌恶

③ spasm [IELTS]:(感情或反应)一阵阵发作,痉挛

is no good and evil, there is only power, and those too weak to seek it... Since then, I have served him faithfully, although I have let him down many times. He has had to be very hard on me." Quirrell shivered suddenly. "He does not forgive mistakes easily. When I failed to steal the Stone from Gringotts, he was most displeased. He punished me... decided he would have to keep a closer watch on me..."

Quirrell's voice trailed away. Harry was remembering his trip to Diagon Alley — how could he have been so stupid? He'd seen Quirrell there that very day, shaken hands with him in the Leaky Cauldron.

Quirrell cursed under his breath.

"I don't understand... is the Stone inside the mirror? Should I break it?"

Harry's mind was racing.

What I want more than anything else in the world at the moment, he thought, *is to find the Stone before Quirrell does. So if I look in the mirror, I should see myself finding it— which means I'll see where it's hidden! But how can I look without Quirrell realizing what I'm up to?*

He tried to edge to the left, to get in front of the glass without Quirrell noticing, but the ropes around his ankles were too tight: he tripped and fell over. Quirrell ignored him. He was still talking to himself.

"What does this mirror do? How does it work? Help me, Master!"

And to Harry's horror, a voice answered, and the voice seemed to come from Quirrell himself.

"Use the boy... Use the boy..."

Quirrell rounded on Harry.

"Yes— Potter— come here."

He clapped his hands once, and the ropes binding Harry fell off. Harry got slowly to his feet.

"Come here," Quirrell repeated. "Look in the mirror and tell me what you see."

Harry walked toward him.

I must lie, he thought desperately. *I must look and lie about what I see, that's all.*

Quirrell moved close behind him. Harry breathed in the funny smell that seemed to come from Quirrell's turban①. He closed his eyes, stepped in front of the mirror, and opened them again.

He saw his reflection, pale and scared – looking at first. But a moment later, the reflection smiled at him. It put its hand into its pocket and pulled out a blood – red stone. It winked and put the Stone back in its pocket— and as it did so, Harry felt something heavy drop into his real pocket. Somehow— incredibly— he'd gotten the Stone.

"Well?" said Quirrell impatiently. "What do you see?"

Harry screwed up② his courage.

"I see myself shaking hands with Dumbledore," he invented.

"I— I've won the House Cup for Gryffindor."

Quirrell cursed again.

"Get out of the way," he said. As Harry moved aside, he felt the Sorcerer's Stone against his leg. Dare he make a break for it?

But he hadn't walked five paces before a high voice spoke, though Quirrell wasn't moving his lips.

"He lies... He lies..."

"Potter, come back here!" Quirrell shouted. "Tell me the truth! What did you just see?"

The high voice spoke again.

"Let me speak to him... face-to-face..."

"Master, you are not strong enough!"

"I have strength enough... for this..."

Harry felt as if Devil's Snare was rooting him to the spot. He couldn't move a muscle. Petrified③, he watched as Quirrell reached up and began to unwrap his turban. What was going on? The turban fell away. Quirrell's head looked strangely small without it. Then he turned slowly on the spot.

---

①turban [TOEFL]：包头巾
②screw up his courage：鼓起勇气
③petrified：恐慌的

Harry would have screamed, but he couldn't make a sound. Where there should have been a back to Quirrell's head, there was a face, the most terrible face Harry had ever seen. It was chalk① white with glaring red eyes and slits for nostrils, like a snake.

"Harry Potter..." it whispered.

Harry tried to take a step backward but his legs wouldn't move.

"See what I have become?" the face said. "Mere shadow and vapor... I have form only when I can share another's body... but there have always been those willing to let me into their hearts and minds.... Unicorn blood has strengthened me, these past weeks... you saw faithful Quirrell drinking it for me in the forest... and once I have the Elixir of Life②, I will be able to create a body of my own... Now... why don't you give me that Stone in your pocket?"

So he knew. The feeling suddenly surged back into Harry's legs. He stumbled backward.

"Don't be a fool," snarled the face. "Better save your own life and join me... or you'll meet the same end as your parents... They died begging me for mercy..."

"LIAR!" Harry shouted suddenly.

Quirrell was walking backward at him, so that Voldemort could still see him. The evil face was now smiling.

"How touching..." it hissed. "I always value bravery... Yes, boy, your parents were brave... I killed your father first, and he put up a courageous fight... but your mother needn't have died... she was trying to protect you... Now give me the Stone, unless you want her to have died in vain."

"NEVER!"

Harry sprang toward the flame door, but Voldemort screamed "SEIZE HIM!" and the next second, Harry felt Quirrell's hand close on his wrist. At once, a needle-sharp pain seared across Harry's scar; his head felt as though it was about to split in two; he yelled, struggling with all his might, and to his

---

①chalk：粉笔
②Elixir of Life：长生不老药

surprise, Quirrell let go of him. The pain in his head lessened— he looked around wildly to see where Quirrell had gone, and saw him hunched in pain, looking at his fingers— they were blistering before his eyes.

"Seize him! SEIZE HIM!" shrieked Voldemort again, and Quirrell lunged, knocking Harry clean off his feet, landing on top of him, both hands around Harry's neck— Harry's scar was almost blinding him with pain, yet he could see Quirrell howling in agony.

"Master, I cannot hold him— my hands— my hands!"

And Quirrell, though pinning Harry to the ground with his knees, let go of his neck and stared, bewildered, at his own palms— Harry could see they looked burned, raw, red, and shiny.

"Then kill him, fool, and be done!" screeched Voldemort.

Quirrell raised his hand to perform a deadly curse, but Harry, by instinct, reached up and grabbed Quirrell's face—

"AAAARGH!"

Quirrell rolled off him, his face blistering, too, and then Harry knew: Quirrell couldn't touch his bare skin, not without suffering terrible pain— his only chance was to keep hold of Quirrell, keep him in enough pain to stop him from doing a curse.

Harry jumped to his feet, caught Quirrell by the arm, and hung on as tight as he could. Quirrell screamed and tried to throw Harry off— the pain in Harry's head was building— he couldn't see— he could only hear Quirrell's terrible shrieks and Voldemort's yells of, "KILL HIM! KILL HIM!" and other voices, maybe in Harry's own head, crying, "Harry! Harry!"

He felt Quirrell's arm wrenched from his grasp, knew all was lost, and fell into blackness, down... down... down...

Questions for Discussion

1. Discuss the reasons why Voldemort failed to win the Stone in the end?
2. Analyse the image of Ron.

Appreciation

"Yeah... We've helped each other out, haven't we? We both got here. Let's take it together."

—— *Harry Potter and the Goblet of Fire*

"我们互相帮助克服了困难,对不对,我们两个一起到了这里,让我们一起去拿吧。"

——《哈利波特与火焰杯》

Brief Introduction

Harry Potter and the Goblet of Fire, written by J. K. Rowling, is the fourth book in the Harry Potter series. It tells the story of Harry Potter in Hogwarts School of Witchcraft and Wizardry after three years of study, gradually growing into an excellent wizard. Rowling Expands the wizarding world beyond Hogwarts and England through two international tournaments, the Quidditch World Cup and the Triwizard Cup. More than 370,000 copies were sold in the UK on the book's first day on July 8, 2000 and three million copies were sold in the United States in the first 48 hours after it went on sale. In 2001, Rowling won the Hugo Award for *Harry Potter and the Goblet of Fire*.

Selected Reading

Harry Potter and the Goblet of Fire

Chapter 31

"Ladies and gentlemen, the third and final task of the Triwizard Tournament is about to begin! Let me remind you how the points currently stand! Tied in first place, with eighty-five points each-Mr. Cedric Diggory and Mr. Harry Potter, both of Hogwarts School!" The cheers and applause sent birds from the Forbidden Forest fluttering into the darkening sky. "In second place, with eighty points—Mr. Viktor Krum, of Durmstrang Institute!" More applause. "And in third place—Miss Fleur Delacour, of Beauxbatons Academy!"

Harry could just make out Mrs. Weasley, Bill, Ron, and Hermione applauding Fleur politely, halfway up the stands. He waved up at them, and they waved back, beaming① at him.

"So... on my whistle, Harry and Cedric!" said Bagman. "Three—two—one"

He gave a short blast on his whistle, and Harry and Cedric hurried forward into the maze.

The towering hedges cast black shadows across the path, and, whether because they were so tall and thick or because they had been enchanted, the sound of the surrounding crowd was silenced the moment they entered the maze. Harry felt almost as though he were underwater again. He pulled out his wand, muttered, "Lumos②," and heard Cedric do the same just behind him.

After about fifty yards, they reached a fork. They looked at each other.

"See you," Harry said, and he took the left one, while Cedric took the right.

Harry heard Bagman's whistle for the second time. Krum had entered the maze. Harry sped up. His chosen path seemed completely deserted. He turned right, and hurried on, holding his wand high over his head, trying to see as far ahead as possible. Still, there was nothing in sight.

Bagman's whistle blew in the distance for the third time. All of the champions were now inside.

Harry kept looking behind him. The old feeling that he was being watched was upon him.

The maze was growing darker with every passing minute as the sky overhead deepened to navy. He reached a second fork.

"Point Me," he whispered to his wand, holding it flat in his palm.

The wand spun③ around once and pointed toward his right, into solid hedge. That way was north, and he knew that he needed to go northwest for the center of the maze. The best he could do was to take the left fork and go right

---

①beam [TOEFL][IELTS]:笑容满面,(通过电子设备)发送,(光)束
②Lumos:荧光闪烁(咒语)
③spin[IELTS]:快速旋转,纺(线)

again as soon as possible.

The path ahead was empty too, and when Harry reached a right turn and took it, he again found his way unblocked. Harry didn't know why, but the lack of obstacles①was unnerving him. Surely he should have met something by now? It felt as though the maze were luring② him into a false sense of security. Then he heard movement right behind him. He held out his wand, ready to attack, but its beam fell only upon Cedric, who had just hurried out of a path on the right-hand side. Cedric looked severely shaken. The sleeve of his robe was smoking.

"Hagrid's Blast-Ended Skrewts③!" he hissed. "They're enormous—I only just got away!"

He shook his head and dived out of sight, along another path. Keen to put plenty of distance between himself and the skrewts, Harry hurried off again. Then, as he turned a corner, he saw... a dementor④ gliding⑤ toward him. Twelve feet tall, its face hidden by its hood, its rotting, scabbed hands outstretched, it advanced, sensing its way blindly toward him. Harry could hear its rattling breath; he felt clammy coldness stealing over him, but knew what he had to do...

He summoned the happiest thought he could, concentrated with all his might on the thought of getting out of the maze and celebrating with Ron and Hermione, raised his wand, and cried, "Expecto Patronum⑥!"

A silver stag erupted from the end of Harry's wand and galloped⑦ toward the dementor, which fell back and tripped over the hem of its robes... Harry had never seen a dementor stumble.

"Hang on!" he shouted, advancing in the wake of his silver Patronus.

---

①obstacle[TOEFL][IELTS]:障碍
②lure[TOEFL]:引诱,诱饵
③Blast-Ended Skrewts:炸尾螺
④dementor:摄魂怪
⑤glide[TOEFL][IELTS]:滑过,(鸟或飞机)滑翔
⑥Expecto Patronum:呼神护卫(咒语)
⑦gallop[IELTS]:飞奔

"You're a boggart! Riddikulus!"

There was a loud crack, and the shape-shifter exploded in a wisp of smoke. The silver stag faded from sight. Harry wished it could have stayed, he could have used some company... but he moved on, quickly and quietly as possible, listening hard, his wand held high once more.

Left... right... left again... Twice he found himself facing dead ends. He did the Four-Point Spell again and found that he was going too far east. He turned back, took a right turn, and saw an odd golden mist floating ahead of him.

Harry approached it cautiously, pointing the wand's beam at it. This looked like some kind of enchantment. He wondered whether he might be able to blast it out of the way.

"Reducio①!" he said.

The spell shot straight through the mist, leaving it intact②. He supposed he should have known better; the Reductor Curse was for solid objects. What would happen if he walked through the mist? Was it worth chancing it, or should he double back?

He was still hesitating when a scream shattered the silence.

"Fleur?" Harry yelled.

There was silence. He stared all around him. What had happened to her? Her scream seemed to have come from somewhere ahead. He took a deep breath and ran through the enchanted mist.

The world turned upside down. Harry was hanging from the ground, with his hair on end, his glasses dangling off his nose, threatening to fall into the bottomless sky. He clutched③ them to the end of his nose and hung there, terrified. It felt as though his feet were glued to the grass, which had now become the ceiling. Below him the dark, star-spangled heavens stretched endlessly. He felt as though if he tried to move one of his feet, he would fall

---

①Reducio:粉身碎骨(咒语)

②intact[TOEFL][IELTS]:完好无损

③clutch[TOEFL][IELTS]:抓紧,(因害怕或痛苦)突然抓住

away from the earth completely.

Think, he told himself, as all the blood rushed to his head, think...

But not one of the spells he had practiced had been designed to combat a sudden reversal of ground and sky. Did he dare move his foot? He could hear the blood pounding in his ears. He had two choices-try and move, or send up red sparks, and get rescued and disqualified from the task.

He shut his eyes, so he wouldn't be able to see the view of endless space below him, and pulled his right foot as hard as he could away from the grassy ceiling.

Immediately, the world righted itself. Harry fell forward onto his knees onto the wonderfully solid ground. He felt temporarily limp with shock. He took a deep, steadying breath, then got up again and hurried forward, looking back over his shoulder as he ran away from the golden mist, which twinkled innocently at him in the moonlight.

He paused at a junction① of two paths and looked around for some sign of Fleur. He was sure it had been she who had screamed. What had she met? Was she all right? There was no sign of red sparks-did that mean she had got herself out of trouble, or was she in such trouble that she couldn't reach her wand? Harry took the right fork with a feeling of increasing unease... but at the same time, he couldn't help thinking. One champion down...

The cup was somewhere close by, and it sounded as though Fleur was no longer in the running. He'd got this far, hadn't he? What if he actually managed to win? Fleetingly, and for the first time since he'd found himself champion, he saw again that image of himself, raising the Triwizard Cup in front of the rest of the school...

He met nothing for ten minutes, but kept running into dead ends. Twice he took the same wrong turning. Finally, he found a new route and started to jog along it, his wandlight waving, making his shadow flicker and distort on the hedge walls. Then he rounded another corner and found himself facing a Blast-Ended Skrewt.

---

① junction [TOEFL][IELTS]：交叉路口

Cedric was right—it was enormous. Ten feet long, it looked more like a giant scorpion① than anything. Its long sting was curled over its back. Its thick armor glinted in the light from Harry's wand, which he pointed at it.

"Stupefy!"

The spell hit the skrewt's armor and rebounded; Harry ducked just in time, but could smell burning hair; it had singed the top of his head. The skrewt issued a blast of fire from its end and flew forward toward him.

"Impedimenta!" Harry yelled. The spell hit the skrewt's armor again and ricocheted off; Harry staggered back a few paces and fell over. "IMPEDIMENTA!"

The skrewt was inches from him when it froze—he had managed to hit it on its fleshy, shell-less underside. Panting, Harry pushed himself away from it and ran, hard, in the opposite direction—the Impediment Curse was not permanent; the skrewt would be regaining the use of its legs at any moment.

He took a left path and hit a dead end, a right, and hit another; forcing himself to stop, heart hammering, he performed the Four-Point Spell again, backtracked, and chose a path that would take him northwest.

He had been hurrying along the new path for a few minutes, when he heard something in the path running parallel to his own that made him stop dead.

"What are you doing?" yelled Cedric's voice. "What the hell d'you think you're doing?"

And then Harry heard Krum's voice.

"Crucio!"

The air was suddenly full of Cedric's yells. Horrified, Harry began sprinting up his path, trying to find a way into Cedric's. When none appeared, he tried the Reductor Curse again. It wasn't very effective, but it burned a small hole in the hedge through which Harry forced his leg, kicking at the thick brambles and branches until they broke and made an opening; he struggled through it, tearing his robes, and looking to his right, saw Cedric jerking and twitching on the ground, Krum standing over him.

---

①scorpion: 蝎子

Harry pulled himself up and pointed his wand at Krum just as Krum looked up. Krum turned and began to run.

"Stupefy!" Harry yelled.

The spell hit Krum in the back; he stopped dead in his tracks, fell forward, and lay motionless, facedown in the grass. Harry-dashed over to Cedric, who had stopped twitching and was lying there panting, his hands over his face.

"Are you all right?" Harry said roughly, grabbing Cedric's arm.

"Yeah," panted Cedric. "Yeah... I don't believe it... he crept up behind me... I heard him, I turned around, and he had his wand on me..."

Cedric got up. He was still shaking. He and Harry looked down at Krum.

"I can't believe this... I thought he was all right," Harry said, staring at Krum.

"So did I," said Cedric.

"Did you hear Fleur scream earlier?" said Harry.

"Yeah," said Cedric. "You don't think Krum got her too?"

"I don't know," said Harry slowly.

"Should we leave him here?" Cedric muttered.

"No," said Harry. "I reckon we should send up red sparks. Someone'll come and collect him... otherwise he'll probably be eaten by a skrewt."

"He'd deserve it," Cedric muttered, but all the same, he raised his wand and shot a shower of red sparks into the air, which hovered[①] high above Krum, marking the spot where he lay.

Harry and Cedric stood there in the darkness for a moment, looking around them. Then Cedric said, "Well... I s'pose we'd better go on..."

"What?" said Harry. "Oh... yeah... right..."

It was an odd moment. He and Cedric had been briefly united against Krum—now the fact that they were opponents came back to Harry. The two of them proceeded up the dark path without speaking, then Harry turned left, and Cedric right. Cedric's footsteps soon died away.

Harry moved on, continuing to use the Four-Point Spell, making sure he

---

①hover[TOEFL][IELTS]：盘旋,(人) 踌躇

was moving in the right direction. It was between him and Cedric now. His desire to reach the cup first was now burning stronger than ever, but he could hardly believe what he'd just seen Krum do. The use of an Unforgivable Curse on a fellow human

being meant a life term in Azkaban, that was what Moody had told them. Krum surely couldn't have wanted the Triwizard Cup that badly... Harry sped up.

Every so often he hit more dead ends, but the increasing darkness made him feel sure he was getting near the heart of the maze. Then, as he strode down a long, straight path, he saw movement once again, and his beam of wandlight hit an extraordinary creature, one which he had only seen in picture form, in his Monster Book of Monsters.

It was a sphinx①. It had the body of an over-large lion: great clawed paws and a long yellowish tail ending in a brown tuft. Its head, however, was that of a woman. She turned her long, almond-shaped eyes upon Harry as he approached. He raised his wand, hesitating. She was not crouching as if to spring, but pacing from side to side of the path, blocking his progress. Then she spoke, in a deep, hoarse voice.

"You are very near your goal. The quickest way is past me."

"So... so will you move, please?" said Harry, knowing what the answer was going to be.

"No," she said, continuing to pace. "Not unless you can answer my riddle. Answer on your first guess— I let you pass. Answer wrongly—I attack. Remain silent—I will let you walk away from me unscathed."

Harry's stomach slipped several notches. It was Hermione who was good at this sort of thing, not him. He weighed his chances. If the riddle was too hard, he could keep silent, get away from the sphinx unharmed, and try and find an alternative route to the center.

"Okay," he said. "Can I hear the riddle?"

The sphinx sat down upon her hind legs, in the very middle of the path, and

---

①sphinx:斯芬克斯

recited:

"First think of the person who lives in disguise, Who deals in secrets and tells naught but lies.

Next, tell me what's always the last thing to mend, The middle of middle and end of the end?

And finally give me the sound often heard During the search for a hard-to-find word.

Now string them together, and answer me this, Which creature would you be unwilling to kiss?"

Harry gaped at her.

"Could I have it again... more slowly?" he asked tentatively. She blinked at him, smiled, and repeated the poem. "All the clues add up to a creature I wouldn't want to kiss?" Harry asked.

She merely smiled her mysterious smile. Harry took that for a "yes." Harry cast his mind around. There were plenty of animals he wouldn't want to kiss; his immediate thought was a Blast-Ended Skrewt, but something told him that wasn't the answer. He'd have to try and work out the clues...

"A person in disguise," Harry muttered, staring at her, "who lies... er... that'd be a-an impostor. No, that's not my guess! A-a spy? I'll come back to that... could you give me the next clue again, please?"

She repeated the next lines of the poem.

"'The last thing to mend,'" Harry repeated. "Er... no idea... 'middle of middle' ... could I have the last bit again?"

She gave him the last four lines.

"'The sound often heard during the search for a hard-to-find word,'" said Harry. "Er... that'd be... er... hang on - 'er'! Er's a sound!"

The sphinx smiled at him.

"Spy... er... spy... er..." said Harry, pacing up and down. "A creature I wouldn't want to kiss... a spider!"

The sphinx smiled more broadly. She got up, stretched her front legs, and then moved aside for him to pass.

"Thanks!" said Harry, and, amazed at his own brilliance, he dashed forward.

He had to be close now, he had to be... wand was telling him he was bang on course; as long as he didn't meet anything too horrible, he might have a chance...

Harry broke into a run. He had a choice of paths up ahead. "Point Me!" he whispered again to his wand, and it spun around and pointed him to the right-hand one. He dashed up this one and saw light ahead.

The Triwizard Cup was gleaming on a plinth a hundred yards away. Suddenly a dark figure hurtled out onto the path in front of him.

Cedric was going to get there first. Cedric was sprinting as fast as he could toward the cup, and Harry knew he would never catch up, Cedric was much taller, had much longer legs—Then Harry saw something immense① over a hedge to his left, moving quickly along a path that intersected② with his own; it was moving so fast Cedric was about to run into it, and Cedric, his eyes on the cup, had not seen it—

"Cedric!" Harry bellowed. "On your left!"

Cedric looked around just in time to hurl himself past the thing and avoid colliding with it, but in his haste, he tripped. Harry saw Cedric's wand fly out of his hand as a gigantic spider stepped into the path and began to bear down upon Cedric.

"Stupefy!" Harry yelled; the spell hit the spider's gigantic, hairy black body, but for all the good it did, he might as well have thrown a stone at it; the spider jerked, scuttled around, and ran at Harry instead.

"Stupefy! Impedimenta! Stupefy!"

But it was no use—the spider was either so large, or so magical, that the spells were doing no more than aggravating③ it. Harry had one horrifying glimpse of eight shining black eyes and razor-sharp pincers before it was upon him.

---

①immense[TOEFL][IELTS]:巨大的
②intersect[TOEFL][IELTS]:交叉
③aggravate[TOEFL][IELTS]:激怒,使严重

He was lifted into the air in its front legs; struggling madly, he tried to kick it; his leg connected with the pincers and next moment he was in excruciating pain. He could hear Cedric yelling "Stupefy!" too, but his spell had no more effect than Harry's—Harry raised his wand as the spider opened its pincers once more and shouted "Expelliarmus!"

It worked—the Disarming Spell made the spider drop him, but that meant that Harry fell twelve feet onto his already injured leg, which crumpled beneath him. Without pausing to think, he aimed high at the spider's underbelly, as he had done with the skrewt, and shouted "Stupefy!" just as Cedric yelled the same thing.

The two spells combined did what one alone had not: The spider keeled over sideways, flattening a nearby hedge, and strewing the path with a tangle of hairy legs.

"Harry!" he heard Cedric shouting. "You all right? Did it fall on you?"

"No," Harry called back, panting. He looked down at his leg. It was bleeding freely. He could see some sort of thick, gluey secretion from the spider's pincers on his torn robes. He tried to get up, but his leg was shaking badly and did not want to support his weight. He leaned against the hedge, gasping for breath, and looked around.

Cedric was standing feet from the Triwizard Cup, which was gleaming behind him.

"Take it, then," Harry panted to Cedric. "Go on, take it. You're there."

But Cedric didn't move. He merely stood there, looking at Harry. Then he turned to stare at the cup. Harry saw the longing expression on his face in its golden light.

Cedric looked around at Harry again, who was now holding onto the hedge to support himself. Cedric took a deep breath.

"You take it. You should win. That's twice you've saved my neck in here."

"That's not how it's supposed to work," Harry said. He felt angry; his leg was very painful, he was aching all over from trying to throw off the spider, and after all his efforts, Cedric had beaten him to it, just as he'd beaten Harry to ask Cho to the ball.

"The one who reaches the cup first gets the points. That's you. I'm telling you, I'm not going to win any races on this leg."

Cedric took a few paces nearer to the Stunned spider, away from the cup, shaking his head.

"No," he said.

"Stop being noble," said Harry irritably. "Just take it, then we can get out of here."

Cedric watched Harry steadying himself, holding tight to the hedge.

"You told me about the dragons," Cedric said. "I would've gone down in the first task if you hadn't told me what was coming."

"I had help on that too," Harry snapped, trying to mop up his bloody leg with his robes.

"You helped me with the egg—we're square."

"I had help on the egg in the first place," said Cedric.

"We're still square," said Harry, testing his leg gingerly; it shook violently as he put weight on it; he had sprained his ankle when the spider had dropped him.

"You should've got more points on the second task," said Cedric mulishly. "You stayed behind to get all the hostages. I should've done that."

"I was the only one who was thick enough to take that song seriously!" said Harry bitterly. "Just take the cup!"

"No," said Cedric.

He stepped over the spider's tangled legs to join Harry, who stared at him. Cedric was serious. He was walking away from the sort of glory Hufflepuff House hadn't had in centuries.

"Go on," Cedric said. He looked as though this was costing him every ounce of resolution he had, but his face was set, his arms were folded, he seemed decided.

Harry looked from Cedric to the cup. For one shining moment, he saw himself emerging from the maze, holding it. He saw himself holding the Triwizard Cup aloft, heard the roar of the crowd, saw Cho's face shining with admiration, more clearly than he had ever seen it before and... then the picture faded, and he found himself staring at Cedric's shadowy, stubborn face.

"Both of us," Harry said.

"What?"

"We'll take it at the same time. It's still a Hogwarts victory. We'll tie for it."

Cedric stared at Harry. He unfolded his arms.

"You—you sure?"

"Yeah," said Harry. "Yeah... we've helped each other out, haven't we? We both got here. Let's just take it together."

For a moment, Cedric looked as though he couldn't believe his ears; then his face split in a grin.

"You're on," he said. "Come here."

He grabbed Harrys arm below the shoulder and helped Harry limp toward the plinth where the cup stood. When they had reached it, they both held a hand out over one of the cup's gleaming handles.

"On three, right?" said Harry. "One-two- three-"

He and Cedric both grasped a handle.

Instantly, Harry felt a jerk somewhere behind his navel. His feet had left the ground.

He could not unclench the hand holding the Triwizard Cup; it was pulling him onward in a howl of wind and swirling color, Cedric at his side.

Questions for Discussion

1. Analyse the image of Harry Potter.
2. Analyse the selected passage with the theory of Archetype.

Terms

1. Modernism
2. Stream of consciousness

Chapter 7 20th-Century English Literature

Reference

[1] DICKENS C. Oliver twist [M]. New York: W. W. Norton & Co, 1992.

[2] BLAKE W. Songs of innocence and experience [M]. London: Penguin Books Ltd. , 2017.

[3] SHAKSPEARE W. Volume editor nicholas brooke [M]. Oxford: Oxford University Press, 2009.

[4] 刘炳善.英国文学简史[M].郑州:河南人民出版社,2017.

[5] [英]戴维·洛奇.治疗[M].罗贻荣,译.北京:新星出版社,2020.

[6] [英]托马斯·马洛礼.亚瑟王之死[M].黄素封,译.北京:人民文学出版社,2005.

[7] [英]亨利·菲尔丁.汤姆·琼斯[M].萧乾,李从弼,译.北京:人民文学出版社,1984.

[8] 马德高.英语专业考研——考点精梳与精炼[M].上海:上海交通大学出版社,2018.

[9] ROWLING J K. Harry Potter and the sorcerer's stone [M]. New York: Scholastic Press, 1998.

[10] ROWLING J K. Harry Potter and the goblet of fire [M]. London: Bloomsbury Children's Books, 2014.

[11] LODGE D. Paradise news [M]. England: Penguin Books,1992.

[12] 罗琳.哈利·波特与魔法石[M].苏农,译.北京:人民文学出版社,2011.

[13] 罗琳.哈利·波特与火焰杯[M].马爱新,译.北京:人民文学出版社,2002.

[14] 戴维·洛奇.天堂消息[M].李力,译.北京:作家学出版社,1998.

[15] 戴维·洛奇.生逢其时:戴维·洛奇回忆录[M].朱宾忠,吴濛,译.郑州:河南大学出版社,2017.

[16] 叶舒宪.《哈利波特》与后现代文化寻根[J].海南广播电视大学学报,2002(2):31-35.

[17] 王守仁.英国文学选读[M].北京:高等教育出版社,2002.

[18] 吴建国.毛姆短篇小说全集[M].北京:人民文学出版社,2020.

[19] 杨熙龄.雪莱政治论文选[M].北京:商务印书馆,1981.

[20]张伯香.英美文学选读[M].北京:外语教学与研究出版社,1999.
[21]张中载.萧伯纳最佳戏剧[M].沈阳:辽宁人民出版社,2014.
[22]王佐良.英国二十世纪文学史[M].北京:外语教学与研究出版社,2000.
[23]西渡.名家读外国诗[M].北京:中国计划出版社,2005.
[24]王佐良.英国浪漫主义诗歌史[M].北京:生活书店出版有限公司,2018.
[25]王佐良.英国诗歌选集[M]上海:上海译文出版社,2012.